Music Therapy in Children's Palliative Care

Giving voice to the perspectives of children and families with lived experience of children's palliative care, *Music Therapy in Children's Palliative Care: Collaborative Family and Practitioner Voices* explores the integral role of music therapy and its benefits for supporting child and family wellbeing within a range of children's palliative care settings. This book places the voices of children and families supported by children's palliative care at the centre as they articulate their own experiences of music therapy alongside music therapists to develop theory and practice in this area.

Through their unique, collaborative writing approach, contributing authors ensure that both perspectives of the therapeutic relationship – those of the families and the therapists – are represented throughout, offering a comprehensive view of their shared journey. Readers will benefit from learning about how music therapy may offer physical, emotional, social and spiritual support, aiming to enhance quality of life for both children and families. Equality, inclusion and belonging operate at the heart of this book, capturing the diversity of families that use palliative care services.

This book is a must read for any music therapist working within a children's palliative care setting. It will also be a compelling text for those with lived experiences, practitioners, educators, students and researchers.

Victoria Kammin is a music therapist from Surrey, UK, who specialises in paediatric palliative care. She is Director of Resonance Creative Therapy, Lecturer on the MSc Music Therapy training at Queen Margaret University and is undertaking her PhD at the University of York with the Paediatric Palliative Care Research Group.

Julie Russell is a freelance illustrator, teacher and lived-experience practitioner from Essex, UK. She has been married for over 25 years, is mother to a teenage son, and a bereaved parent to a toddler. Julie has given motivational talks about her family's experiences with paediatric palliative care and is a member of the Family Advisory Board at The Paediatric Palliative Care Research Group, University of York, and Cicely Saunders Institute, Kings College London.

'The authors have uniquely captured the role of music therapy at all points of children and their families' journeys through paediatric palliative care and beyond. They genuinely place the voices of children and families at the centre, capturing their narratives in a truly meaningful way. The value of meaning-making through collaborative song shines through and it is a privilege to read such intimate stories'.
Julia Hackett, *Associate Professor, Paediatric Palliative Care Research Group, University of York, UK*

'An incredible assemblage of sensitive and close to heart topics and scenarios etched under research, involving both service users and service providers reflecting their lived experiences of the therapeutic role of music in children's palliative care. This book will expand the horizons of readers, enabling them to have insight into an emotionally turbulent world of families of children with life-shortening conditions facing multifaceted challenges on a daily basis with music helping them in its management and playing a soothing role. A must read!'.
Riffat Iqbal, *a full-time carer now, after being a teacher, interpreter, playscheme deputy manager for special needs children, a tutor of Urdu language and customer service adviser. A cancer survivor, a proud mother of an 11-year-old son with complex needs and a bereaved parent to an adult daughter.*

'The value of memory-making when you are caring for a child who you know is going to have a short (and complex) life is incredibly difficult. We weave therapies and activities into our day to day. Clarity often only comes after the event. Vicky and Julie have gathered together the threads, from first-hand experiences, how music and music therapy plays a part in giving meaning and purpose to both child and parent. It was Shakespeare who said, "If music be the food of love, play on"'.
Tussie Myerson, *bereaved mother and advocate and campaigner for families caring for children with life-limiting conditions*

'Collaboration and reciprocity are at the heart of this book. The co-authored stories integrate voices from parents and music therapists to offer unique and valuable insights into the role that music and music therapy play in children's palliative care. In sharing the stories of families and therapists, the authors highlight the development of music therapy in children's palliative care and celebrate the mutual growth and learning that can occur through music, listening, dialogue and relationships'.
Dr Philippa Derrington, *Music Therapist and Programme Lead, MSc Music Therapy, Queen Margaret University*

Music Therapy in Children's Palliative Care

Collaborative Family and Practitioner Voices

Edited by Victoria Kammin and Julie Russell

LONDON AND NEW YORK

Designed cover image: Getty

First published 2025
by Routledge
605 Third Avenue, New York, NY 10158

and by Routledge
4 Park Square, Milton Park, Abingdon, Oxon, OX14 4RN

Routledge is an imprint of the Taylor & Francis Group, an informa business

© 2025 selection and editorial matter, Victoria Kammin and Julie Russell; individual chapters, the contributors

The right of Victoria Kammin and Julie Russell to be identified as the authors of the editorial material, and of the authors for their individual chapters, has been asserted in accordance with sections 77 and 78 of the Copyright, Designs and Patents Act 1988.

All rights reserved. No part of this book may be reprinted or reproduced or utilised in any form or by any electronic, mechanical, or other means, now known or hereafter invented, including photocopying and recording, or in any information storage or retrieval system, without permission in writing from the publishers.

Trademark notice: Product or corporate names may be trademarks or registered trademarks, and are used only for identification and explanation without intent to infringe.

British Library Cataloguing-in-Publication Data
A catalogue record for this book is available from the British Library

Library of Congress Cataloging-in-Publication Data
Names: Kammin, Victoria, editor. | Russell, Julie (Mother of Fraser) editor.
Title: Music therapy in children's palliative care : collaborative family and practitioner voices / edited by Victoria Kammin and Julie Russell.
Description: [First.] | New York, NY : Routledge, 2025. | Includes bibliographical references and index.
Identifiers: LCCN 2024047826 (print) | LCCN 2024047827 (ebook) | ISBN 9781032657318 (hardback) | ISBN 9781032657288 (paperback) | ISBN 9781032664378 (ebook)
Subjects: LCSH: Music therapy for children. | Hospice care. | Palliative treatment.
Classification: LCC ML3920 .M897815 2025 (print) | LCC ML3920 (ebook) | DDC 615.8/5154083--dc23/eng/20241009
LC record available at https://lccn.loc.gov/2024047826
LC ebook record available at https://lccn.loc.gov/2024047827

ISBN: 978-1-032-65731-8 (hbk)
ISBN: 978-1-032-65728-8 (pbk)
ISBN: 978-1-032-66437-8 (ebk)

DOI: 10.4324/9781032664378

Typeset in Times New Roman
by KnowledgeWorks Global Ltd.

Dedication

Vicky and Julie would like to express their sincere gratitude to the children, families and professionals who have shared their time, enthusiasm and voices in helping create this book. It would be nothing without you.

To my boys.

Iain, for all your encouragement, belief and support for me in creating this book.

To my son Dan for being my daily joy and no. 1 fan.

And to my son Fraser, may the ripples from your beautiful life go on. XXX

Julie

To my boys.

T, for your continuous love, support and unwavering belief in me, 30 years with you by my side makes everything possible.

To my sons Sammy and J, my heart melts at the kind, loving, talented young men you have grown into. Being your mother has enriched my life in ways I will never be able to express or thank you for. Can't wait for the next chapter. XXX

To my dearest Ma, you have inspired me throughout my life, guiding me with your compassion, understanding and love for everyone. Thank you for everything. You are the best mother, grandmother and mother-in-law we could ever wish for.

Vicky

Contents

Foreword		ix
LESLEY SCHATZBERGER		
List of Contributors		xiii
List of Digital resources		xiv
Introduction		1
JULIE RUSSELL AND VICTORIA KAMMIN		
1	**The Need for Belonging**	11
	JULIE RUSSELL AND VICTORIA KAMMIN	
2	**Lines of Communication: Creating Continuing Bonds on the Neonatal Unit**	31
	MARIAM TITUS, DEVANG RAM MOHAN AND KIRSTY JANE	
3	**Sophie's Wonderful World: The Impact of Music Therapy on a Family Caring for a Life-Limited Child**	42
	WENDY DE ST PAER AND SOPHIE NGUYEN'S PARENTS	
4	**Freya's Light**	56
	SARAH-JAYNE DAWES AND CERIDWEN REES	
5	**The Power of Connection: Family-Centred Virtual Music Therapy Groups**	72
	TOM GREY AND VICTORIA SWAN	
6	**'Alive, brave and free. That's what music means to me': Celebrating the Diverse Voices of a Children's Hospice Community through Collaborative Songwriting**	86
	RACHEL DRURY, POLLY HARRIS AND JANET MCLACHLAN	

7 **Music Therapy in Paediatric Palliative Care: A Link between the Hospice and Hospital** 100
CATHY IBBERSON, MUSIC THERAPIST, WITH A REFLECTION BY JOANNA CHAMBERS

8 **'Things change, and that's the way it is': Therapeutic Songwriting with Young Adults Transitioning from Paediatric Palliative Care** 114
GIORGOS TSIRIS AND DAPHNE RICKSON

9 **The Gods of Music** 132
NICKY HALE AND VICTORIA KAMMIN, WITH CONTRIBUTIONS FROM JOCELYN WATKINS, JANE WOOD, ADAM GORB AND MEGAN STEINBERG

Index *151*

Foreword

Lesley Schatzberger

When we plan to bring children into the world, we tend to imagine their steady development through childhood and into independence, with all the wonderment, joys, challenges, frustrations and hopes involved. For the first 11 years of our parenting journey, my husband and I enjoyed all those emotions, and more. When our first child, Hannah, was two years old, we were thrilled to welcome Jessica into the family, and as the two girls grew, they showed us how very different and complementary siblings' characters could be.

Our children were born into a family steeped in music, both their parents being professional musicians. Singing our way through daily activities was the norm in our household, and even before they could walk, the children would often come on tour with us. Jessie was learning to play the violin and then a little later also started piano lessons. When she was eight years old, she indicated that she would like to be in a professional orchestra one day: only a few months later our world was turned upside down, and that became a pipe dream.

Shortly after her ninth birthday Jessie started to say she was getting dizzy, which she found quite amusing. A visit to the doctor resulted in a course of antibiotics to treat a supposed middle ear infection, but a week later she was also reporting double vision. She was admitted to hospital, and within two days we were given the devastating diagnosis of a tumour in the brain stem. By this stage she was no longer able to walk: the change in her had been incredibly rapid. Neither surgery nor chemotherapy were possible, so the single treatment available to her was radiotherapy, and we knew that this would almost certainly only give her just a limited period of improvement.

The likelihood is that you are reading this as someone who has, or has had, direct involvement with a child whose life will be, or has been, shortened through a medical condition. You might be a family member, a music therapist, another health professional or simply interested in the power of music to transform lives. You will no doubt be inspired by the skill of the music therapists in their work with the babies, children and young people, by the courage of the children and young people and by the infinite love evident in every chapter.

When a child receives a life-shortening diagnosis, it is as if the whole family receives that diagnosis, and their world will never be the same again.

> *We need a sense of hope for something beyond ourselves, which helps to give our lives proportion and direction. Music lives and breathes to tell us just that: who we are and what we face.... it is a path between ourselves and the infinite.*[1]
>
> Yehudi Menuhin

As the great violinist Yehudi Menuhin implies here, music can help us to ground ourselves, to know who we are and to face what we must face. It can give us respite from our fears and connect us with both the past and the future. As Sophie's mum says in Chapter 3, 'For us parents, despite the paralysing fear and anxiety that we were experiencing while trying to adapt to a new life after the diagnosis, those music sessions seemed to be a wonderful escapism'.

Within six months of our first visit to the doctor, we were spending the last four days of Jessie's life in a children's hospice. Three months earlier, during the short period of respite afforded her by radiotherapy, it had been suggested to us that we consider visiting Martin House, the children's hospice nearest to our home in York. At that time, we were in denial, and fearful about the implications of being referred to a hospice – we had no idea that a hospice is a place where the most is made of *living*. Had our experience been recent, we might have benefited from the helpful link between hospital and hospice which we can read about in Chapter 7: 'Music therapy has in part provided a bridge for families referred to Martin House in demystifying the perception of a children's hospice…'.

As parents of a child living with a life-shortening condition, we can feel helpless. Our primal instinct is to protect our child from every danger, to preserve their life, to nurture their development, to prepare them for independence. But how can we respond when the ability to do this is taken away from us? To stand by and watch a precious young life ebbing away is agonising; to know that health professionals rather than we, as parents, are the only people who may be able to alleviate their pain, suffering or confusion; and to feel that we have been robbed of the future we had hoped for – we can feel completely disempowered. And yet, through music we find that we do have a powerful form of connection with our offspring, which is unique to the relationship we have with that child. In Chapter 2, we hear from parents who say that, through song, 'it felt like we could be competent, we could bring him joy, we could be his parents'.

The loss of a child is often acknowledged as being harder to bear than any other. One might be left with enduring recollections of anxiety, crises or medical procedures. To cope with the shattering grief, we need positive memories, but there might have been little time to build them in the short lives of some children. Families often remark on the importance of memories made during music therapy sessions, some of which are crystalised through recordings. The beautiful recording of the collaborative song described in Chapter 6 has provided a legacy which will forever comfort bereaved families, and in other chapters, we learn about memories made by music, and particularly song.

Throughout this book there is a sense of the power of music to transcend physical limitations, and to allow a child to grow and to thrive, whatever their condition. This is supremely evident in Fraser's story in Chapter 1. Fraser's parents knew that he would never be able to participate in the school activities and performances which most families take for granted, but the relationship he and Music Therapist Vicky had built together, and the opportunities she had provided, enabled him to play an important role in a concert in which he shone – an incredibly powerful moment for his parents, who experienced 'so, so much pride'.

In Chapter 4 we hear that our music story doesn't end when we die. It is difficult to imagine how this might be better illustrated than by Lucy's story, in Chapter 9. This extraordinarily talented young woman, with a little help from those who nurtured her development as a musician, not only left a body of wonderful and varied compositions, but also demonstrated how music defies perceptions of Dis/ability. Both her music and her influence live on.

Our experience with Jessie opened our eyes to the need for good palliative care for children, and we certainly received that care at Martin House back in 1994. Almost everything had been considered, not only for the children who were ill, but also for their siblings, parents, and even grandparents. However, we did think there was something extra that could enhance the quality of life for the children there. Children's hospices at that time had never had access to music therapy, and we felt that this would have so much to offer, particularly as so many children with life-shortening conditions cannot communicate verbally.

So it came about that our musical little girl gave rise to Jessie's Fund, which set about establishing posts for music therapists in all eight children's hospices across the UK at that time (www.jessiesfund.org.uk). That number grew exponentially over the next 25 years or so, and Jessie's Fund grew alongside it, with the aim of helping, through music, all children destined to have short lives. Jessie never got the chance to be in that professional orchestra she dreamed of, but her life and music has had a profound impact for thousands of children who do not reach adulthood.

Music is, and always has been, an integral element of rituals across all cultures. It helps us to celebrate, it soothes, it aids our mourning, it emboldens us. It is not a luxury – it is a functional necessity. Why else would billions be spent on army bands around the world? In the short lives of the children we meet in this book, and in their wider families' lives, music is a crucial aspect of their care, and of their very humanity. To quote, once again, Yehudi Menuhin, 'I can only think of music as something inherent in every human being – a birthright. Music coordinates mind, body and spirit'.[2]

xii Foreword

Figure 0.1 Jessie, age 6, playing the piano.

Notes

1 Menuhin, Y. and Curtis, D. W. *The Music of Man.* Macdonald and Jane's Publishers, 1979, p. 159.
2 Minto, D., quoting Yehudi Menuhin. *Classroom Gems: Games, Ideas and Activities for Primary Music.* Longman, 2009, p. 4.

List of Contributors

Editors

Julie Russell, Patient and Public Involvement Partner University of York and Cicely Saunders Institute, King's College London

Victoria Kammin, Queen Margaret University, University of York, Resonance Creative Therapy

Authors

Cathy Ibberson: Artforms Leeds, Martin House Children's Hospice, Northern Ballet Leeds, Jessie's Fund, Jazz Leeds

Ceridwen Rees: Children's Hospice South West

Daphne Rickson: ONZM, Te Heranga Waka – Victoria University of Wellington

Giorgos Tsiris: St Columba's Hospice Care and Queen Margaret University

Kirsty Jane: Kings College London, University College London Hospital, Noah's Ark Children's Hospice (at the time of writing and publication, Kirsty was in receipt of NIHR fellowship award NIHR303074)

Lesley Schatzberger: Tutor, School of Arts and Creative Technologies (Music), University of York, Founder, Jessie's Fund

Polly Harris: Nordoff & Robbins Music Therapy, in partnership with Children's Hospices Across Scotland (CHAS) and Kilpatrick School

Rachel Drury: Children's Hospices Across Scotland (Music Specialist) and Royal Conservatoire of Scotland (Research lecturer)

Janet McLachlan: Nordoff & Robbins Music Therapy, in partnership with Children's Hospices Across Scotland (CHAS) and Scottish Centre for Children with Motor Impairments (SCCMI)

Victoria Swan: Demelza Hospice Care for Children

Wendy de St Paer: Chroma, RLPO/MerseyCare NHS trust (at the time of writing Claire House Children's Hospice)

List of Digital resources

Chapter 1, The Need for Belonging: https://soundcloud.com/transcendentale/sangwanwasa

Chapter 2, Lines of Communication: https://www.instagram.com/soundorigins.mt?igsh=MW8xdWswZ2N1ZWZtbg

Chapter 6, Alive, brave and free: https://www.youtube.com/watch?v=NRp0ZW0ragY

Chapter 9, The Gods of Music https://soundcloud.com/lucyhalecomposer

Introduction

Julie Russell and Victoria Kammin

In our book, *Music Therapy in Children's Palliative Care: Collaborative Family and Practitioner Voices*, families and music therapists work together using a dialogic, co-authorship approach to explore experiences of music therapy in paediatric palliative care and inform future practice. This method ensures that both voices – those of the families and the therapists – are heard together through their shared engagement in the therapeutic and co-authorship process. By drawing on the lived experiences and expertise of both groups, this book highlights the mutual growth and learning that occurs, offering unique perspectives that illuminate the multifaceted role of music therapy in children's palliative care.

Paediatric palliative care

Paediatric palliative care, as defined by the World Health Organisation (2023), focusses on the 'active total care of the child's body, mind, and spirit' as well as support for their families. Central to the ethos of paediatric palliative care is to enhance the quality of life for both the children and their families through physical, emotional, and psychosocial support (Lindenfelser et al., 2008, 2012; Kammin et al., 2024).

The prevalence of life-limiting conditions in children and young people has risen, increasing from 26.7 per 10,000 to 63.2 per 10,000 between 2001 and 2018 in England (Fraser et al., 2021). Many of these children are dependent on medical technologies such as ventilators (Mann et al., 2019) or gastrostomy feeds (Taylor et al., 2019; Fisher et al., 2023) and might require numerous medications for treating their primary condition or managing pain and other symptoms (Fisher et al., 2023).

Parents or guardians are often expected to provide complex and extensive care with limited external support (Ronan et al., 2020; Fisher et al., 2023). This caregiving role includes a broad spectrum of responsibilities including delivering personal, emotional, and medical care, advocating in educational and healthcare settings, researching to make informed medical decisions, organising daily activities and transportation as well as providing usual parental care (Verberne et al., 2017; Fisher et al., 2023). Paediatric palliative care plays a crucial role for many of these children and families, often beginning at the time of diagnosis through to post-bereavement (Chambers, 2018; Fisher et al., 2023).

Music therapy in paediatric palliative care

The World Federation of Music Therapy defines music therapy as the 'professional use of music and its elements as an intervention in medical, educational and everyday environments with individuals, groups families or communities who seek to optimise their quality of life and improve their physical, social, communicative, emotional, intellectual and spiritual health and wellbeing' (World Federation of Music Therapy, 2011). Research indicates that goals outlined by the World Health Organisation for palliative care can be addressed through music therapy, including reduction of anxiety, pain, increasing emotional expression and improving family interactions (Kammin et al., 2024). However, current music therapy literature in palliative care is predominantly focussed on adult palliative care, bereavement, end of life or oncology patients (Clark et al.,2014; Daveson &Kennelly, 2000; Kammin et al., 2024; Zuckerman, 2019).

While the benefits of music therapy in paediatric palliative care are recognised, there is a paucity of evidence in this area, leading to considerable variability in its provision within and across countries. There is an urgent need for high-quality research to develop and sustain these services, particularly research that involves children and families articulating their own experiences with music therapy. Positioning lived experience and service user perspectives as central to service provision and development is essential. Currently, these voices, along with other stakeholder experiences, are underrepresented in the existing literature, and as a result, do not significantly contribute to service development (Kammin et al., 2024).

Lived experience

Lived experience refers to the knowledge gained through direct, personal engagement with a particular condition or situation (Gov.uk, 2024). Individuals with lived experience are considered experts by experience, offering a deep understanding derived from their own experiences which cannot be replicated by theoretical knowledge (Byrne et al., 2018; Bibb, 2022).

Lived experience has emerged as a distinct discipline, becoming a recognised and valued profession (Byrne & Wykes, 2020). This field is grounded in its own unique philosophy and values, which emphasises the significance of personal narratives in shaping practice and policy. Lived experience work is inherently emancipatory and values-based, rooted in a commitment to social justice (Gillard et al., 2017). It highlights the pivotal role of individuals with lived experience as catalysts for change, advocating for systemic improvements and greater inclusivity in service provision (Gillard et al., 2015). By integrating lived experience into service development, the relevance and impact of services are enhanced while ensuring that the voices of those directly affected are heard and valued.

Lived experience in music therapy practice and research

The music therapy profession is critically examining the power dynamics between therapists and clients, advocating for a shift from changing individuals to transforming systems (Hadley, 2013). Viewing music therapy as an intervention applied to service users can create inherent power imbalances (Pickard, 2020; Davies, 2022). Instead, a client-centred approach that values and incorporates the expertise and lived experiences of clients should be prioritised. This approach challenges the traditional notion of the therapist as the expert and promotes a collaborative model where client and therapist co-create the therapeutic process (Baines, 2013). Promoting lived experience as a guiding principle in music therapy practice, theory, research, and training is essential. Baines (2021) highlights the importance of placing client expertise and lived experience at the forefront, advocating for a collaborative approach that addresses the power imbalances inherent in traditional therapeutic relationships.

Origins of the book: our story

Julie Russell (co-editor)

Vicky was my son Fraser's music therapist at the children's hospice in which we were supported. We have stayed in touch since Fraser's passing, and I've supported Vicky with raising awareness of music therapy in children's palliative care with information, photographs and videos that she has needed for presentations. We have contributed a chapter about Fraser's musical story to a music therapy book (*Music Therapy in Children and Young People's Palliative Care*, Ludwig, 2019).

It was in November 2022, when we both had chance to meet up for the first time in several years, that we discussed how we could spread the word about the positive elements of music therapy for the whole family within a variety of paediatric palliative care settings. We began to consider a potential book, where the voices of the children and families supported by children's palliative care services would be heard, explaining how music therapy had affected them and what legacy it leaves in their lives. We were keen to get a broad spectrum of contributors from a diversity of backgrounds, cultures and experiences for the book and ensure their stories were at the forefront of every chapter.

Vicky Kammin (co-editor)

Julie and I met again in November 2022 over lunch in my hometown, and hers during childhood. As we reminisced and caught up on our lives, it was clear that our profound connection forged through our shared experiences with her son Fraser remained at the core of our relationship. During our animated discussions, I shared my research on child and family experiences of music therapy in paediatric palliative care and involvement with the Paediatric Palliative Care Research Group at the University of York. We talked about how this role had introduced me to Patient and Public Involvement and their Family Advisory Board and how it had resonated deeply with my collaborative approach with families developed over the years working in children's hospice care.

The seeds of our book began to take root as I tentatively suggested we might co-edit a book together and provide an opportunity to amplify these voices through a book written collaboratively by families and music therapists. Our shared commitment to highlighting lived experiences and shaping music therapy practice where our relationship had begun found a home in this collaboration, placing lived experience at the centre of practice development.

This book has had many ripple effects in our personal and professional lives: Julie is now an active member of the Paediatric Palliative Care Research Group, Patient and Public Involvement Family Advisory Board at the University of York, where I'm undertaking my PhD on child and family experiences of music therapy in children's palliative care. She is also undertaking considerable work with researchers, professionals and families in paediatric palliative care as well as collaborating with me on different projects.

Diversity

In crafting this book, we sought to capture a wide range of voices and experiences to reflect the rich diversity of families supported by children's palliative care services and the multitude of ways music therapy might provide support. The narratives presented span a wide range of backgrounds and highlight the importance of culturally responsive practices in music therapy which acknowledge and respect the individuality of each child and their family.

This book recognises the intersectionality of identities, understanding how factors such as race, ethnicity, gender, sexuality, disability and socioeconomic status can intersect to uniquely influence each person's experience. Through inclusive storytelling and collaborative authorship, we strive to illuminate these intersections and advocate for more personalised, diverse and equitable approaches to music therapy in paediatric palliative care.

Music therapy as a discipline is increasingly recognising and addressing issues related to diversity and minority identities within professional practice (Langford et al., 2020; Davies, 2022). However, at present the profession lacks significant diversity stemming from systemic barriers. For example, learning an instrument, which is a foundational requirement for music therapists, has increasingly become a privilege with increasing governmental cuts to the arts and the high costs associated with private lessons and purchasing instruments (McFerran & Rickson, 2014). Furthermore, currently the training required to become a qualified music therapist is expensive and might be inaccessible to many individuals, particularly those from lower socioeconomic backgrounds (Hadley, 2013).

The British Association for Music Therapy (BAMT) is engaged in a process of critical self-reflection and action concerning diversity and minority identities within professional practice. The BAMT Diversity Survey and subsequent Diversity Report in 2020 (Langford et al., 2020) exemplify these efforts, which highlight the need for increased representation across race, disability, gender, sexual orientation, and other marginalised identities (Davies,2022). By bringing these issues to light and working towards more inclusive practices, the music therapy profession must continue to strive to evolve into a profession that better reflects and serves the diverse populations it supports.

It is important to acknowledge that the diversity of the music therapist authorship in this book unfortunately does not match the diversity represented in the family voices. However, the collaborative, co-authorship approach in this book encourages active listening to and learning from families with diverse backgrounds and their lived experiences. This method not only enriches the content with a wide array of perspectives but also demonstrates the profound value of including multiple voices in therapeutic discourse. By integrating these authentic narratives, the book becomes a richer, more nuanced resource, reflecting the spectrum of experiences in paediatric palliative care. This inclusive approach serves as a call to action for the music therapy profession, urging it to continue evolving towards greater inclusivity and representation, ensuring that all voices are heard and valued in the therapeutic process. Ultimately, this book aims to contribute to a more inclusive and equitable future for music therapy in paediatric palliative care, where every individual's unique story is valued, and every voice can be heard.

Readership

We have been mindful to create an accessible text that speaks to a broad audience, including families, practitioners, allied health professionals, educators, researchers and policymakers. By doing so, we hope to foster a valued, understanding and appreciation of the role that music therapy can play in supporting children and their families in paediatric palliative care. We have encouraged authors to write using Plain English as much as possible, ensuring that this text is accessible to a broad and diverse readership. The intended audience includes, but is by no means limited to:

- Families supported by children's palliative care, who can find validation and understanding of their experiences through shared narratives.
- Music therapists, who can gain new insights to enhance their practice.
- Arts and Play therapists, who may find interdisciplinary approaches and ideas applicable to their work.
- Allied health care professionals, who can better understand the role and benefits of music therapy in holistic care.
- Educators, who can incorporate these findings into their teaching to inform future practitioners.
- Researchers, who may explore new research opportunities and theoretical frameworks.
- Service lead employers of music therapists, who can see the value and impact of these services.
- Service leads considering music therapy provision, who may be inspired to integrate these practices into their programmes.

- Funders, in the provision of evidence for the importance and effectiveness of music therapy in paediatric palliative care.
- Communications teams, fundraisers and trustees working in children's palliative care, who can better advocate for and support these services.
- Arts Therapies training courses, which can use this text as a resource for educating future therapists.
- Allied Health Professionals training courses, which can integrate these insights into their curriculum.
- Paediatric Palliative Care training courses, which can enhance their programmes with real-world applications and interdisciplinary collaboration.
- Special education training courses, which can draw on these experiences to support students in special education.

By making this book accessible to such a wide audience, we hope to foster a deeper understanding and appreciation of music therapy's role in paediatric palliative care. This inclusivity aims to inspire a broader support network, encourage interdisciplinary collaboration, and ultimately lead to more comprehensive and compassionate care for children and their families.

Collaborative co-authorship

Co-authorship and collaborative writing form the main premise of this book, permeating every aspect from the editorship to the individual chapters. This collaborative writing approach integrates both the professional and personal perspectives of music therapists and the lived experiences of families, adopting a dialogic approach which allows for both voices to be heard simultaneously. This facilitates mutual growth and change for both the client and therapist through their engagement in the therapeutic process. This method creates a shared space where personal narratives and professional insights converge, fostering a deeper exploration of the therapeutic relationship. As Thompson and Harris (2024) note, 'the meeting points of these narratives can be a catalyst for creativity and change in both the client and therapist', highlighting the transformative power of dialogical practice.

Through this publication and its recommendations for future practice, we aim to empower families with lived experience of children's palliative care, granting them the voice, autonomy, and confidence to articulate their views and shape the services that impact their lives. By embracing a more inclusive and collaborative approach, we aspire to foster equity of voice and ensure that the therapeutic process is truly client-centred and empowering.

The co-authorship process was carefully and sensitively crafted by the editors and authors to ensure it was accessible, meaningful, supportive and fulfilling for all participants. Each chapter reflects a unique mode of collaboration, tailored to the individual preferences and circumstances of the contributors. These methods included traditional writing, interview styles, walking and talking, recording voice notes and employing different creative mediums. The goal was to foster a joint collaboration, where both parties found the process enriching and could learn from one another to inform practice.

In some chapters of the book, there are very intimate stories from just one family member telling their story alongside the music therapist that had supported them. And in others we hear of larger scale projects, involving multiple children and/ families with the voices of some of those contributors being heard through statements that were made during or shortly after the project was carried out. The strong sense of collaboration between all parties whether it be from a music therapist and a small family to multiple music specialists within a large group has shone out in the writing of this book, giving a very real and true sense of the journey all participants have been on during their time together and beyond.

In this collaborative endeavour, therapists were encouraged to engage deeply, embracing vulnerability and reflecting on their own life experiences and how these shaped their therapeutic encounters. This introspective process contributed to the creation of narratives that are both personal and professionally insightful, echoing Hadley's (2013) concept of 'an intimate partnership of mutual giving, learning, and growth'.

This approach resonates with Yalom's (2002) idea of 'fellow travellers', where the traditional boundaries and power dynamics between therapists and clients are challenged. By moving from the roles of therapist and client to collaborators and co-authors, the book seeks to flatten the hierarchical structure often present in therapeutic settings. Yalom (2002) suggests that deeper, more authentic connections might emerge when both parties acknowledge their shared humanity:

> 'Perhaps the real therapy occurred at the deathbed scene, when they moved into honesty with the revelation that they were fellow travellers, both simply human, all too human'.

This shift enabled a dynamic interplay between the personal and professional dimensions of the therapeutic relationship, resulting in first-person, highly interactive accounts of therapeutic work from dual perspectives.

Through this collaborative writing approach, the book not only documents practice but also highlights the personal transformations experienced by both therapists and clients. The co-authorship process illuminates the notion that both parties evolve as a result of their engagement in psychotherapeutic processes and collaborative writing. A key contribution of this book lies in its exploration of how dialogical practices and shared narratives can drive creativity, change and growth in the field of paediatric palliative care music therapy.

We aimed to create an authentic, personal and intimate text while developing music therapy theory collaboratively with families and music therapists. Each chapter reflects a balance between personal narratives and professional insights that was negotiated between each co-author pair. Music therapists were encouraged to support families in finding this balance, while we, as co-editors with different perspectives of lived experience and professional expertise, provided guidance, support and containment throughout the process.

From the outset, we acknowledged the potential challenges and discomforts that might arise. We reflected together on how to sit with these, strategies for management and how to ensure families and music therapists felt as comfortable as possible throughout the process. We emphasised that participation was entirely voluntary and that anyone could withdraw from the project at any time.

We encouraged families to be open and honest, engaging with the process as it felt right for them. We were mindful throughout the process of families not feeling obliged to participate as can be a common dynamic in therapeutic relationships, in particular third-sector settings. By fostering an environment of mutual respect and genuine collaboration, we hoped to create a meaningful and impactful resource that was enriching for everyone involved.

Co-editor partnership

Our partnership as co-editors, each bringing a unique blend of lived experience and music therapy expertise, was integral to the collaborative process. From the onset, we established ground rules to foster openness, honesty and transparency, ensuring the protection of both our personal and professional relationships. This approach enabled us to navigate challenges together, supporting one another every step of the way.

In many ways the collaborative writing felt like an extension of our therapeutic relationship. The strong foundations of our relationship allowed us to co-author and co-edit effectively and made us especially mindful of taking care of this relationship, free from any power dynamics. The trust we built years ago facilitated the telling of our stories, and the process of writing deepened our connection and understanding.

Our distinct strengths and perspectives complemented each other well. Whether managing spreadsheets or communicating with different stakeholders, our diverse backgrounds enabled us to tackle tasks effectively, ensuring a balanced and comprehensive approach to the project. This mutual understanding also allowed us to empathise with the lived experiences of contributors from different angles, enriching the depth and authenticity of our collaboration.

As co-authors of a chapter ourselves, we experienced first-hand the vulnerability inherent in sharing personal perspectives. This first-hand experience deepened our appreciation for the courage shown by our contributors and reinforced the importance of creating a safe and containing space for all voices to be heard. We were exceptionally mindful of maintaining our strong relationship, however, rather than compromising it as we initially feared, this experience liberated and strengthened it. This theme of growth and connection was evident among our contributors, and we are profoundly grateful for the courage they displayed in sharing these intimate, moving and powerful stories.

Throughout the journey, we remained committed to fostering an environment where families and therapists felt empowered to share their stories authentically, embracing a collaborative mindset and collective expertise. Our collaborative journey as co-editors and co-authors was marked by mutual learning, respect and growth.

We extend our deepest gratitude to all the contributors whose bravery and openness enriched this project immeasurably. Your voices have made a lasting impact, and we are honoured to have been part of this transformative journey together.

Concluding thoughts

Our journey began with a commitment to amplifying the voices of families, inviting them to co-author their experiences alongside music therapists and shape the future of music therapy practice in paediatric palliative care.

We acknowledge the impactful role of music therapy in providing holistic support to children and their families in paediatric palliative care. However, despite its recognised benefits, the field still lacks comprehensive research and faces considerable variability in service provision. Our book, grounded in the lived experiences of children and families, aims to address this gap by prioritising their voices in the conversation. Through their narratives and insights, we seek to enrich the discourse surrounding music therapy in paediatric palliative care, offering a more comprehensive understanding of its impact and potential.

As our book unfolds, we invite readers to embark on this journey with us, exploring the multifaceted role of music therapy and embracing the power of collaboration where every voice is heard, and every story is valued.

References

Baines, S. (2013). A brief anti-oppressive analysis of music pedagogy, the professional musician and the music business: A case for Music therapy. *Music: Social impacts, health benefits and perspectives*, 167–182.

Bibb, J. (2022). Embedding lived experience in music therapy practice: Towards a future of co-designed, co-produced and co-delivered music therapy programs in Australia. *Australian Journal of Music Therapy*, *33*(2), 25–36.

Byrne, L. & Wykes, T. (2020). A role for lived experience mental health leadership in the age of Covid-19. *Journal of Mental Health*, *29*(3), 243–246.

Byrne, L., Stratford, A. & Davidson, L. (2018). The global need for lived experience leadership. *Psychiatric rehabilitation journal*, *41*(1), 76.

Chambers, L. (2018). A Guide to Children's Palliative Care. 4th ed. Together for Short Lives.

Clark, B. A., Siden, H. & Straatman, L. (2014). An integrative approach to music therapy in paediatric palliative care. *J Palliative Care*, 30, 179–187.

Daveson, B. A. & Kennelly, J. (2000). Music therapy in palliative care for hospitalized children and adolescents. *J Palliative Care*, *16*, 35–38.

Davies, H. (2022). 'Autism is a way of being': An 'insider perspective 'on neurodiversity, music therapy and social justice. *British Journal of Music Therapy*, *36*(1), 16–26.

Fisher, V., Fraser, L. & Taylor, J. (2023). Experiences of fathers of children with a life-limiting condition: a systematic review and qualitative synthesis. *BMJ Supportive & Palliative Care*, *13*(1), 15–26.

Fraser, L. K., Gibson-Smith, D., Jarvis, S. et al. Estimating the current and future prevalence of life-limiting conditions in children in England. *Palliative medicine* 2021; 35, 1641–1651.

Fraser, L. K., Miller, M., Hain, R. et al. (2012). Rising national prevalence of life-limiting conditions in children in England. *Paediatrics*, 129, e923–9299.

Gillard, S., Foster, R., Gibson, S., Goldsmith, L., Marks, J. & White, S. (2017). Describing a principles-based approach to developing and evaluating peer worker roles as peer support moves into mainstream mental health services. *Mental health and social inclusion*, *21*(3), 133–143.

Gillard, S., Holley, J., Gibson, S., Larsen, J., Lucock, M., Oborn, E., ... & Stamou, E. (2015). Introducing new peer worker roles into mental health services in England: comparative case study research across a range of organisational contexts. *Administration and Policy in Mental Health and Mental Health Services Research*, *42*, 682–694.

Gov.uk (2024). https://openpolicy.blog.gov.uk/2024/03/13/launching-the-lived-experience-in-policymaking-guide-reflections-on-the-principles-behaviours-and-mindsets-that-underpin-lived-experience-work.

Hadley, S. (2013). Dominant narratives: Complicity and the need for vigilance in the creative arts therapies. *The Arts in Psychotherapy*, *40*(4), 373–381.

Kammin, V. (2019). Balancing the Public and the Private. *Music Therapy in Children and Young People's Palliative Care*, *31*, 38–42.

Langford, A., Rizkallah, M. & Maddocks, C. (2020). British Association of Music Therapy diversity report.

Lindenfelser, K., Hense, C. & McFerran, K. (2012). Music therapy in pediatric palliative care: Family-centered care to enhance quality of life. *American Journal of Hospice and Palliative Medicine*, 29, 219–226.

Lindenfelser, K. J., Grocke, D. & McFerran, K. (2008). Bereaved parents' experiences of music therapy with their terminally ill child. *Journal of Music Therapy*, 45, 330–348.

Mann, K., Alvey, J. C., Marty, C., & Murphy, N. A. (2019). Health-Related quality of life and family functioning of parents of children with medical complexity. *Current Physical Medicine and Rehabilitation Reports*, 7, 23–29.

McFerran, K. S. & Rickson, D. (2014). Community music therapy in schools: Realigning with the needs of contemporary students, staff and systems. *International Journal of Community Music*, *7*(1), 75–92.

Pickard, B. (2020). A critical reflection on the Health and Care Professions Council Standards of Proficiency for music therapists: A critical disability studies perspective. *British Journal of Music Therapy*, *34*(2), 82–94.

Ronan, S., Brown, M. & Marsh, L. (2020). Parents' experiences of transition from hospital to home of a child with complex health needs: a systematic literature review. *J Clin Nurs*, 29, 3222–35.

Taylor, J., O'Neill, M., Maddison, J., Richardson, G., Hewitt, C., Horridge, K., ... & Fraser, L. K. (2019). 'Your Tube': the role of different diets in children who are gastrostomy fed: protocol for a mixed methods exploratory sequential study. *BMJ open*, *9*(10), e033831.

Thompson, T. & Harris, D. X. (2023). *Collaborative Writing and Psychotherapy: Flattening the Hierarchy Between Therapist and Client*. Taylor & Francis.

Verberne, L. M., Kars, M. C., Schouten-van Meeteren, A. Y. N. et al. (2017). Aims and tasks in parental caregiving for children receiving palliative care at home: a qualitative study. *Eur J Pediatr*, *176*, 343–54.

World Health Organisation (2023). Paediatric Palliative Care. www.who.int/europe/newsroom/fact-sheets/item/palliative-care-for-children.

World Federation of Music Technology. www.wfmt.info.

Yalom, I. D. (2002). The gift of therapy: An open letter to a new generation of therapists and their patients. *(No yitle)*.

Chapter 1

The Need for Belonging

Julie Russell and Victoria Kammin

Figure 1.1 Fraser playing the Chimes.
Photograph provided by parents.

Co-authoring process

The writing journey evolved through various forms of communication, including email, phone, online, face to face over coffee, lunch and walks as the authors reflected on shared experiences which began 18 years ago. Julie's narrative provided the foundations into which Vicky's perspectives were interwoven with supporting literature to help provide further insight into their experiences.

Through iterative exchanges, the writing process mirrored the dynamics of a therapeutic relationship. Just as therapists and clients engage in expression, listening, attuning and collaborating to facilitate growth, the authors listened to each other's ideas, attuned to one another's perspectives, and worked together to craft a cohesive and meaningful narrative. This collaborative effort not only enriched the final product but also deepened the understanding and connection between the co-authors.

Throughout this chapter, we use terms such as 'motherhood', 'family' and 'parenting' to inclusively refer to all primary caregivers and diverse family configurations. By doing so, we aim to acknowledge and celebrate the diversity of caregiving roles and family structures.

'Joining a club you never thought you'd want to be part of': New reality and beginnings

Julie

We came to Christopher's hospice in Guildford when our son Fraser was about ten months old. Fraser was born with a rare metabolic condition which meant he had both physical and developmental issues and was life-limited.

Fraser was our first child, and it came as a complete shock that he was born with his condition, as there were no signs that he was poorly during my pregnancy, and there were no known members of the family having had children with this condition.

Fraser was extremely poorly at the beginning of his life but had amazing care at various hospitals to keep him alive. But it was thought that although the medical staff were not able to identify the exact condition he had, it came under an umbrella of conditions that meant he would not survive past infancy and was therefore life-limited.

My husband Iain and I were devasted by this news. Fraser, a beautiful boy, our first child who carried hopes and dreams of a new future together, would be taken away from us, at a time not known by the professionals. His life, our lives had become a waiting game.

After the Metabolic Teams from the hospitals that had been looking after Fraser announced this outcome for him, it was a couple of months later we had a home visit from a nurse at Christopher's Children's Hospice CHASE (now part of Shooting Star Children's Hospices), just outside of Guildford in Surrey. We were living in Guildford, so the hospice was only a ten-minute drive from our house.

She came to explain what Christopher's were able to offer us, a community support worker that could be by our side throughout Fraser's life, assisting us with activities at the hospice and offering us respite care if we needed it. That was it, the moment of total reality, like joining a club you never thought you'd want to be part of but handled in such a kind, supportive and encouraging way that we realised that this was an opportunity for Fraser and one we were grateful to accept.

Vicky

I began my new post in the children's hospice where Fraser was supported as a relatively newly qualified music therapist, navigating the early days of motherhood with my eight-week-old baby and mourning the recent loss of my father. Despite the complexity of emotions I experienced, I felt passionate about working in a setting where the ethos of children's palliative care, emphasising quality of life and support for the whole family (World Health Organisation, 2023), was so unmistakably present, and the ripple effects of music therapy extended beyond the children and young people to encompass their siblings, parents, grandparents, staff and the wider community.

My role was established through the remarkable charity Jessie's Fund, which has profoundly impacted children, young people, families and professionals fortunate enough to work with them over the last thirty years. Recognising the significant opportunities that music therapy offers for emotional expression, quality family time, strengthening familial bonds, developing coping mechanisms and enhancing well-being both pre- and post-bereavement, (Amadoru & McFerran, 2007; Kammin el al., 2024; Lindenfelser et al., 2008, Lindenfelser et al., 2012; Steinhardt et al., 2021; Zuckerman, 2019) Jessie's Fund has been pivotal in establishing music therapy positions in children's hospices and hospitals in the UK and providing invaluable support to these music therapists throughout their careers.

I was learning how to be both a mother and a music therapist in a children's hospice in what felt like a symbiotic relationship. The significance of the maternal role is well-documented in the literature, with mothering reported to significantly impact child development both physically and emotionally, and to influence the psychological wellbeing of future healthy adults (Borg, 2013). Psychotherapeutic and psychoanalytic theories emphasise the importance of the maternal role and maternal elements within the therapeutic relationship (Borg, 2013).

In psychodynamic music therapy literature, the use of music to establish a therapeutic relationship is closely likened to mother-infant interaction (Dindoyal, 2017; Sobey & Woodcock, 1999). Research by Trevarthen and Malloch (2009) illustrates how infants utilise innate 'communicative musicality' to non-verbally share experiences, describing this as the 'source' of the therapeutic experience. This connection became strikingly clear through the act of musically attuning to both my baby and my clients, engaging in reciprocal interactions characterised by 'initiating, complementing, and responding to one another' (Pavlicevic, 1997).

Over time, I became increasingly aware of how the intersecting roles of mother and therapist have the potential to enrich one another when paired with robust support.

The reciprocal influence of these roles, both in training and practice, is well documented in the literature (Derry, 1992; Godfrey-Djundja, 2019; Parker et al., 2024). Recent research emphasises how this dynamic can enhance therapists' understanding and empathy towards children and their caregivers, fostering deeper relational connections (Parker et al., 2024). Additionally, Derry (1992) suggests that therapists' own children might develop into 'empathic, introspective individuals' as a result of their parents' dual role (Godfrey-Djundja, 2019)

However, Parker et al. (2024) shed light on therapists' experiences of guilt, particularly concerning the enjoyment of ordinary comforts and pleasures related to pregnancy and motherhood. With knowledge gained from training and practice in child development, attachment, and mental health (Culross et al., 2008), therapists often grapple with feelings of guilt as they navigate the delicate balance between work and parental responsibilities (Basecu, 1996; Dindoyal, 2017; Grossman, 1990; MacNab, 1995; Robinson, 2013; Zackson, 2013).

Considerable research has focused on the pregnancy period itself (Fenster et al., 1986; Fuller, 1987; Rosenthal, 1990; Parker et al., 2024), highlighting the profound impact of the pregnant therapist for both the therapist and their clients. Pregnant therapists might have questions regarding disclosure, transference, and countertransference feelings, navigating the evolving nature of therapeutic relationships from dyadic to triadic while making sense of the therapeutic process. The dual role of therapist and mother offers opportunities for personal and professional growth but also presents unique challenges that require careful reflection and support.

In the context of paediatric palliative care, therapists who might have, be expecting or hope to have children in the future, inhabit a distinctive realm where they work alongside other parents confronting their 'greatest fear' – the potential loss of a child (Parker et al., 2024). The pregnant therapist symbolises the complexity of this situation, embodying both hope and vulnerability. A well-supported pregnant therapist in this clinical context holds potential to address complex issues within therapeutic practice, including separation, loss, envy, and sibling rivalry (Fenster et al., 1986; Grossman, 2013). However, without adequate support, these therapists risk encountering emotional overwhelm and diminished therapeutic presence, negatively impacting both their well-being and the quality of support provided (Fenster et al., 1986; Grossman, 2013). Therefore, the significance of robust support systems for pregnant therapists in paediatric palliative care cannot be overstated as they navigate the delicate equilibrium between personal and professional identities in their practice.

Working in a children's hospice offers a unique perspective that can be both life-affirming and anxiety-inducing, requiring continuous personal and professional reflection and support. The framework established by Jessie's Fund, initially offering two three-hour music therapy sessions per week to children's hospices, enabled me in the early stages of motherhood to work while my husband cared for our baby. This arrangement in the main alleviated feelings of guilt or conflict stemming from my dual roles as a therapist and a mother (Basecu, 1996), allowing me to devote myself to fostering relationships with the children, young people, and families at work. Witnessing first-hand the fierce love and protective instincts of these families towards their children, alongside constant reminders of life's fragility in this setting profoundly influenced my approach to motherhood. Through the lens of paediatric palliative care, I gleaned invaluable insights about both living and dying from children and families in this context, profoundly shaping my perspective as a therapist-mother.

Rowley (2021) highlights the importance of developing personal self-care strategies to mitigate burnout and maintain well-being among therapists in palliative care settings. I was mindful of the emotional impact of the work, my own experiences of loss and grief and the constant strive to be good enough both as a mother and a therapist (Lyndon, 2014) and recognised the significance of self-care, supportive structures, and clinical supervision in this context (Hermann et al., 2018). Over the years I have worked on developing individualised self-care practices and support systems that are sustainable and effective for me. These practices encompass writing clinical and process notes diligently before leaving work, using my commute as a transitional period between work and home, participating in regular clinical supervision and accessing support systems like debriefs and peer support.

Alongside this I seek solace in mindfulness and nature-oriented activities like open air swimming, walking, and cycling, which provide a sense of freedom and rejuvenation, 'unrestricted by physical boundaries' (Rowley 2021). Surrounding myself with supportive networks of family, friends and parent groups also reinforce my sense of adequacy and resilience.

Reading Julie's poignant description of entering a club she never wished to join provided me with a lens through which to articulate a narrative that has been ever present for me throughout my journey in paediatric palliative care, especially during the formative years of my own children. While Julie and her husband, Iain, adapted to their new reality, I made a deliberate choice to pursue a career in paediatric palliative care despite being a young mother with unchanged hopes and dreams for their own child. This difference felt stark, I had control over my decision to work in this field, whereas these families had no choice but to face the reality that their child was dying. This profound contrast heightened my awareness of life's fragility, deepening my empathy and commitment to providing compassionate and meaningful support to these children and families.

Conversations surrounding my work often elicit societal discomfort, offering me insights into the initial apprehension families might experience when seeking palliative care services. However, my close involvement with children and families in this setting have significantly deepened my understanding of life, loss, grief and death. Julie, Iain, Fraser and all the families I've had the privilege to work alongside have taught me so much more about living and quality of life than dying.

Engaging with the community and fostering discussions that destigmatise death and dying, while being mindful of individual circumstances, cultural nuances, and past bereavements, is essential. Societal discomfort surrounding discussions of death often stems from fear, uncertainty and a lack of familiarity with the end-of-life process. By addressing these topics with empathy and sensitivity, we can help create a more supportive environment for those navigating palliative care and foster broader societal awareness of death and dying. Embracing these conversations has the potential to empower individuals and communities to navigate end-of-life experiences with greater understanding and compassion.

'A BIG HUG': Community and belonging

Julie

I have described Christopher's as a 'BIG HUG', as every time we visited; we were so warmly welcomed by all the staff. It was clear that it was going to be a sanctuary for us, away from the ever-progressing world. When your life changes so utterly profoundly, you find yourself on the other side of the train track. Life doesn't stop; it keeps moving along at the same speed as the life you were meant to have, the life that your friends and family and indeed strangers are having around you, but you are witnessing it from the other side. Because of Fraser's medical needs and fragility, I knew that trying to fit in with a daily and weekly routine of baby activities with other new mothers in the local area was not going to work. This was to me and is to any new mother in this situation a complete loss and such an isolating experience. It was important to both my husband and I that we found a place in our local community for Fraser, that he had somewhere to belong.

Christopher's and in particular our hospice community worker Tanya were fantastic at understanding that. She helped us to 'shape our week' around activities for Fraser that gave us a reason to get out of the house, go somewhere he could experience positive activities in an environment that could support him and me. I believe that this tailor-made approach to hospice care was quite unique at the time, but it is something I am forever grateful for.

Fraser's week turned out to be a busy one with activities like hydrotherapy, supported by a wonderful volunteer Jan, a small playgroup where Fraser could play with other children similar in age and where I got to spend time with other parents and music therapy.

Vicky

Julie's description of the hospice as a 'big hug' resonates deeply with the ethos of paediatric palliative care in supporting the whole family (World Health Organisation, 2023; Together for Short Lives 2024). This sentiment echoes my own experience upon entering the hospice, where both families and staff were enveloped by a nurturing environment akin to a family, providing a sense of belonging and community. Under the guidance of an inspirational director of care at this time, characterised by care, warmth, and compassion, the multidisciplinary team evolved into a supportive unit. Our shared mission of supporting children and families facing adversity united us, fostering a culture of collaboration, innovation, creativity and mutual support.

This collaborative ecosystem exemplifies the principles of Person-Centred Practice (McCormack et al., 2021) within the hospice setting, where each member is valued and contributes to a holistic approach to care. By prioritising these principles, hospices aim to empower staff to deliver individualised care tailored to the unique needs and preferences of each child and family, while also ensuring that staff members are well-supported, enabling them to effectively fulfil their caregiving roles. This holistic approach not only enhances the quality of care provided but also cultivates a sense of belonging and camaraderie among staff members, despite their diverse roles and responsibilities.

'Person-centredness is an approach to practice established through the formation and fostering of healthful relationships between all care providers, service users and others significant to them in their lives. It is underpinned by values of respect for persons (personhood), individual right to self-determination, mutual respect and understanding. It is enabled by cultures of empowerment that foster continuous approaches to practice development' (McCormack et al., 2013).

By the time I met Fraser my eldest son was two-and-a-half, and my youngest was 12 months old, the same age as Fraser. I remember going to visit Julie and Fraser in their home for my initial visit alongside Tanya their community team key worker. I was struck by Fraser, his blond hair and big blue eyes, his resemblance to my youngest son and his loving mother who welcomed me, yet another, professional, another stranger, into their home. We chatted and played with Fraser, spoke about music and reflected together on whether music therapy might be something that they would like to try. Julie's enthusiasm was palpable, perhaps stemming from their family's musical background and the potential of this medium to offer non-medical, holistic support in the hospice at a time when the family were seeking community and a sense of belonging.

The potential of music therapy to foster a sense of community within palliative care settings, thereby enhancing family well-being and quality of life, is well-documented (Bradt & Dileo, 2010; Dileo & Loewy, 2005; Heath & Lings, 2012; Hilliard, 2003; Lindenfelser, 2005; Lindenfelser et al., 2012; Nall & Everitt, 2005; McConnell & Porter, 2016; O'Kelly & Koffman 2007; Vanstone-Howe, 2019; Vedel et al., 2014). I was hopeful that music therapy, the hospice and its community could provide this support and sense of belonging to the family as they began to process their new reality.

'Monday mornings were something to look forward to': Routine and reprieve

Julie

Monday mornings were something to look forward to, and I don't know if I had ever felt that before coming to Christopher's. This was our music therapy time with our Music Therapist, Vicky Kammin. Fraser started having sessions with her at about a year old. Both my husband and I are musical and could see Fraser responded well to music at home. So when we were offered to have music therapy sessions with Vicky, we jumped at the chance.

Vicky would come to the lounge to meet us, just before the session. Full of happiness and enthusiasm, Vicky brightened up our day immediately and having this regular start to our week was so important, especially if we had spent the weekend in our local hospital dealing with Fraser's unstable condition.

Fraser would respond immediately when he saw Vicky and heard her voice. It would be smiles all round when we had a little catch up before each session, just to see how Fraser was and how he was doing that day.

After that, Vicky and Fraser went off to the Music Therapy room for their session and I was given the time to relax, have a cup of tea and chat to all the wonderful staff and volunteers, knowing I could relax for that precious time.

Upon Fraser's return, he would be so animated and full of smiles, I just knew he'd had the best time. It was also interesting to see just how alert he was after each session, sort of switched on to the environment around him, taking things in. This is where the therapy extended outside of the therapy room, not just for him but also for me. The world might have been progressing, but so were we.

Vicky

Families supported by paediatric palliative care express a strong desire for normalcy, (Aasgaard, 2002; Beecham et al., 2019; Hynson, 2012; Namisango et al., 2019; McFerran & Sheridan, 2004) as illness significantly disrupts their daily lives. It is recognised that parents are often expected to become 'providers of healthcare for children with very complex needs' (Fraser et al., 2021), with higher incidences of physical and mental health challenges reported in mothers (Fraser et al., 2020) and fathers needs becoming increasingly considered (Fisher et al., 2023).

Music therapy is acknowledged for its role in providing access to these much-needed normalised experiences (Amadoru & McFerran, 2007; Zuckerman, 2019) in its ability to meet the individual needs of children with life-limiting conditions (Amadoru & McFerran, 2007; Lindenfelser et al., 2008; Lindenfelser et al., 2012; Zuckerman, 2019). This is attributed to the accessibility and adaptability of music therapy (Amadoru & McFerran, 2007; Lindenfelser et al., 2008; Lindenfelser et al., 2012; Zuckerman, 2019), which can be delivered at the most suitable time and setting for children and their families. Kammin et al., (2024) highlight the capacity of music therapy to address the emotional and physical needs of both children and parents, providing reprieve from the demands of caregiving (Amadoru & McFerran, 2007; Groen, 2007; Lindenfelser et al., 2008; Lindenfelser et al., 2012; McConnell & Porter, 2016; Steinhardt et al., 2021; Zuckerman, 2019).

Reflecting upon my transition from a career-oriented lifestyle to one centred around family, I gained a profound appreciation for the importance of routine and communal support in parenthood. The camaraderie found in parenting groups provided crucial structure, support and respite. Families supported by palliative care services face significant challenges such as managing complex medical needs, navigating emotional distress and coping with the uncertainties of their child's condition (Hain et al., 2021). These responsibilities often extend beyond traditional caregiving roles (Fraser et al., 2020), placing immense physical, emotional and psychological strain on parents and caregivers (Fraser et al., 2021; Hain et al., 2021). Consequently, the provision of respite becomes imperative for families in paediatric palliative care, offering them much-needed relief from the demands of their caregiving duties (Whiting, 2021). However, challenges such as fear of leaving home, heightened infection risks, and limited inclusive opportunities or specialist provisions make accessing this essential support very difficult (Kirk & Glendinning, 2002; Steele & Davies, 2006). This highlights the necessity of ensuring that respite care is accessible and tailored to the unique needs of families with life-limited children, providing a vital lifeline that sustains their well-being and capacity to care.

Keeping this in mind, Julie and I deliberated on the optimal structure for Fraser's sessions, recognising the importance of finding the best time for the family and providing much-needed routine and structure. We agreed that adopting a schedule similar to traditional psychotherapeutic norms – weekly sessions held at the same time and place when Fraser was well – could provide a regular, consistent, and safe space for therapy while also offering much-needed routine. This approach not only provided physical and emotional reprieve for Julie but also allowed her and Fraser to gradually explore moments of independence. This is akin to the concept of a secure base proposed by Bowlby (1969), where the caregiver serves as a source of safety and support for exploration. We scheduled sessions for Monday morning, providing structure after the weekend, followed by a hydrotherapy session with a volunteer healthcare assistant and opportunities for socialisation over coffee or lunch with other parents, if they felt like it.

I eagerly anticipated my Monday morning sessions with Fraser and still remember them vividly. He was one of the first children I worked with over an extended period, providing me with the opportunity to build strong therapeutic relationships with him, Julie and later his father, Iain. Fraser radiated a gentle curiosity and a quiet charm that touched everyone around him. He often evoked profound maternal sentiments in me, strengthened further perhaps by his likeness to my youngest son, who was the same age. As we explored the potential of music therapy together, it became evident that individual sessions allowed Fraser to express himself using a medium that was accessible and to develop a relationship without the need for words.

When I recall my sessions with Fraser, the image of the chimes percussion instrument immediately comes to mind. The reflective surface of the chimes caught and played with the light, drawing Fraser's attention and sparking his curiosity. The instrument's design allowed it to be positioned close to his dominant movements, enabling independent play. The gentle, resonant tones produced by even the slightest touch provided immediate auditory feedback, which seemed to excite Fraser every time he sounded them. I vividly remember how hard he tried to make them ring. Although he sometimes got frustrated, the challenge and anticipated reward seemed to spur him on to keep trying, his face lighting up with excitement each time he successfully made them sound. Fraser quickly grasped that his movements not only produced sounds but also influenced my musical responses, and he seemed to delight in the opportunity for interactive musical dialogues where he held agency and control.

Fraser's palpable excitement, determination and strength of character during our sessions was infectious, I found myself eagerly returning to the lounge afterwards to share anecdotes with Julie from our session. Witnessing their reunion and observing the joy and pride radiate from Julie's expression upon hearing about Fraser's experiences was profoundly moving. I felt compelled to celebrate his ability to thrive despite his life-limiting condition, recognising the importance of a parent hearing about their child's successes in comparison with the continual reports of limitations and uncertain futures that often characterise the landscape of children's palliative care.

Kammin et al. (2024) highlight the unique benefits of music therapy for this population, emphasising that children not only engage with the intervention but also thrive in unexpected ways (Amadoru & McFerran, 2012; Lindenfelser et al., 2008; Lindenfelser et al., 2012; Steinhardt et al., 2021; Walden et al., 2020; Zuckerman, 2019). Music therapy has the potential to identify and promote children's healthy aspects and their capacity to flourish despite illness or disability (Amadoru & McFerran 2012; Kammin et al., 2024; Lindenfelser et al., 2008; Lindenfelser et al., 2012; Walden et al., 2020; Zuckerman, 2019). By supporting children in developing their identity beyond their life-limiting condition, music therapy can facilitate moments of celebration and foster lasting memories which hold particular significance in this context (Amadoru & McFerran 2012; Kammin et al., 2024; Lindenfelser et al., 2008; Lindenfelser et al., 2012). Kammin et al. (2024) illustrate the transformative perspectives gained through music therapy, where families' experiences are reframed from focusing on losses to recognising strengths, thereby enhancing their resilience (Amadoru & McFerran, 2012; Zuckerman, 2019).

'Our moment to be proud parents to our son and for Fraser to shine': Performing and Thriving

Julie

Thanks to Vicky's ongoing programme of Music Therapy at Christophers, a couple of opportunities arose for Fraser during the following year to be included in bigger music therapy projects, based at the hospice. He was invited to a three-day workshop with players from the Royal Philharmonic Orchestra to create music in small groups with other children who attend the hospice. Fraser had a wonderful hospice carer Kylie look after him during the day and care for all his needs while joining in the workshops and enabling him to create his own music on various instruments. At the end of the three days, a performance of the music was performed by the players, the children and their workshop carers. As parents were not involved in the workshop, we had the very exciting prospect of seeing our child perform (and on a stage!). This was so important to us as we knew Fraser would never be Joseph or a star or even a sheep in a Nativity play at school – just another one of those reasons for grieving what might have been; but this was our moment to be proud parents to our son and for Fraser to shine. And shine he did, what an incredible evening of music, achievement, love, determination and pride – so, so much pride.

Another opportunity for Fraser was to take part in a music session that was filmed and included in a TV programme called 'Over The Rainbow', a charity fundraising programme highlighting the need for musical experiences for not just life-limiting children but children with special needs. It was an uplifting experience to be a part of, and I think Fraser loved just a little the attention he got that day from the wonderful Anneka Rice!

Music Therapy at Christopher's gave our family so many things it's hard to convey them all. The special relationship that Fraser and Vicky had – developed through trust, understanding and a joint love of music. The ability to see our son as a child with abilities greater than was first thought possible achieve and enjoy music and all it can provide. To give my husband and I the chance to include our love of music into Fraser's life in a way that was accessible to him and sit proudly in the audience and quietly cry with pride and love for his achievements.

Figure 1.2 Fraser full of smiles at the garden reception after the Festival of Music.
Photograph provided by parents.

Vicky

As our therapeutic relationship developed, significant opportunities arose to include the family and wider community in the music therapy work. I am acutely aware of the multiple opportunities I have had to share my own children's successes, celebrate them and create lifelong memories through school assemblies, nativity plays and similar events. Children and young people in paediatric palliative care often do not have the same opportunities to perform in formal arenas as other children, thereby missing important and memorable experiences for both child and family that are perhaps taken for granted in other environments. These lack of opportunities could compound the losses experienced by children and families in a children's hospice, making these moments of celebration and performance even more essential for this life-limited population, as they create lasting memories and support continuing bonds (Kammin, 2019).

Research highlights the therapeutic potential of performance-based interventions in enhancing self-expression, social interaction, and emotional well-being (Ansdell, 2005; Kammin, 2019; Kildea, 2007; Pavlicevic & Ansdell, 2004; O'Grady, 2008; Stige et al., 2010; Tsiris et al., 2022). There was an opportunity to include Fraser in two music therapy projects collaborating with orchestral musicians, one of which was televised. This provided Fraser with the opportunity to lead a composition that focused on and celebrated his individual ability while expressing himself musically within a group setting and sharing this through performance with his family. The benefits of performance for this population include opportunities for self-expression, sharing, developing a sense of pride and self-esteem, celebrating life, normalised experiences, and memory making (Kammin, 2019). Performance in this setting has the potential to frame significant and important moments and create lasting memories when balanced with robust ethical consideration (Kammin 2019; Farrant, C., et al., 2014). Central to the use of performance in this context is carefully considering boundaries, monitoring client consent and prioritising safe practice (Kammin, 2019).

These collaborative initiatives allowed for engagement with the wider community, offering two-fold benefits. Integrating children's hospices into the community can support children, young people and families in palliative care by fostering a sense of belonging, inclusion in their local communities and feelings of being understood and welcomed. This engagement can also help raise societal awareness of the experiences of those supported by children's palliative care, quality of life and living as well as death and dying (Froggatt et al., 2007). Additionally, such engagement provides opportunities to identify barriers to accessing services, challenge perceptions of hospice care, and increase awareness and uptake of these services (Kirk & Fraser, 2014).

'He was a boy who had a full life and a life full of music': Our Final Goodbye

Julie

Vicky was there when Fraser's health declined unexpectedly one night in hospital, and Iain and I decided to take Fraser to Christopher's for end-of-life care. Although we thought we might lose him on the short car journey there, he rallied when we carried him through the front doors, sensing where he was, in the place he loved so much. Fraser was with us for another five days and during that time Vicky was able to come and see Fraser, giving adapted music therapy sessions to our little boy.

These were poignant and moving times as we were trying to process what was happening to our family, and how we were saying goodbye to Fraser. Those sessions continue to be held close in our hearts, and we are forever grateful to Vicky for her involvement during that time.

The recording of the chimes that Fraser played during the Royal Philharmonic Orchestra performance was played at his funeral, for everyone to hear. You see, Fraser was so much more than a little sick boy, to us and those special, wonderful people that choose to support children like Fraser, he was a boy who had a full life and a life full of music.

Vicky

I received a phone call from Tanya, Fraser's community team member from the hospice, informing me that Fraser had very suddenly deteriorated and had been admitted to the hospice for end-of-life care. The news shocked me deeply. In the context of children's hospice care, where we support children and young people from diagnosis to end-of-life or transition to adult services, uphold the hospice ethos of focusing on quality of life and often witness fragile young lives defy medical predictions, there can be an institutional culture of death avoidance (Barnett et al., 2021; Hawley, 2017; Wong et al., 2011). While this culture might help to develop coping mechanisms addressing the presence of mortality, there is a delicate balance between necessary and healthy psychological defences and those that constitute barriers to essential emotional processing, posing a risk for burnout (Stensland & Landsman, 2017). This can lead to challenges when faced with the reality of death.

Fraser, Julie and Iain found themselves thrust into a new reality as they entered a different phase of their journey. The phone call afforded me time to grasp the situation, process my own emotions and contemplate the role of music therapy – what I could offer, how I could support them and what potential music therapy held in this context. Though I had previous experience working with children at the end of life, facing this with a child and family I had been working so closely with was an entirely new challenge.

I reflected on how I could best support Fraser, Julie and Iain. Our familiar, trusting relationship felt key to guiding moments of musical expression and solace, listening to and containing their emotions, and helping to co-create enduring memories. The therapeutic relationship, the therapist's interpersonal skills and experience in paediatric palliative care are reported as integral to the success of music therapy (Kammin et al., 2024). Contro et al. (2002) highlight the pivotal role of therapeutic relationships in providing emotional and psychological support during end-of-life transitions from the family's perspective. For Fraser, music had been a medium of joy and connection, and I wanted to ensure it continued to be a source of comfort and strength for him and his family.

The literature on music therapy in end-of-life care outlines many benefits, including symptom relief, providing a medium for emotional expression and processing, facilitating communication, addressing spiritual needs and supporting the emotional and psychological well-being of service users and caregivers alike (Bradt & Dileo, 2010; Graham-Wisener et al., 2018). Tsiris et al. (2022) suggest that music can create a space conducive to embracing, expressing and celebrating the 'unknown tensions and resolutions of living and dying'. However, Bradt and Dileo (2010) and McConnell et al. (2016) highlight a lack of robust evidence supporting the efficacy of music therapy in this context, highlighting the urgent need for further research.

I was acutely aware of the importance and responsibility attached to the support families receive at the end of life, as these moments are often recalled with vivid clarity (Barrett et al., 2022). The manner in which a child dies directly influences parents' ability to cope during and after the child's death (Barrett et al., 2022). Professionals involved with the family at this time have the potential to enhance the grieving process through their care and support (Barrett et al., 2022).

During Fraser's final week, we had three music therapy sessions at the hospice with the whole family. These sessions were profoundly moving, intimate, and deeply meaningful, and I felt truly privileged to be part of them. Each session commenced and ended with Fraser's customary hello and goodbye songs, establishing a sense of familiarity and comfort. The remainder of the time was spent improvising all together, with profound moments of connection and expression. Our last session took place just hours before Fraser died, there was an unspoken awareness that this was our final goodbye. These memories remain vivid in my mind even after all these years, a testament to the profound impact of those moments shared with Fraser and his family.

Before conducting end-of-life sessions, I take time to reflect on what I can offer both personally and professionally. Where appropriate, I engage with families beforehand to co-create the session, select suitable musical instruments, and arrange the room setup. Familiarising myself with the child's physical and emotional state, gaining insight into family dynamics and observing their coping mechanisms aid in my preparation and self-regulation. The availability of trusted colleagues for post-session support is crucial in assisting me with the regulation of my emotions in the moment. This combined personal and professional support provides containment and helps me navigate the emotional intricacies of the session. Centering my focus on the child and family and grounding myself through breathing techniques and the music form the cornerstone of my approach. This enables me to remain emotionally connected while keeping the family at the forefront, ensuring that their experience and grief are at the centre.

Julie and Iain invited me to see Fraser in the cold bedroom after he had died – this is a dedicated space in the hospice where children and young people can stay for a few days after their death, or until their funeral, if the family desires. Families are invited to adorn the room with their child's possessions, including cards, photographs, toys, balloons and to play music, creating a personalised and comforting environment (Forrester, 2008). The availability and manner of this support is individualised based on cultural and religious considerations. This practice, now a standard component of routine bereavement support, facilitates a transitional period that assists families in navigating the initial stages of grief, which are known to significantly impact long-term outcomes (Hackett & Beresford, 2021).

I felt deeply honoured when Julie and Iain invited me to join them in Fraser's cold bedroom after he died. I recognised the significance of this moment for both the family and me in confronting the finality of his death. Understanding the importance of preparation, both personally and professionally, I took the time needed to best support and contain their emotions while managing my own. As I entered the room, I saw Fraser resting peacefully in his lovingly prepared bed, surrounded by his treasured belongings.

What I hadn't prepared myself for was seeing Fraser in the same check pyjamas my child had been wearing when I tucked him into bed the night before. The striking resemblance between them in that moment took my breath away in the cold of the room. This shock was quickly replaced by a need to be present and supportive for Julie and Iain. This was their son, their grief, and I wanted to ensure I could support them the best way I could in this moment and in its memory. I quickly regained my composure, determined to be fully present and supportive. This time with Fraser, Julie and Iain is etched in my memory, creating an unspoken bond between the three of us – a shared experience that feels ever-present and driving our experiences in writing this chapter and co-editing this book.

Dindoyal (2017) describes the intense countertransference feelings that can be experienced linked to maternal identities. She reports on her study findings of a music therapist working with a child who shared the same name and age as her own and how these close parallels can evoke a painful, personal response. In their poignantly titled book *When Professionals Weep*, Katz et al. (2016) explore emotional and countertransference responses in end-of-life care, validating these emotional responses and emphasising the importance of processing them to prevent compassion fatigue and burnout.

Rowley (2021) illustrates the unique aspects of working in palliative care and the challenge of maintaining clear boundaries with clients, particularly when clinicians identify with their clients. Abendroth and Flannery (2006) explored the risk of compassion fatigue in palliative care nurses, revealing that a significant portion faced moderate to high risk, with a substantial number in the high-risk category. This highlights the challenge practitioners face in navigating their own emotional landscapes while delivering high-quality care. Consequently, supportive structures within professional environments and robust self-care practices are essential. In my experience, clinical supervision, self-reflection, peer support and self-care have been crucial in maintaining this balance.

Concluding thoughts

Together we explored the profound experiences of music therapy within a children's hospice through the lens of motherhood, capturing the journey from referral to end of life and post-bereavement. The chapter has illuminated the reciprocal nature of therapeutic practice, highlighting how music therapy has the potential to foster mutual growth among children, young people, families and therapists alike. Through personal experience and professional practice, this chapter delved into the complex landscape of children's palliative care and the potential of music therapy to provide connection and comfort, helping families create lasting memories. While the need for robust evidence to substantiate its benefits remains pressing, the stories shared here illustrate the transformative power of music therapy in paediatric palliative care settings.

Families supported by paediatric palliative care can help shape society's understanding of life, loss, and grief and reinforce the critical importance of compassionate, person-centred care. Music therapists working in this field require a commitment to self-care, professional support and ongoing reflection to navigate the emotional complexities involved. The resilience and love shown by these families inspire and guide professionals working in this setting and illustrate the profound impact of truly empathetic and meaningful support. Through this shared journey, we are reminded that the power of music and human connection can transcend the most challenging circumstances, leaving an indelible mark on all who are touched by it.

Vicky

I am deeply grateful to Fraser, Julie and Iain for the profound and memorable experiences we shared. These moments have significantly influenced my work with many other children and families, as well as my own mothering. Introducing Julie to Patient and Public Involvement as part of the Paediatric Palliative Care Research Group at the University of York and witnessing the profound impact she and her family's experiences bring, as well as the meaning this has brought to her, has highlighted her invaluable contributions. Today, Julie is rightly sought after by many researchers, professionals and families in paediatric palliative care, and I am proud to have witnessed and shared in her profound contributions. My sincerest thanks go to you Julie for co-editing this book with me; it has been an incredible experience to work with you again, relive our shared story and curate the moving and powerful narratives of children and families' journeys through music therapy.

Julie

Little did I know the first day I met Vicky when she and our community worker Tanya came to our home from the hospice to introduce the idea of music therapy sessions for Fraser, that this would be the start of an extremely fulfilling relationship that has grown over the years, during Fraser's life and to this day. In Vicky's true professional manner, my family didn't know about her family life and the impact having a family of her own and looking after others in a palliative setting might have on her. Her reliability, creativity and enthusiasm to support Fraser and my husband and I through a musical journey together was only ever at the forefront of her mind. Over the years since Fraser's passing, we have worked together to share that musical journey with others. In doing so, this has deepened our friendship and understanding of each other's perspective of those sessions and experiences with Fraser but in the wider sense, broadened our understanding of the legacy of that experience for both families and music therapists alike. It has been a great privilege over the years to see Vicky's enthusiasm and drive to improve access and understanding in developing family centred practice in music therapy in paediatric palliative care settings and I am so proud of all her achievements during this time. When Vicky tentatively suggested co-editing a book about the lived experience of children and families receiving music therapy in various paediatric settings I was, I confess a little nervous. This was definitely new territory to me. But of course, that ever constant, enthusiasm, reassurance and support that I have always received from Vicky has been there to help guide both of us in this 'new chapter' of our lives. I have always said that the ripples of Fraser's life will go on, and they do every day, in many different ways. This, thanks to Vicky has led me to have the great pleasure of meeting and working alongside all the collaborators in this book and to feel close to the families and the children that are represented in it. So, Vicky, my compassionate friend, thank you.

References

Aasgaard, T. (2002). *Song creations by children with cancer: Process and meaning.* Aalborg University.

Abendroth, M., & Flannery, J. (2006). Predicting the risk of compassion fatigue: A study of hospice nurses. *Journal of Hospice & Palliative Nursing, 8*(6), 346–356.

Amadoru S & McFerran K. (2007). The role of music therapy in children's hospices. *European Journal of Palliative Care, 14*, 124–127.

Ansdell, G. (2005, November). Being who you aren't; Doing what you can't: Community music therapy & the paradoxes of performance. In *Voices: A world forum for music therapy, 5*(3).

Barnett, M. D., Reed, C. M. & Adams, C. M. (2021). Death attitudes, palliative care self-efficacy, and attitudes toward care of the dying among hospice nurses. *Journal of clinical psychology in medical settings, 28*, 295–300.

Barrett, L., Fraser, L., Noyes, J., Taylor, J. & Hackett, J. (2023). Understanding parent experiences of end-of-life care for children: a systematic review and qualitative evidence synthesis. *Palliative Medicine, 37*(2), 178–202.

Basescu C. (1996). The ongoing, mostly happy 'crisis' of parenthood and its effect on the therapist's clinical work. In: Gerson B and Gerson B (Eds) *The Therapist as a Person: Life Crises, Life Choices, Life Experiences, and their Effects on Treatment.* Hillsdale, NJ: Analytic Press, Inc, pp. 101–117.

Beecham E, Langner R, Hargrave D. et al. (2019). Children's and parents' conceptualization of quality of life in children with brain tumors: a meta-ethnographic exploration. *Qualitative health research, 29*, 55–68.

Borg, L. K. (2013). Holding, attaching and relating: a theoretical perspective on good enough therapy through analysis of Winnicott's good enough mother, using Bowlby's attachment theory and relational theory. Master's thesis, School for Social Work, Smith College.

Bowlby, J. (1969). *Attachment and loss* (No. 79). Random House.

Bradt, J. & Dileo, C. (2010). Music therapy for end-of-life care. *Cochrane Database of Systematic Reviews*, (1).

Bunt, L. & Stige, B. (2014). *Music therapy: An art beyond words*. Routledge.

Contro, N., Larson, J., Scofield, S., Sourkes, B. & Cohen, H. (2002). Family perspectives on the quality of pediatric palliative care. *Archives of pediatrics & adolescent medicine*, *156*(1), 14–19.

Derry, P. S. (1994). Motherhood and the importance of professional identity to psychotherapists. *Women & therapy*, *15*(2), 149–163.

Dileo, C. & Loewy, J. V. (2005). *Music therapy at the end of life*. Jeffrey Books.

Dindoyal, L. (2018). 'In the therapist's head and heart': An investigation into the profound impact that motherhood has on the work of a music therapist. *British Journal of Music Therapy*, *32*(2), 105–110.

Farrant, C., Pavlicevic, M., & Tsiris, G. (2014). *A guide to research ethics for arts therapists and arts & health practitioners*. Jessica Kingsley Publishers.

Fenster, S., Phillips, S. B. & Raporport, E. R. G. (1986). The Therapist's Pregnancy: Intrusion in the Analytic Space. Hillsdale, NJ: Analytic Press, Inc.

Fisher, V., Fraser, L. & Taylor, J. (2023). Experiences of fathers of children with a life-limiting condition: a systematic review and qualitative synthesis. *BMJ Supportive & Palliative Care*, *13*(1), 15–26.

Flower, C. (2008). Living with dying: Reflections on family music therapy with children near the end of life. *Music therapy with children and their families*, pp. 177–189.

Forrester, L. (2008). Bereaved parents' experiences of the use of 'cold bedrooms' following the death of their child. *International journal of palliative nursing*, *14*(12), 578–585.

Fraser, L. K., Gibson-Smith, D., Jarvis, S., Norman, P. & Parslow, R. C. (2021). Estimating the current and future prevalence of life-limiting conditions in children in England. *Palliative Medicine*, *35*(9), 1641–1651.

Fraser, L. K., Murtagh, F. E., Sheldon, T., Gilbody, S. & Hewitt, C. (2020). Health of mothers of children with a life-limiting condition: a protocol for comparative cohort study using the Clinical Practice Research Datalink. *BMJ open*, *10*(7), e034024.

Froggatt, K., Hockley, J., Parker, D. & Brazil, K. (2007). *A Good Death: Researching the End of Life*. Open University Press.

Fuller, R. L. (1987). The impact of the therapist's pregnancy on the dynamics of the therapeutic process. *Journal of the American Academy of Psychoanalysis*, *15*(1), 9–28.

Godfrey-Djundja, K. (2019). *Motherhood in the therapy room: An interpretative phenomenological analysis of the experience of mother-therapists who work with mothers who grieve for their child* (Doctoral dissertation, Middlesex University/Metanoia Institute).

Graham-Wisener, L., Watts, G., Kirkwood, J., Harrison, C., McEwan, J., Porter, S., ... & McConnell, T. H. (2018). Music therapy in UK palliative and end-of-life care: a service evaluation. *BMJ supportive & palliative care*, *8*(3), 282–284.

Groen, K. M. (2007). Pain assessment and management in end of life care: A survey of assessment and treatment practices of hospice music therapy and nursing professionals. *Journal of music therapy*, *44*(2), 90–112.

Grossman, H. (1990). The pregnant therapist: Professional and personal worlds intertwine. In: Chester N and Grossman H (Eds) The Experience and Meaning of Work in Women's Lives. Hillsdale, NJ: Lawrence Erlbaum Associates, pp. 57–82.

Grossman, H. Y. (2013). The pregnant therapist: Professional and personal worlds intertwine. In *The experience and meaning of work in women's lives*. Psychology Press, pp. 57–81.

Hackett, J. & Beresford, B. (2021). 'Cold bedrooms' and other cooling facilities in UK children's hospices, how they are used and why they are offered: A mixed methods study. *Palliative Medicine*, *35*(3), 603–610.

Hain, R., Goldman, A., Rapoport, A. & Meiring, M. (Eds). (2021). *Oxford textbook of palliative care for children*. Oxford University Press.

Hawley, P. (2017). Barriers to access to palliative care. *Palliative Care: Research and Treatment*, *10*, 1178224216688887.

Heath, B. & Lings, J. (2012). Creative songwriting in therapy at the end of life and in bereavement. *Mortality*, *17*(2), 106–118.

Hermann, M. A., Walsh, R. L. & Underwood, J. W. (2019). Experiences of school counselor mothers: A phenomenological investigation. *Professional School Counseling*, *22*(1), 2156759X19844491.

Hilliard, R. E. (2003). The effects of music therapy on the quality and length of life of people diagnosed with terminal cancer. *Journal of Music therapy*, *40*(2), 113–137.

Hynson, J. L. (2012). The child's journey: Transition from health to ill-health. *Oxford textbook of palliative care for children*, 2nd ed. Oxford: Oxford University Press, pp. 13–22.

Kammin, V., Fraser, L., Flemming, K. & Hackett, J. (2024). Experiences of music therapy in paediatric palliative care from multiple stakeholder perspectives: A systematic review and qualitative evidence synthesis. *Palliative Medicine*, *38*(3), 364–378.

Katz, R. S. & Johnson, T. A. (Eds). (2016). *When professionals weep: Emotional and countertransference responses in palliative and end-of-life care*. Routledge.

Kildea, C. (2007, July). In your own time: A collaboration between music therapy in a large pediatric hospital and a metropolitan symphony orchestra. In *Voices: A World Forum for Music Therapy*, *7*(2).

Kirk, S. & Fraser, C. (2014). Supporting Parents Caring for a Technology-Dependent Child at Home: A Research Synthesis. Child: Care, Health and Development, *40*(6), 761–774.

Kirk, S. & Glendinning, C. (2002). Supporting 'expert' parents – professional support and families caring for a child with complex health care needs in the community. *International journal of nursing studies*, *39*(6), 625–635.

Lindenfelser, K. J., Hense, C. & McFerran, K. (2012). Music therapy in pediatric palliative care: Family-centered care to enhance quality of life. *American Journal of Hospice and Palliative Medicine®*, *29*(3), 219–226.

Lindenfelser, K. J., Grocke, D. & McFerran, K. (2008). Bereaved Parents' Experiences of Music Therapy with their Terminally Ill Child. *Journal of music therapy*, *45*(3), 330–348.

Lyndon, L. G. (2013). *Pregnancy, motherhood, and career: Negotiating maternal desires and professional ambition*. The Wright Institute.

MacNab, S. S. (1995). Listening to your patients, yelling at your kids: The interface between psychotherapy and motherhood. In M. B. Sussman (Ed.), *A Perilous Calling: The Hazards of Psychotherapy Practice*. Oxford: John Wiley & Sons, pp. 37–44.

Malloch, S. & Trevarthen, C. (2009). *Communicative musicality*. Oxford: Oxford University Press.

McConnell, T., Scott, D. & Porter, S. (2016). Music therapy for end-of-life care: an updated systematic review. *Palliative medicine*, *30*(9), 877–883.

McCormack, B., Manley, K. & Titchen, A. (Eds). (2013). *Practice development in nursing and healthcare*. John Wiley & Sons.

McCormack, B., McCance, T., Bulley, C., Brown, D., McMillan, A. & Martin, S. (Eds). (2021). *Fundamentals of person-centred healthcare practice*. John Wiley & Sons.

McFerran, K. & Sheridan, J. (2004). Exploring the value of opportunities for choice and control in music therapy within a paediatric hospice setting. *Australian Journal of Music Therapy*, *15*(2004), 18–32.

Nall, K. & Everitt, E. (2005). From hospice to home: Music therapy outreach. *Music therapy in children's hospices: Jessies fund in action*, pp. 147–158.

Namisango, E., Bristowe, K., Allsop, M. J., Murtagh, F. E., Abas, M., Higginson, I. J., ... & Harding, R. (2019). Symptoms and concerns among children and young people with life-limiting and life-threatening conditions: a systematic review highlighting meaningful health outcomes. *The Patient-Patient-Centered Outcomes Research*, *12*, 15–55.

O'Grady, L. (2008). The role of performance in music-making: An interview with Jon Hawkes. In *Voices: a world forum for music therapy*, *8*(2).

O'Kelly, J. & Koffman, J. (2007). Multidisciplinary perspectives of music therapy in adult palliative care. *Palliative medicine*, *21*(3), 235–241.

Oldfield, A. & Flower, C. (2008). *Music Therapy with Children and their Families*. Jessica Kingsley Publishers.

Parker, M. M., Glickman, C., Carnes-Holt, K. & Meany-Walen, K. (2024). Qualitative exploration of the duality of mothers who are play therapists: A feminist perspective. *International Journal of Play Therapy*, *33*(1), 40–51. https://doi.org/10.1037/pla0000211.

Pavlicevic, M. & Ansdell, G. (2004). *Community music therapy*. Jessica Kingsley Publishers.

Robinson, L. C. (2013). Therapist as Mother, and Mother as Therapist: The Reciprocity of Parenting and Profession for Female Psychoanalytic Psychotherapists. Ann Arbor, MI: ProQuest Information & Learning.

Rosenthal, E. S. (1990). The therapist's pregnancy: Impact on the treatment process. *Clinical Social Work Journal*, *18*(3), 213–226.

Rowley, A. (2021). Don't forget your oxygen mask! Caring for ourselves so that we can better care for our clients. *British Journal of Music Therapy*, *35*(1), 27–33.

Sobey, K. & Woodcock, J. (1999). Psychodynamic music therapy. *Process in the arts therapies*, 132–154.

Steele, R. & Davies, B. (2006). Impact on parents when a child has a progressive, life-threatening illness. *International journal of palliative nursing*, *12*(12), 576–585.

Steinhardt, T. L., Mortvedt, S. & Trondalen, G. (2021). Music therapy in the hospital-at-home: A practice for children in palliative care. *British Journal of Music Therapy*, *35*(2), 53–62.

Stensland, M. & Landsman, M. (2017). Burnout among Iowa hospice workers: a test of the job demands-resources model. *Journal of social work in end-of-life & palliative care*, *13*(4), 219–238.

Stige, B. (2017). *Where music helps: Community music therapy in action and reflection*. Routledge.

Together for Short Lives (2024). www.togetherforshortlives.org.uk/about-us.

Tsiris, G., Hockley, J. & Dives, T. (2022). Musical care at the end of life: Palliative care perspectives and emerging practices. In N. Spiro & K. R. Sanfilippo (Eds), *Collaborative insights: Interdisciplinary perspectives on musical care throughout the life course*. Oxford University Press, pp. 119–145.

Vanstone-Howe, N. (2019). Fostering the Relationship between Parent and Child using Music Therapy. *Music Therapy in Children and Young People's Palliative Care*, 99.

Vedel, I., Ghadi, V., Lapointe, L., Routelous, C., Aegerter, P. & Guirimand, F. (2014). Patients', family caregivers', and professionals' perspectives on quality of palliative care: a qualitative study. *Palliative Medicine*, *28*(9), 1128–1138.

Whiting, L., O'Grady, M., Whiting, M. & Petty, J. (2021). Factors influencing nurse retention within children's palliative care. *Journal of Child Health Care*, *25*(4), 587–602.

Wong, P. T. & Tomer, A. (2011). Beyond terror and denial: The positive psychology of death acceptance. *Death studies*, *35*(2), 99–106.

World Health Organisation (2023). Paediatric Palliative Care. www.who.int/europe/news-room/fact-sheets/item/palliative-care-for-children.

Zackson, J. (2013). The Impact of Primary Maternal Preoccupation on Therapists' Ability to Work with Patients. Ann Arbor, MI: ProQuest Information & Learning.

Zuckerman, K. (2019). *Parents' Experiences of Music Therapy with Paediatric Palliative Care Patients* (Doctoral dissertation).

Chapter 2

Lines of Communication: Creating Continuing Bonds on the Neonatal Unit

Mariam Titus, Devang Ram Mohan and Kirsty Jane

Parent and Therapist Collaboration

This chapter has been written collaboratively between music therapist Kirsty Jane, and parents, Mariam and Devang, to provide insight into the value of music therapy in neonatal intensive care and to highlight the challenges for both parents and therapist in accessing and providing music therapy in this setting. Kirsty spent time with both Mariam and Devang in Great Ormond Street and University College London Hospital (UCLH) neonatal units. The trio have worked collaboratively to depict their journey together, reflecting on their shared experience. At the start of the chapter development, parents and therapist met to discuss the writing process and jointly decided that Mariam and Devang would provide Kirsty with a journal style reflection of their experience to then weave through her reflections of her experiences with the family. The chapter was sent between parents and therapist to edit on reflection of what each other had written. Theory has been drawn upon to consider these experiences in greater depth and develop areas for further reflection to increase the accessibility and availability of neonatal music therapy. Mariam and Devang continued to receive emotional support via a children's hospice during and after the writing process. Due to copyright law we have been unable to print lyrics of songs Mariam and Devang chose to depict each stage of their experience. We instead, invite the reader to listen to the playlist created by parents in the digital resource list and listen to the songs where mentioned.

Therapist: Kirsty Jane

When I was approached about writing a chapter in collaboration with parents this felt like an exciting opportunity to reach out to parents I had worked with closely to share their experiences. My hope was that through sharing parent experiences, collaboratively we could help shape the development of neonatal music therapy in the United Kingdom and increase its availability for parents, particularly for those with infants who met hospice criteria. At the time of writing this chapter there was no standardised practice for neonatal music therapy in the UK and no training requirements for music therapists practicing on the units other than a MA

Music Therapy and the Health and Care Professions Council registration. While training programmes and neonatal music therapy research are available worldwide (Haslbeck, 2014; Loewy et al., 2013; Shoemark, 2018; Standley, 2003), these are not easily transferable to the NHS system, and therefore many units become wary about funding music therapists on their units. This has resulted in the availability of music therapy for parents on neonatal units in the UK being a rarity. Through my work with seriously unwell infants on the neonatal unit and supporting transition to hospice care either during life or post death, I reached out to parents to develop a parent advisory group, Mariam and Devang were part of this group. I hoped to improve my understanding of parental experience of the neonatal unit and music therapy and begin to consider how neonatal music therapy could be developed. Parents expressed an overwhelming sense of devastation and loss of hope when describing time on the unit and identified time in music therapy as a positive experience. This chapter aims to reflect on the potential for music therapy on the neonatal intensive care unit from both parent and therapist's perspective.

Parents: Mariam and Devang

As strange as it might sound to anyone who is unfamiliar with the workings of a Neonatal Intensive Care Unit (NICU), we came away from our experience there with an overwhelming feeling of gratitude. Gratitude for the people there and the care with which they work, gratitude for the three months we got to spend with our son, gratitude for the indelible memories we were able to create. When we heard from Kirsty during a reflection session that music therapy is not part of the default care for all babies on all NICUs, we were surprised and saddened. As the rest of this chapter will detail, it had given us some of the most precious memories with our little boy. To think that there might be other families who, while going through this immensely challenging time, might not have such an opportunity felt like something we wanted eagerly to help redress.

So when Kirsty reached out about collaborating on this, there wasn't a moment's hesitation. Would it be hard? Undoubtedly. Would we struggle to convey everything we wanted on a topic that was so immensely intimate and private? Undeniably. Would we try to if it meant there was the smallest chance it might help another family? Unquestionably.

And selfishly, while our journey didn't pan out the way we had envisaged, we were like so many other parents in this one way: how could we not take on the chance to talk about our Little King?

Admission to the Neonatal Unit

When a baby is born prematurely parents are faced with a sudden loss of pregnancy and a change in the dream of life with their baby (Loewenstein, 2019). Often the non-birthing parent will follow the baby and stand by as they watch professionals striving to maintain the life of their child moving into a highly medicalised environment, detached from the world outside, before eventually being joined by the birthing parent when they are well enough to visit. The ability to be physically close to their baby is now compromised, owing to medical equipment, providing parents with a stark reminder that they alone are not enough for their baby. Parents are expected to take on an identity as parent not only sooner than expected (if premature) but also with barriers challenging their potential to connect with this new life. When a baby is reliant on complex medical care, parents additionally become aware of the possibility and proximity of loss (Valizadeh et al., 2013). Many parents express feelings of guilt and responsibility for their baby requiring neonatal admission continually questioning how they have ended up in the neonatal environment (Rihan, 2021).

In the United Kingdom there are three levels of neonatal units. In intensive care on a level 3 unit (highest level of support) there are likely to be at least four babies in the nursery with nurses providing care at a ratio of 1:2. This is a public environment for parents to find themselves in while managing the emotional challenges of neonatal admission. However, parents are encouraged to stay in their 'bay' and use headphones provided to maintain confidentiality of information on other babies in the room. Parents are in an environment where they are aware of the alarms and health of other babies in the nursery but also isolated. Visiting hours and restrictions, particularly since the COVID-19 pandemic, result in the family often feeling disconnected from their family and community. Additionally, babies in intensive care rely on a high level of medical support, including ventilation, medication, monitoring of heart rate, respiratory rate and oxygen saturation and, in premature cases, incubation to maintain body temperature and look after the baby's skin. Many parents find that these images and sounds, particularly of a baby desaturating, continue to haunt them at home, entering into their sleep.

One of the primary strategies to support parents during their baby's stay on the neonatal unit is the implementation of Family Integrated Care (Craig et al., 2015). This model aims to make parents equal partners in the care of their baby. Music Therapy was set up on the neonatal unit at UCLH to provide support for parents in managing the neonatal admission. In 2020 music therapy became integrated into standardised care available for all babies and their families on the unit. The aim is to provide parents and family members with a musical bubble that creates time to focus on connecting as a family rather than focusing on the baby's diagnosis or care requirements.

Starting music therapy

Mariam and Devang

Music plays a huge role in our lives. What we lack in any apparent skill, we try to make up for in enthusiasm. It manages to connect to something deep within, something quite primitive; a connection that we were wishing to foster and nurture in our son Reiaan.

Reiaan was born into the clinical chaos of a NICU ward. Amidst the dangling wires and beeping monitors, we felt inessential. The harsh reality of our situation weighed heavy: we were the least qualified people in the room to parent this baby, our baby. And in the first few days, as strange as it might sound, we submitted to that feeling.

When Kirsty first reached out to us about music therapy for Reiaan, we were circumspect. He was recovering from surgery, and this felt like a rogue tangent to his prescribed recovery plan. The lightness of music felt at odds with our cold and austere surroundings. 'Could this in any way hamper his recovery?', we asked nervously. "If anything, quite the opposite" came the reply.

<Bob Dylan 'Forever Young', Verse 1>

Kirsty

When I met Mariam and Devang, Reiaan had required specialist intestinal surgery and suffered a significant bleed on his brain. This and his young age, required him to have minimal handling and made him more susceptible to being sensitive to light, touch and sound. Reiaan was Mariam and Devang's first baby, and I could feel the complete love they had for him as well as their anxiety around not wanting to hurt him. We looked together through Reiaan's incubator at his tiny, delicate body and I began to explore with them what they had noticed about the way he was expressing himself in the world. Here were parents faced with a very fragile life that they cared about so deeply and there was also an overwhelming sense of fear. I am very aware on the neonatal unit, in particular when the infant requires complex medical care, that there are many professionals involved giving opinions or medical advice, so I am very fortunate if parents allow time for me to speak with them. Parents are already navigating a hugely stressful environment and experience, how would it make them feel to have another professional offering suggestions for how they might spend their time together? I was not there to teach Mariam and Devang anything, I was there to bring their parental identity and expressive capabilities to their awareness. And so, we started by looking at their baby together. We discussed his reactions to touch and sound, reflected together on their time so far on the unit and considered what Reiaan might be experiencing. We then began to explore Mariam and Devang's connections with music and ways music expressed their identities. If we were going to be making music together, ultimately this needed to be something that parents themselves could see their potential in creating, not something that they required a professional to carry out.

The development of parental self-efficacy

One of our main aims as therapists is to develop therapeutic growth in our clients and to arrive at a point where they are not reliant on us to navigate the world (Blatt et al., 2010). On the neonatal unit therefore, it would seem valuable to ensure that parents understand that they hold the skills to look after and engage with their baby and that they are their baby's preferred voice to listen to. This will increase the likelihood of parents continuing to engage with their baby through using their voice between sessions and post-discharge. There are several mechanisms in the development of self-efficacy including gaining experiences but perhaps most importantly being able to imagine experiences, witnessing the positive effects of these and receiving positive feedback (Gallagher, 2012). In neonatal music therapy we might consider this process to support parents in using their voice with their baby. First, understanding ways they can use their voice and being able to imagine themselves doing this will be beneficial and create motivation. Secondly, to receive positive feedback from their baby and professionals that confirms that they have this ability will be empowering.

For parents with healthy infants in familiar environments they begin to receive feedback from their infant that confirms their parental identity and skills early on. Through multiple attempts to connect with one another, parent and infant develop a unique connection (Bruschweiler-Stern, 2002). This includes the sing-song, infant directed speech that parents naturally engage their infant with (Malloch, 1999). On the neonatal unit this process becomes challenged. Owing to parents' increased likeliness of experiencing symptoms of Post Traumatic Stress Disorder as a result of neonatal admission, the parent's capacity to process support from professionals is likely to be compromised. Furthermore, parents availability for their infant and their expressive capability are likely to be impacted, owing to parents managing their emotions as a result of trauma and their heightened awareness of the possibility of loss (Flaks, 2014). Additionally, the infant's capability to express themselves is likely to be compromised, particularly if they are sedated or requiring ventilation, making it harder for parent and infant to engage in expressive dialogue. This in turn can impact on the parent's potential to bond with their baby. In music therapy we can provide opportunities for parents to connect with their infant through the use of the voice (Shoemark, 2011) and modelling musical interaction. However, it is also our responsibility as music therapists to assist parents in noticing and understanding the minute forms of infant expression in order for parents to begin to enter into a dialogue with their baby.

My sessions with Reiaan and his parents began by exploring together their experiences of the unit so far and developing their understanding of Reiaan's communication. This communication included looking at physical and autonomic responses to touch and sound. These small forms of communications were reframed from warning signs or dislike, to Reiaan's first conversations with them. They were entering into a dialogue where parents offered something to Reiaan, paused, waited and observed his response and then responded to him in a way that acknowledged that they had seen, listened and understood. This form of interaction would be beneficial for him developmentally (Milgrom et al., 2013) and made a clear distinction between why their live interaction would be more beneficial than a non-responsive music playing device. I modelled how they could use their voice, thinking about ways of varying the level of stimulation and adjusting their voices according to what they saw Reiaan was communicating. For example, if he began to yawn or stretch out his hand to as if blocking interaction, I suggested pausing before offering a lower level of stimulation such as moving from singing with words to humming. These were gestures that parents had already noticed and drew upon to think about ways they could use their voices to enter into conversation with Reiaan. Parents were then left to process this and try it out for themselves.

Connecting through music

Mariam and Devang

Kirsty guided us through those initial interactions. She told us that directly playing music would be over-stimulating for a baby of his age, but that he would really enjoy us singing/humming. We asked Kirsty if she should sing instead; after all, if music was to help his recovery, she was the most qualified in the room! She repeated herself: he would really enjoy *us* singing. Our voices. His Amma and Dada. How grateful we were.

And so it was, that we scraped the bowl of our meagre talents, hunched over his cot and sang; settling him down by gently humming *Summertime (Heyward, 1959)*; lulling him to sleep with the soft notes of Erik Satie; channelling our inner Timon and Pumba as he was looking around at the world with his big, sparkly eyes. Mariam was Timon, and Devang was Pumba in case you were wondering! We'd like to think Reiaan found this terribly amusing.

Kirsty

Reiaan's parents began to connect with him through drawing on their previous experiences and connections to music. They were developing their bond with Reiaan and this was being strengthened through sharing music. Each week I returned and spent time with the family sharing their music with Reiaan through simplified versions of the songs that parents shared with me. Mariam and Devang had considered what was important to them as a family and had begun to share these songs with their little boy. They developed confidence to use their voice between sessions. Our time together moved from me modelling and assisting them in interpreting Reiaan's cues to us spending time in music together, using our voices to connect. Through music, a space was created that separated them from the neonatal unit environment and held them together in sound.

Figure 2.1 Reiaan communicating in his own special way.
Photograph provided by parents.

Music for connections

Our experiences with music are unique. When we share our experiences of music or use our voice we are expressing a unique part of our identity. It may express our culture, our experiences and our beliefs. Loewy's 'Songs of Kin' intervention (Loewy, 2015) promotes the approach of using music identified by parents rather than therapist, through taking songs that parents bring to sessions. The intervention aims to support parents in processing their grief while creating a sense of security which can hold them through their neonatal journey and beyond and enable them to communicate their hopes for their baby. Parent's experiences with music will also influence their willingness to sing to their infant (Custodero, 2003) and their engagement with music on the neonatal unit (Shoemark & Arnup, 2014).

On a neonatal unit, a baby's life is considered at its most vulnerable and therefore parents will do everything to protect their child's future. This might be both developmentally and spiritually. The term 'music' in some cultures will promote images of performance, in some cases be considered a sinful activity and therefore would not be something that parents would wish to experiment with for fear of tainting their child in their God's eyes. In some faiths it will be inappropriate for a female therapist to sing to a male infant for a similar reason. It is therefore vital that music therapists, particularly on neonatal units, have cultural awareness and demonstrate this to parents in order to develop a relationship where parents feel able to celebrate and share their cultural identities with both the therapist and their baby, and that their beliefs are respected and valued. It might therefore be vital to consider speaking to parents about the use of their voice rather than offering the term 'music'. This small adjustment can open possibilities for identifying areas within parent's lives where the voice is used and considered for use on the neonatal unit to connect the baby with their family's cultural identity. In this form it could be considered that music will connect the baby to their community and wider family who are unable to visit but, in many cultures, will continue to be a significant part of the baby's care when discharged. Additionally, by supporting parents to engage with their infant through using their voice in a way that is acceptable to their community, they are provided with something that they can share with their wider support network to help them understand their neonatal experience.

Becoming parents

Mariam and Devang

We were actively participating in Reiaan's care. And the more we saw him responding to it, the more it gave us in return. It gave us something to anchor ourselves to in the maelstrom that is a day in the NICU. We could connect with him. The lyrics often felt so appropriate, like the songs were really dedications from us to him. And when combined with the melody, it felt like our own special language.

One in which we could convey all of our love; our hopes and dreams; our fears and worries; and convey them so intimately and gently. For this first time, we felt like we could be competent, we could bring him joy, we could be his parents.

<Bob Dylan 'Forever Young', Verse 2>

Parental identity established

Mariam and Devang began to experience moments where they could see Reiaan recognised and understood their voices. He knew them and they knew him. Moreover, they could bring him comfort. These experiences supported them in knowing that even though Reiaan was reliant on complex medical care, their relationship was special because they were his parents and always would be and that connection was unique to them alone.

An unpredictable journey

Kirsty

I returned to the unit one week to find that Reiaan and his parents were no longer there. In the week since I had last visited, Reiaan had suddenly become unwell and died. In his space was a new admission, Reiaan's name removed from my caseload without explanation. One of the biggest challenges I have experienced on the neonatal unit is how quickly things can change and that while relationships are built they can also end without warning. When a music therapist is only visiting once a week, they might find out that a baby has died only by noticing that the name is no longer there. While the physical space will be occupied by a new baby, the impact of the time with this family continues with the therapist and is processed. After time passes and the music shared is heard again and the therapist is reminded of the time shared together, the legacy of the baby lives on.

Mariam and Devang

When someone passes away, the knowledge of not being able to communicate with them is a wrench that tightens the chest. And so it was with Reiaan who, although only a few months old, was the most communicative little fellow. His big eyes would sparkle in wonderment as he heard his favourite songs, his fingers would dance expressively as he reached out to the world, his forehead would crease in annoyance if we went too far off-key. A little human, in every sense of the word.

This nagging fear persisted, that because his experiences here with us were complete, dedicating to him a new song, with new meaning, would become progressively harder. And so we clung on ever tighter to songs we sang to him; holding on to the memory, fearing that our special language would slip away if we did any different.

But one day, listening to one of his songs we realised: the melody, the meaning, it's all the same; it's all still there. All that has changed is that now it's him singing to us, his love for us; his hopes and dreams for us; his fears and worries about us. And that will always be true. Whatever new experiences we have; and whatever new music we listen to. With the crackle and pop of the record player, that line of communication will always be kept alive.

<Bob Dylan 'Forever Young', Verse 3>

Reflections

Kirsty

One of the fears that professionals have when I speak about using songs from parents' own lives to share with their babies is of a song becoming tainted by sadness and pain. However, my experience in working with parents and their babies during life through to end of life and beyond is that the music takes on a new meaning and comfort. For those who have had music therapy during end of life, it might be difficult to listen to the music but it maintains a source of connection to the life of the person with whom they shared it (Ormston et al., 2022). For Reiaan's parents, music connected them during his life and continues to provide connection to him since his death. It provided 'moments of meeting' (Gotthold & Sorter, 2006) which for parents confirmed their identity as his parents rather than by-standers. These moments create a bond which is internalised (Bowlby, 1969) and might be considered as providing support in a similar way to a transitional object (Winnicott, 1953): a song can create a connection to the baby when physical proximity is not possible. We might therefore consider the value of this transitional object post death in supporting the parents' continuing bond with their baby (Field et al., 2005); creating a feeling of closeness and comfort when physical closeness is no longer possible.

Mariam and Devang

Music plays a huge role in our lives. Even before Reiaan was born, in order to reveal the gender to ourselves and our families, we made a musical game out of it. We created two 'gendered' playlists curated by our family: one with songs with references to 'boy' and another with references to 'girl'. We asked a cousin who was in the know to shuffle play from the applicable list. We, along with our family, raced to guess we were having a boy to the starting notes of 'Here comes the Sun' (The Beatles, 1969). It was The Beatles, it was a pun, and it was a simple game that reflected us.

In the NICU, after we graduated from the familiar songs and our confidence grew, we asked the wider family to start curating a playlist for Reiaan once again. We got everyone from across the world to send in their dedications, hopes and dreams for him. On his last day, we played and sang out loud the songs from this playlist. Our son took his last breath with the words in the hook of Kermit's Rainbow Connection (Williams and Ascher, 1979) trailing in the background and in some small way we didn't feel so alone in the loneliest moment of our lives, because we had those words, curated by those who loved him, around with us. Holding on to the belief that some day, one day, we will find the rainbow connection.

After he passed away, for a while music was the only thing that helped us really connect with Reiaan again. It was something felt by us but also our wider family. So, we turned to what we knew best. At his funeral, in the order of the service we included a QR code to an open playlist called 'For Reiaan' where our friends and family could add songs to it. To this day, it's a playlist that plays not just in our house and the ever-evolving list fills our hearts and ears with shared love for Reiaan.

Final thoughts

Time on the neonatal unit is something which few parents can speak about and feel other people can understand or relate to. The medical environment is unimaginable to those who have not lived in it. Music Therapy can provide moments that the wider population can connect with. This might not only aid wider family and communities to support parents on the unit but also provide parents with moments they can continue to talk about post discharge or after the death of their baby. These are experiences that hold moments where parents have confidence that they truly knew their baby.

Reiaan's parents describe the challenges and the value of music therapy for parents with life-limited infants on the neonatal unit. Through music therapy, parents can be supported in connecting with their baby and creating moments that will be treasured forever. Creating a *'line of communication'* that will forever keep parents and their babies close.

References

Blatt, S. J., Zuroff, D. C., Hawley, L. L. & Auerbach, J. S. (2010). Predictors of sustained therapeutic change. *Psychotherapy Research, 20*(1), 37–54. https://doi.org/10.1080/10503300903121080

Bowlby, J. (1969). *Attachment and Loss. Vol. 1: Attachment. Attachment and Loss*. Basic Books.

Bruschweiler-Stern. N., Harrison, A. M., Lyons-Ruth. K., Morgan. X. C., Nahum. J. P., Sander. L. W., Stern. D. N. & Tronick. E. Z. (2002). Explicating the Implicit: The local level and the microprocess of change in the analytic situation. *Int. J. Psychoanal., 83*, 1051–1062.

Craig, J. W., Glick, C., Phillips, R., Hall, S. L., Smith, J. & Browne, J. (2015). Recommendations for involving the family in developmental care of the NICU baby. *J Perinatol, 35*(Suppl 1), S5–8. https://doi.org/10.1038/jp.2015.142.

Custodero. L. & Johnson-Green, E. A. (2003). Passing the Cultural Torch: Musical Experiences and Musical Parenting of Infants. *Sage Journals, 51*(2), 102–114.

Dylan, B. (1974). *Forever Young*.[1] Asylum.

Field, N. P., Gao, B. & Paderna, L. (2005). Continuing bonds in bereavement: An attachment theory based perspective. *Death Studies, 29*(4), 277–299. https://doi.org/10.1080/07481180590923689.

Flaks M. K., M. S., Almeida P. P., Bueno, O. F., Pupo, M. C., Andreoli, S. B. et al. (2014). Attentional and executive functions are differentially affected by post-traumatic stress disorder and trauma. *J Psychiatr Res., 48*(1), 32–39.

Gallagher, M. W. (2012). Self-Efficacy. *Encyclopedia of Human Behaviour (second edition).*
Gotthold, J. J. & Sorter, D. (2006). Moments of Meeting: An Exploration of the Implicit Dimensions of Empathic Immersion in Adult and Child Treatment. *International Journal of Psychoanalytic Self Psychology, 1*(1), 103–119. https://doi.org/10.2513/s15551024ijpsp0101_6.
Haslbeck, F. B. (2014). Creative music therapy with premature infants: An analysis of video footage†. *Nordic Journal of Music Therapy, 23*(1), 5–35. https://doi.org/10.1080/08098131.2013.780091.
Heyward, D. (1959). Summertime. *On Porgy and Bess.* Verve.
John, E. & Rice, T. (1994). Hakuna Matata. Walt Disney.
Loewenstein, K. et al. (2019). An Integrative Review of Qualitative Studies Within the Transactional Model of Stress and Coping. *Journal of Perinatal and Neonatal Nursing, 33*(4), 340–349. https://doi.org/10.1097/JPN.0000000000000436.
Loewy, J. (2015). NICU music therapy: song of kin as critical lullaby in research and practice. *Annals of the New York Academy of Sciences, 1337*(1), 178–185. https://doi.org/10.1111/nyas.12648.
Loewy, J., Stewart, K., Dassler, A. M., Telsey, A. & Homel, P. (2013). The effects of music therapy on vital signs, feeding, and sleep in premature infants. *Pediatrics, 131*(5), 902–918. https://doi.org/10.1542/peds.2012-1367.
Malloch, S. N. (1999). Mothers and infants and communicative musicality. *Musicae Scientiae, 3*(1_suppl), 29–57. https://doi.org/10.1177/10298649000030S104.
Milgrom, J., Newnham, C., Martin, P. R., Anderson, P. J., Doyle, L. W., Hunt, R. W., Achenbach, T. M., Ferretti, C., Holt, C. J., Inder, T. E. & Gemmill, A. W. (2013). Early communication in preterm infants following intervention in the NICU. *Early Hum Dev, 89*(9), 755–762. https://doi.org/10.1016/j.earlhumdev.2013.06.001.
Ormston, K., Rose, E. & Gallagher, K. (2022). George's Lullaby: A case study of the use of Music Therapy to support parents and their infant on a palliative pathway. *Journal of Neonatal Nursing, 28*(3), 203–206. https://doi.org/10.1016/j.jnn.2022.01.011.
Rihan, S., Mohamadeen, L. & Zayadnes, S. A. et al. (2021). Parents' Experience of Having an Infant in the Neonatal Intensive Care Unit: A Qualitative Study. *Cureus, 13*(7). https://doi.org/10.7759/cureus.16747.
Shoemark, H. (2011). Frameworks for using music as a therapeutic agent for hospitalized newborn infants. In N. S. Rickard & K. McFerran (Eds), *Lifelong Engagement with Music.* Nova Science Publishers, Inc, pp. 3–22.
Shoemark, H. (2018). Time Together: A Feasible Program to Promote parent-infant Interaction in the NICU. *Music Therapy Perspectives, 36*(1), 6–16. https://doi.org/10.1093/mtp/mix004.
Shoemark, H. & Arnup, S. (2014). A survey of how mothers think about and use voice with their hospitalized newborn infant. *Journal of Neonatal Nursing, 20*(3), 115–121. https://doi.org/10.1016/j.jnn.2013.09.007.
Standley, J. (2003). Music therapy with premature infant: Research and developmental interventions. *Music Therapy Perspectives, 23*(1), 76–78. https://doi.org/10.1093/mtp/23.1.76.
The Beatles (1969). Here Comes the Sun. On *Abbey Road.* EMI.
Valizadeh, L., Zamanzadeh, V. & Rahiminia, E. (2013). Comparison of anticipatory grief reaction between fathers and mothers of premature infants in neonatal intensive care unit. *Scandinavian Journal of Caring Sciences, 27*(4), 921–926. https://doi.org/10.1111/scs.12005.
Williams, P. & Ascher, K. (1979). Rainbow Connection. On *The Muppet Movie: Original Soundtrack Recording.* CBS.
Winnicott, D. W. (1953). Transitional Objects and Transitional Phenomena. *The International Journal of Psychoanalysis, 34.*

… Chapter 3

Sophie's Wonderful World: The Impact of Music Therapy on a Family Caring for a Life-Limited Child

Wendy de St Paer and Sophie Nguyen's parents

Introduction

Parents who have received a life-limiting diagnosis for their child face an abundance of challenges. In addition to the immediate shock and grief, families must juggle multiple appointments, learn new skills in order to provide their child with care and make decisions about the manner and extent of treatments. Timescales are often uncertain, so they might face day-to-day challenges around work and finances, and whether it is in the child's best interests to keep attending school while they are well enough. They might experience guilt and will already be mourning a future their child will not have. All while trying to support their child and any siblings.

Claire House Children's Hospice is based in the North West and supports over 400 families across the region. The hospice provides whole family support, incorporating respite care in hospice or at home, as well as sibling support, counselling and specialised nursing care at end-of-life. Within the hospice, alongside the care team there is a team of complementary therapists, play specialists, physiotherapists, counsellors, a psychologist and a music therapist. Many children supported by Claire House have complex life-long conditions and they, along with their families, form an extended relationship with the hospice lasting many years. Others have a briefer relationship, often after end-of-life diagnosis, which will last until the child dies and might include post-bereavement support. Families can use one of two dedicated bedrooms in the 'Butterfly Suite' as an alternative to a funeral home. Here, in the first stages of bereavement they can remain close to their child while continuing to receive support from the care team.

The hospice currently funds a day and a half of music therapy, and this time is split between providing sessions for children residing 'in-house' for respite, and community-based sessions for children who have been referred by staff or families.

Although the music therapy service is, officially, to provide therapy for the children under Claire House, the wider family often becomes part of the sessions. This therefore raises the question of who is receiving therapy; is it for the child alone or the family? And are the family aware that they might be recipients of music therapy and not simply observers? The ethics of this have been raised by other music therapists (Flowers, 2019) and are perhaps not sufficiently considered in the hospice

DOI: 10.4324/9781032664378-4

setting. Within this ambiguity there is a degree of role changing in the therapy process. The therapist adjusts their focus between child and parents (and sometimes siblings), and all present take their turn in the roles available – participator, observer, leader, follower, supporter and recipient of support. In the following description of music therapy with Sophie and her family, we can see how these roles change.

Writing together

When approaching Sophie's parents, I was highly conscious that the process would involve delving into their thoughts around the loss of their daughter. The emotional and psychological burden needed to be considered. In early meetings we acknowledged this but Sophie's parents, who were still deeply immersed in grief, were hopeful the writing would be helpful in processing this grief, while helping others and providing a tangible legacy for Sophie's short but special life.

We met on two occasions before beginning to write and used our time to consider how we would collaborate. Sophie's parents were keen to have perspectives from all of us, including Sophie, and it was decided that we would all tell our 'story' and then consider what could be learnt from this triangulation of perspectives. Sections in italics were contributed by Sophie's parents.

Throughout the process, it was extremely emotional for us to write. Our grief for Sophie is still immeasurably raw, it might always stay like that. From the start Wendy was aware of this and discussed with us how to lessen it. What helped us get through the process of writing was being aware and accepting these feelings as an integral part of the process and working towards a result worthy of that journey.

Sophie

Five-year-old Sophie, an only child, was referred to music therapy in February 2021. Three months earlier she had been diagnosed with a rare mitochondrial condition for which there was no treatment. Progression of the disease was uncertain, and her doctors were unable to predict whether she would experience a gradual decline or a sudden 'event' leading to death, but there were already concerns about her swallow and respiratory drive.

Sophie and her family would go on to have seven music therapy sessions with me before she died at Claire House Wirral in July 2021. Following her death, she remained in the Butterfly Suite at Claire House for several days where, at her parents' request, I delivered a further two sessions for the whole family.

A famous American poet and civil activist Maya Angelou once said, 'Be a rainbow in someone else's cloud'. Not only is Sophie a rainbow in our cloudiest moments but her unconditional love brings out the best colours and depths in us. That is how it feels to be in Sophie's wonderful world.

Sophie started music therapy sessions shortly after we had been given the devastating news that shattered our little perfect world with Sophie in the centre of it. We are the type of family that puts quality time first; laughing, playing together, appreciating little things. So when we were told about the news, it felt like a sledgehammer dropping down on a tiny pin into a small plank of wood. Not only did it nail that little pin in, but also destroyed everything in the process, our little world broken into million pieces.

We come from a multicultural background, including South East Asia and Eastern Europe, which provides us with different perspectives of health care from other countries. We feel that the care we have received was exceptional, particularly the link between hospitals, hospices and charities. Had Sophie been diagnosed in other countries, we would highly doubt whether she would have received the same quality care throughout.

One of those highlights was music therapy with Wendy. Not only did it bring much joy to Sophie and our life, but it also left us something so invaluable of Sophie's – a beautiful song.

First meeting

Sophie was a confident, engaging little girl, unusual for Claire House in that she could walk with little support and express herself easily through speech. I recall her voice being slightly breathless, as though it was hard for her to coordinate breath and speech, and she had some balance difficulties, preferring to move around with one hand on the furniture or the support of an adult hand.

Although I had planned only to introduce myself and explain a little about music therapy, we did end up doing some impromptu music therapy during this first meeting. Sophie's parents were quietly spoken and courteous, keen for Sophie to 'do well' in her music making. I showed her the instruments available in the room, including some small percussion, a piano, a guitar and my violin. When Sophie and I sat at the piano, Sophie's parents encouraged her verbally and her dad helped her to play 'Twinkle, Twinkle, Little Star' by moving her hands to the correct keys. I explained that my aim was not to help Sophie create a polished musical product or to perform, but to enable self-expression and to build some trust between Sophie and myself. After this we continued with Sophie free to play as she wished and with her parents no less engaged in the process. They watched their daughter explore her section of our shared piano as I contained her musically with open chords. Sophie led and I followed, with my playing, and her parents quickly seemed to understand the value of our interaction.

After around 20 minutes Sophie became more interested in the toys on display and I took the opportunity to speak to both parents. They spoke with love and pride about her intelligence, creativity and kindness, her achievements at school and her love of music. A year previously she had been fit and well with no indications of the illness to come.

We arranged to meet weekly, and I saw Sophie on seven further occasions before she died in July that year. Five of these meetings were at Claire House and two were in her family home. She was usually supported by her Mum, but on one occasion her Dad brought her.

So there we were, coming to Sophie's first music therapy session. We did not know what to expect, all we hoped for was to give Sophie more positive, quality moments. We were nervous, but we met with a welcome introduction from Wendy. Once

Sophie seemed more comfortable in Wendy's presence, we sat back, giving Sophie and Wendy some distance while they got to know each other as they sat by the piano.

For a brief moment, our little beautiful picture reappeared, framing around Sophie smiling and talking to Wendy. She was laughing as she pressed some keys while Wendy improvised, turning random sounds into a fun melody. Sophie's singing voice filled up our hearts with warmth and for that precious short moment it reminded us how lucky we were still to be a part of Sophie's wonderful world.

The sessions took place in a large, light room that held a digital piano and drum kit, a guitar and a range of small percussion instruments. Sessions were framed with a hello and goodbye song. During each session the supporting parent moved between various roles as observer, supplier of information, facilitator (when Sophie lacked confidence or needed physical support) and musical participant.

Initially I had intended for the sessions to be unstructured and child-led, but it soon became clear that Sophie preferred some structure. In contrast to our first meeting, she displayed some uncertainty when improvising at the keyboard with me. After this I made the sessions semi-structured, incorporating songs that were familiar to Sophie and repeating activities from week to week while trying to facilitate moments of choice and self-expression.

Sessions with Wendy were the highlight of Sophie's week. During our 15-minute drive to Liverpool, Sophie would sit in the front, and we would sing our favourite songs. Sophie had this joyous passion for singing and dancing. Music was always a significant part of our life and while we tried to introduce Sophie to as many interesting things as possible, music was undoubtedly one of Sophie's first loves. It was evident how much she looked forward to the sessions. As we sat in the car, I couldn't stop smiling seeing how excited my little girl was and once more I wished I could have frozen time to cherish Sophie's precious smile forever.

I never counted the number of sessions we did together. Maybe counting meant getting to the end and I did not want the end. Wendy introduced us to her musical instruments and was always so patient and nurturing with Sophie, giving her time and space and letting her decide what she wanted to do. I did not really know what to expect nor what these sessions would be like. All I had in my mind was enriching Sophie's life. Most days I just wanted to wrap her up in cotton wool and erase that horrifying diagnosis in my head.

The details of the sessions are somehow blurry in my memory now. It did not matter to me what we did but how it made Sophie feel. Seeing her pure joy and engagement was everything I could have wished for. Most of the time, Wendy would follow Sophie's lead and adjust the sessions so they would be appropriate for Sophie as her energy levels fluctuated. For us parents, despite the paralysing fear and anxiety that we were experiencing while trying to adapt to new life after the diagnosis, those music sessions seemed to be a wonderful escapism.

The second session was the only one attended by Sophie's Dad. I noted that Sophie remained physically close to him, perhaps using him as a secure base as she continued to try to understand the 'rules' of music therapy. Sophie's Dad joined in with activities, provoking amusement from her when he made mistakes-on-purpose in an action song.

One session it was me, Sophie's Dad, who took Sophie to Claire House. I was nervous, actually I was scared. I wanted everything to be as good as possible for Sophie, but I was not certain what I needed to do.

Sophie was a little bit reserved that day and I was not sure whether it was because she was more tired, or she sensed my crippling anxiety. Sophie was always extremely sensitive to other people's emotions, such a special girl.

Wendy did the hello song, and I think Wendy also could feel Sophie was a little more coy that day. She started gently and encouraged Sophie to try out various small instruments. I was just sitting there observing my little girl, my world, and then Wendy asked me to get involved, to pick up a small instrument and make a sound. I picked up something, I don't remember exactly what it was and slowly, it seemed like everyone started to become more relaxed and settled. I was being my goofy self, which Sophie seemed to enjoy. And there she was, my little girl smiling, singing and playing, and for a short moment, everything was all right again.

The song

During this session a piece of work started which formed a thread that ran through the remainder of our sessions, stretching beyond the time I spent with Sophie and her family. I had asked about music which Sophie and her parents enjoyed. They told me that they often listened to 'What a Wonderful World'. It seemed to represent the happiness of their family unit, reaching back to the period before Sophie's diagnosis. I suggested that we could alter the lyrics to reflect the things that were important to Sophie. The process was begun during this session and drew on aspects of family life as replacement lyrics – cooking, cuddles, TV programmes that Sophie enjoyed. They included 'jacken wings', Sophie's childish mispronunciation of 'chicken' which had become a family phrase. Despite the cheerful nature of the lyrics I noted afterwards that it 'felt quite painful'.

Our Sunday mornings were usually slow and laid-back as we enjoyed our lie-in and cuddles. One time, we turned on some music in the background and chose Louis Armstrong's 'What a Wonderful World'. Sophie immediately loved the melody and hummed along with us in bed. Sometimes, we would film the three of us in bed while listening to the song. Sophie loved staring at herself, she would make silly faces and laugh. It became our weekly ritual, serene and full of happiness.

So when Wendy asked about Sophie's favourite songs, this song came up. Over a few sessions we discussed different things that Sophie loved doing. I helped with suggesting some of the things that could go onto the list as Sophie seemed to be unable to make up her mind. As I was suggesting the list to Wendy, the flashback of those beautiful moments came alive and unexpectedly I felt my grief crushing me. I realised that those moments were finite, and my heart was crumbling inside as I listened to Wendy and Sophie's singing voices echoing across the room.

The next sessions all included play, led at last by Sophie, who formed a game of make-believe around the theme of food and cooking. I played along, using instruments as ingredients and eventually recalled a rhyme which involved chopping up 'vegetables' to a steady beat, ostensibly to make soup. Sophie based her ingredients on the shape or colour of the instrument-vegetable and joined in with the rhyme until we had created the soup which she then offered to her mother. After this, food and play remained an important part of each session. They found their way into Sophies song and seemed to be a central part of family life.

On one occasion we used the song, 'If you're happy and you know it', as a way of exploring emotions. The song started with trying out different ways of playing (If you're happy and you know it play it loudly) and then moved to different feelings. Sophie and I both suggested various feelings (excited, sleepy, hungry) and Sophie told me what she would do if she experienced them. Eventually I suggested sad, and Sophie's answer was 'Talk to Mummy or cuddle Mummy', and then immediately wanted to cuddle her. I sang 'If you're sad and you know it cuddle Mummy', as they remained together. In my notes I remarked on the apparent intensity of feeling at this point and wondered if Sophie felt sad for herself or was somehow aware of her Mum's sadness. Or maybe she was simply tired and wanting a cuddle.

Over the next couple of sessions Sophie's confidence grew. She helped me plan activities, and we completed her song. It was difficult to obtain direct answers from Sophie about her preferences and she seemed content for her Mum to suggest answers and then to agree with them. At the time I worried that I might not be hearing Sophie's voice.

At home

Eventually we moved the sessions to the family home at parents' request. I took a small selection of instruments with me, and Sophie once again helped to plan activities. In the first session I tried to incorporate a marching game, but Sophie was fearful of falling. I wondered if her symptoms were progressing.

The next session was the last time I would see Sophie before she died. When I arrived at the house, she was extremely tired, and I wondered whether she would be able to participate. During our 'Hello' song she chose to listen rather than join in but after this I was able to entice her into active participation through play. Our food-based game reached a new level when Sophie's Mum fetched her wooden sushi set! We made meals together which Sophie generously shared with her Mum and me. I sang about this, borrowing a nursery rhyme melody and changing the words to reflect Sophie's game.

We sang Sophie's Wonderful World (now completed), with me playing the violin. Despite her fatigue, Sophie declared that this was a show, and she wanted to sing it again. In our second performance I played pizzicato (plucking the strings) to give greater space for Sophie's voice and afterwards she expressed satisfaction at our efforts. The performance was captured by Sophie's Mum on her phone.

After this Sophie's fatigue took a greater hold and she elected to listen rather than play or sing and lay with her head on her Mum's lap. I noticed that she held her head slightly turned to the left, as though her centre of vision had shifted, and I felt a sense of unease.

We were terrified of what was lying ahead in the near future, but we also knew that each day with Sophie was precious and we treasured every one. When Wendy started the sessions at home, Sophie's song had taken shape and we had already sung it a few times together. That day, during the last home session Sophie sang her song while Wendy played an instrument in the background. Her beautiful voice made me feel incredibly proud and fulfilled that there were so many things she loved in her life. I managed to film Sophie singing the song on the phone and we used the audio for her memorial service. Since then, the original song gained a new dimension with so many intense emotions. To this day, we are still unable to listen to Sophie's version or the original.

Post-bereavement work

The following day Sophie began to have seizures and was admitted to hospital. Here she became unresponsive and attempts to treat her were unsuccessful. After thirteen days she was transferred to Claire House Wirral for end-of-life care. At the hospice she was looked after by experienced nurses who helped manage her symptoms as life-supporting treatment was withdrawn. Sophie died later that day.

I was working at the hospice the following day and went to see Sophie's parents. They spoke to me for some time, sharing their philosophy that Sophie continued to be with them in a metaphysical sense and then asked if I would do a music therapy session with her. They told me that they wished to feel happy in her presence.

This short session took the format of previous sessions, starting with the 'Hello' song and incorporating many of the songs we had used, including Sophie's Wonderful World. Sophie's parents behaved as though she were still living, addressing her directly and stroking her affectionately. They declined my offer of singing the 'Goodbye' song that we had always used, perhaps fearing this was too great a test of their determination to be happy.

Two days later I visited them again. This time they showed me a number of pictures and videos of Sophie and asked me to sing to her again, this time just the 'Hello' song. We talked about music for Sophie's funeral, and I suggested that they listen to potential choices before the event, so they were not caught unawares by misremembered lyrics or unexpected emotions caused by the music. Sophie's Dad said later that this had been valuable advice. I was conscious of referring to Sophie in the past while they spoke about her in the present but felt this was a natural part of their transition from being parents of an unwell child to becoming bereaved parents.

Wendy provided more sessions when Sophie was moved to Claire House's Butterfly Suite, we did not realise the importance and significance of those two sessions until they took place. When Sophie stopped, our world stopped, everything stopped. But those two extra sessions created a bridge to help the transition between the two worlds. As we three were standing around Sophie, singing and playing music to her felt in parts familiar and in some others something completely different, almost unreal and beyond our logical comprehension.

Discussion

In considering our perspectives of music therapy with Sophie, several themes have become apparent.

For Sophie, her parents believe that music therapy provided opportunities for pleasure and self-expression. They recall her 'smiling, singing and playing', describing her excitement and laughter as she engaged during the sessions. Outside the sessions they noted a benefit too, describing music therapy as 'the highlight of Sophie's week' and something she anticipated with pleasure.

For Sophie's parents, anxiety and the desire to freeze or shift time feature significantly. They use powerful imagery when writing of their previously happy world being 'shattered' by Sophie's diagnosis and seem to be seeking to recapture the time before diagnosis. They write of wanting to 'cherish Sophie's precious smile forever', recalling that 'for a short moment, everything was alright again' as music therapy provided moments of reprieve (Kammin et al., 2024; Zuckerman, 2019). There is an eagerness and urgency around providing 'enriching' and 'quality' moments for Sophie. They reflect on the struggle to draw their focus away from the progression of time and illness to be in the here-and-now with Sophie and her enjoyment.

From the music therapist perspective, the focus of the work alternated between Sophie's immediate needs and her parents' ongoing and future needs as they coped with Sophie's illness and imminent loss. Retrospectively I came to understand that this change of focus was subconscious, and I was not always fully aware of which family member was at the centre of the therapy (Flower, 2019).

Sophie was blessed with thoughtful, loving parents who were able to provide safety and stability for her as they navigated their own difficult journey. But at times she seemed to be affected by the strong challenging emotions experienced by each parent. Her Dad and I sensed her anxiety as he battled with his own anxiety in our second session. Later Sophie responded to a question about sadness by seeking comfort from her Mum. Sitting in the middle of these feelings I tried to balance the need to acknowledge them with the need for Sophie, a young child, to play and have fun.

The song, Sophie's Wonderful World, largely met both these needs. It provided a fun, creative activity that was highly relevant for Sophie. She could engage with the song on different levels, either actively by contributing to its content and performance, or receptively by listening to it or acknowledging other people's contributions.

'Sophie's Wonderful World' was also a piece of legacy work for Sophie's parents, allowing a life review within a contained supportive environment and leaving them with a 'product' of their time with their daughter in music therapy. The benefits of such work are well documented within music therapy literature (Kirkwood et al., 2019; Reid, 2007).

Legacy work can result in a tangible creation and the creation process might help families to initiate the process of life review (Allen et al., 2008). Benefits to this can include strengthening of social bonds (Kirkwood et al., 2019), expressing values and beliefs and a sense of continued connection to a loved one during bereavement (Cadrin, 2006).

It was within this aspect of the work that I had experienced the painful counter-transference (the therapist's emotional response to the client – Hough, 2014) from Sophie's Dad. In asking Sophie and her Dad to consider what was most important to her, I was also asking him to review and summarise Sophie's life, with the unspoken subtext that it was approaching its end.

I had initiated the work with the aims of self-expression and enjoyment for Sophie in mind. Subconsciously however, I had transferred my own focus to her parents and had enabled them to lead this part of the creative process, resulting in my concern about not hearing Sophie's voice. I wonder now whether my anxiety was caused by the mismatch between my conscious aims and my subconscious change of focus. There is something to be learnt from this for me about how such changes occur and how I can develop my awareness of this within my practice.

At the start of this journey with Wendy, we always thought that we were the observers; mum and dad taking little one to music therapy sessions to watch and smile at the things our little girl did. But as we experienced these sessions, slowly we started to realise that all of us were actively involved by being there utilising the tools, knowledge and experience we had to help Sophie express herself.

As for us, the sessions also brought positivity and much needed escapism. For 45 minutes each week, we were submerged into this world of sounds and Sophie's sweet voice. It was magical being in those sessions, especially when Sophie's song was in the making. When we finished the session that meant going back out to the reality that we were not ready to face.

As the sessions went on, we came to a realisation that perhaps it did not matter what will happen, we cannot control the future but what we could control was how we lived in the present. It is a privilege to be part of Sophie's wonderful world and even though it was far too short, every single day was a beautiful gift that we will always treasure.

Therapist emotional processing

When it comes to supporting children and young people, the focus is on the service users and very little on the practitioners. Hence why I (Sophie's dad) thought it would be a new insight to hear Wendy's reflections on working with Sophie and our family. Undoubtedly, there was also a small part of me seeking for a reassurance of Sophie's significance in other people's perspective.

In early discussions, Sophie's Dad said that he felt my emotional process through the loss of a client would also be a helpful thing to include. He was sure I had been affected by Sophie's death, and he was correct, but I also wondered whether he was seeking assurance that I had experienced some of the grief they had endured. I was not sure I could give this assurance.

Kubler-Ross's (1969) five stages of grief have been part of public consciousness for several decades now, despite the author's own misgivings at their widespread misinterpretation. The stages include denial, anger, bargaining, depression and acceptance, but were not intended to be understood as a linear process. Rather than experiencing each stage in a prescribed order, Kubler-Ross meant them as descriptions of stages commonly experienced when grieving. Not everyone will experience every stage. Stroebe and Schut's (1999) Dual Process Model of coping with bereavement is now accepted as a more accurate model of grief (Fiore, 2021) among professionals. This describes a process of oscillation between 'loss-oriented' behaviours, focusing on grief and the cause of it, and 'restoration-oriented behaviours' which allow distraction from loss and the continuation of daily life.

Children's hospice care is typically offered to children who have a 'condition that means they are not expected to reach adulthood' (Hospice UK, 2024). At Claire House, when children are assessed for eligibility for hospice support, one of the questions is 'Would you be surprised if this child died before their 18th birthday?'

This means that when I meet a Claire House child, I have already accepted that they are unlikely to survive to adulthood. So how does this affect my emotional process and how do I cope with the repeated bereavement of clients?

When I first met Sophie and her family, I had already accepted her diagnosis and the likely outcome of her condition, thus bypassing most of Kubler-Ross's stages. For me there was no denial – I trusted the medical professionals and did not wonder about second opinions or alternative treatments. I was not left feeling angry or clinically depressed that such a terrible thing was happening to this family. This might appear 'cold' but the absence of a true grief response in me, despite experiencing sadness, allowed me to continue to work therapeutically with the whole family without being emotionally overwhelmed.

After Sophie's death, my sadness was already tempered with acceptance and there was no Dual Process for me to navigate as my daily life continued. What did remain with me however was an intense sadness for her parents and their enduring grief at her loss. Strong feelings around the pain experienced by survivors of the death of a child have been a consistent part of my experience of working with families who have lost, or are about to lose, a child. Such feelings are explored and processed in clinical supervision and through a strong professional support network within the hospice. Without this structured support (supervision) and semi-structured support (in-hospice) it is doubtful whether I would have the capacity to sit with, and contain the anguish experienced by families as they lose a child.

Language

Within the hospice we are strongly encouraged to use direct language around death and dying; euphemisms are generally avoided. Bearing this in mind I used direct language in an early draft when describing Sophie's music therapy sessions. After reading this material Sophie's parents told me they found my written use of 'death' and 'died' deeply painful and almost too hard to read. I was taken aback – while I was aware that reading my draft would be emotionally gruelling, I recalled Sophie's Mum using these very words when talking to me. I had not anticipated this response to my 'professional' language.

We explored this further, and she spoke of her difficulty in telling people about what had happened to Sophie. It seemed as though this direct language was bearable when both protagonists knew the history – here it was used to orient the conversation in place or time. But the language was too painful when used unexpectedly or when it was necessary to inform someone 'what' had happened to Sophie. Perhaps control of the narrative is the issue here and unpredictable use of, and responses to, such language by others is overwhelming.

We discussed how to continue – would they prefer me to use different terminology for the publication? They both said they would like to consider their options but to leave my original wording as the writing process continued. Control was handed back to Sophie's parents.

We struggle with using the word 'die'. We know that our daughter has died. The heartbreak and grief that follow are indescribable but one could imagine it is like an ocean wave, constantly going forth and back. Most days it is so fierce it tosses us around and pulls us under with its consumingly loud force like a tsunami crashing down making everything in this world small and insignificant, but we know she has died.

Despite this, the life she led was full of happiness, laughter and love, and she truly shared that with those she met. So we would rather focus on how she has lived than emphasise her death. That is how we are able to manage our grief, the awareness of what has happened. Just like the wave it bounces forth and back, but this way we have less thunderstorm and lightning, less tsunami waves, this way we are able to carry Sophie's legacy and our grief closer to our chest and move forward in a positive way.

We can understand that within clinical settings, it is encouraged to use direct language around death and dying. This might be useful in order to prevent parents from being in a state of denial. However, cultures around the world show how approaches to death can be vastly different. Added to this is the extra layer of complexity of child loss, and how each parent's grief could be very different. Bearing this in mind, it is healthy for both practitioner and parents to discuss this openly so they can have a better understanding and find the right balance. This is something we are very grateful that we were able to do with Wendy.

Summary

The adaptation of a family chosen song became a central part of music therapy with Sophie and her family. The song acted as a dual-process therapeutic tool, addressing the needs of both child and parents. During its creation the therapy focus moved between all three participants, increasingly becoming directed to Sophie's parents. This leads to questions over how music therapy is offered to hospice families and whether in future it should be offered as a family-centred rather than child-centred process.

During the collaboration with Sophie's family for this chapter, questions around use of language and therapist emotional processing arose. For me it now seems clear that control of language must remain in the hands of families, as long as this does not result in avoidance or lack of clarity. Most importantly, families' own use of certain words and phrases does not mean they will always be comfortable with that use by others.

Finally, for Sophie's parents, post-bereavement sessions were not only a transition from parenthood to bereaved parenthood, but a statement of intent, as Sophie will never be in the past for her parents. She continues to exist for them and is present every day, in all that they do.

Receiving a terminal diagnosis for your 5-year-old child is a surreal experience. A myriad of emotions flooded in immediately and got trapped in our mind every second of our day while we tried to navigate with new reality. One of the most dominant emotions was fear that paralysed us and at times prevented us from thinking clearly. But after having recovered from the initial shock we tried to settle into this new life – life full of possibilities in a limited timeframe. We tried to let fear become the background instead of the driving force.

Music therapy was one of those beautiful possibilities. Seeing Sophie's pure joy during those music sessions was healing and comforting. What was more, we realised as we worked on this chapter with Wendy, that Sophie's world was constant. Our world changed with the diagnosis, but Sophie's remained a happy and carefree one full of love. She enjoyed life and everything it had to offer, she felt our undying love every day and perhaps at the end love is all that matters in the face of impermanence and fragility of life.

Sophie's Wonderful World

Mummy's cooking, Daddy's too,
Jacken Wing for me and you,
And I think to myself
What a wonderful world

I like Number Blocks, and bubble tea,
Building sandcastles on the beach,
And I think to myself
What a wonderful world

Sunbathing in sunglasses and watching Peppa Pig,
Playing with baby Mia and going to Legoland,
I see friends shaking hands
Saying, "How do you do?"
They're really saying, "I love you"

Cuddles with Daddy, and Mummy too,
Playing tag in the flowers so blue,
And I think to myself
What a wonderful world

Yes, I think to myself
What a wonderful world

Figure 3.1 Sophie playing her ukulele. *Ba mẹ yêu con nhiều nhiều -* meaning *Daddy Mummy love you lots lots.*

Photo taken by Sophie's parents.

References

Allen, R. S. et al. (2008). Legacy activities as interventions approaching the end of life. *Journal of Palliative Medicine*, *11*(7), 1029–38. doi: https://doi.org/10.1089/jpm.2007.0294

Flower, C. (2019). *Music Therapy with Children and Parents: Toward an Ecological Attitude*. Doctoral thesis. Goldsmiths, University of London. https://research.gold.ac.uk/id/eprint/26132 (Accessed: 20 October 2023).

Kammin, V., Fraser, L., Flemming, K. & Hackett, J. (2024). Experiences of music therapy in paediatric palliative care from multiple stakeholder perspectives: A systematic review and qualitative evidence synthesis. *Palliative Medicine*, p.02692163241230664.

Kirkwood, J. et al. (2019). The MusiQual treatment manual for music therapy in a palliative care inpatient setting. *British Journal of Music Therapy*, *33*(1), 5–15.

Kübler-Ross, E. (1969). *On Death and Dying*. New York: Macmillan.

Koodiyedath, B. & Miller, M. (2012). End of life or short break care – outcome of children referred to a children's hospice in the UK. *Archives of Disease in Childhood*, 97, A172. doi: https://doi.org/10.1136/archdischild-2012-301885.405.

Magill, L. (2009). The spiritual meaning of pre-loss music therapy to bereaved caregivers of advanced cancer patients. *Palliative & Supportive Care,* *7*(1), 97–108. doi: https://doi.org/10.1017/S1478951509000121.

Reid, J. (2007). Music therapy in improving the quality of life of palliative care patients: does it work?. *BMJ blog,* 8 May 2017. https://blogs.bmj.com/ebn/2017/05/08/music-therapy-in-improving-the-quality-of-life-of-palliative-care-patients-does-it-work (Accessed 20 October 2023).

Stroebe, M. & Schut, H. (1999). The dual process model of coping with bereavement: rationale and description. *Death Studies*, *23*(3), 197–224. doi: https://doi.org/10.1080/074811899201046.

Zuckerman, K. (2019). Parents' Experiences of Music Therapy with Pediatric Palliative Care Patients.

Chapter 4

Freya's Light

Sarah-Jayne Dawes and Ceridwen Rees

Introduction

Bob Heath (2021), music therapist and author writes in the introduction to his book, 'Songs from a Window':

> 'It's surely no accident that the world is full of songs? They identify us as individuals … they help us celebrate our victories and mourn our losses; they capture our history and secure it for generations to come'.

When I first qualified as a music therapist, I attended one of Bob Heath's songwriting courses. It had a profound effect on me and has shaped much of my approach as a music therapist in children's hospices for the last 25 years. I did of course learn some skills around how to facilitate songwriting, but the biggest lesson I learnt was how to just 'be' with people, to walk alongside them and to use the music space as a blank canvas to support people in their journey through life and into death, often using song-writing as a tool. In other conversations with Bob, who acted as something of a mentor to me in my early years, and in my supervision sessions for over 20 years with the wonderful music therapist and psychotherapist, Hilary Wainer, I have found that this notion of the music-story being something of a legacy has been confirmed time and time again; our music story doesn't just end when we die.

This chapter tells the story of Freya, who I met at Helen House Children's Hospice, Oxford, in the year 2000 when she was one year old. The song that I wrote for her funeral in 2004, 'Freya's Light', is integral to this chapter, and the power of the song and its influence, some twenty-four years on from when I first met Freya will be uncovered as you read on. Freya's Mum and I decided that the best way to capture the essence of who Freya was and her impact on all those who knew her, would be through a recorded conversation, with myself asking a few key questions and then just letting SJ tell her story. SJ is such an eloquent speaker who loves to talk about her daughter and so I just sat down with her one evening with a glass of Prosecco and we just chatted. The conversation as

DOI: 10.4324/9781032664378-5

Figure 4.1 Freya enjoying playing the drum. Photograph provided by parents, edited by AP Bailey at TL Media.

a whole was some 59,000 words! I simply extracted all the most relevant parts of the conversation and documented them here. Neither SJ's nor my words have been edited at all; you are reading this as if you were in the room with us, bearing witness to this wonderful family and their love for their daughter. As you read on, you will see how Freya's Light still shines on and will continue to shine bright, as I help make memories for families to cherish in years to come. SJ's words are in italics for clarity.

Freya's Light

It's such a privilege to be sitting down with you SJ (Sarah-Jayne) and talk about your beautiful Freya.

Well, you know me, I never miss an opportunity to talk about my gorgeous Freya!

So, starting at the very beginning, I was trying to think of a title for the chapter, and I had several ideas floating around in my head; and then suddenly I thought, 'Hang on a minute?! 'Freya's Light'! – the song I wrote for her funeral – surely that's got to be the title?!'

Oh gosh – Yes!!

Because we had candles at her service, which is why I wrote 'Freya's Light' in the first place, and Freya *was* light, and she *is* light, and because she is *still* shining her light on all of us, which will become clear as we chat.

Yes – that absolutely was her, Freya spreading her light, I love it!

You've always said that lights and music were a 'constant' in her life.

Absolutely, lights and music were her two main things: fairy lights, candles, add music into the mix and she was a very happy girl!

These two elements are key to Freya's story then really, and they underpin everything we're going to talk about.

Yes, completely...

SJ's Music Story

So, before we talk more about Freya, tell me a bit about *your* first memory of music?

Well, I did all the usual stuff, recorder at school and so on, and I did have piano lessons for a while, but they fizzled out eventually...

Did you stop playing the piano altogether?

No, not at all, because I thought, 'Actually, I do like music, and I can still play piano', because we had a piano at home, 'so I will carry on playing...'

And when did you start to learn the Saxophone?

Oh, not until 1990 when I was about 30. I just remember seeing one in the window of a music shop and I would walk past and think to myself, 'That looks like a really sexy instrument, I'd love to learn to play it!' Anyway, one day I bought it, came home and then thought, 'How on earth do I put it together?!'

Tricky!

I know! But I got myself some lessons and actually I became quite good, and I even played in a local restaurant for a while.

So, music has always been a thread in your life?

It has... I don't think I'd really thought about it until now, but yes...

Freya

Now then, tell me a little bit about your girl? What was she like?

Ok, well I just want to say 'love' when I think of Freya. She was always smiling, full of joy, and she had complete trust in anyone who was kind to her, and she would really pick up on that with a smile, or a cheeky giggle!

Sooo cheeky!

I know, and I feel really blessed to have had her in my life, because with Freya there were never any feelings of guilt over any arguments with her.

I never had to tell her off, or say, 'no Freya, you can't do that' or 'you can't have that'. How lucky we are that we have no memories like that? So, in a way our relationship and our love for her was free from any bad feeling; all she ever knew was pure love.

That is such a beautiful way of looking at it...

What did they tell you at the hospital about Freya's condition, and did you find out when you were pregnant?

It was at a late scan that something first was flagged up, but they only said that there might be something wrong with her kidneys, and I cried the whole way home. Now I look back and I think, 'Please, if it had only been that...' So we were kind of expecting a problem, but nothing remotely like what actually happened.

Tell me what happened during labour, and did you choose any music for the birth?

Well, that's a funny story because I had chosen 'Enya' to have Freya by, but Steve was a big cricket fan, so he asked if we could dip into the cricket for a while, and one of the anaesthetists said: "Well I wouldn't mind knowing the score too!" So for a while, 'Enya' was off, and the cricket was on!

And that's your first memory of music with Freya: 'Enya' – and cricket as a rival factor!

Yes! I always smile when I hear Enya or any cricket scores now!

And what happened when she was born?

Well, there was suddenly a lot of panic – people were rushing around – Steve started crying...

Steve was crying... because of... the way Freya looked?

Absolutely, it was a real shock: She was bright, bright red, and her head was very large...

And she had a white mark on her forehead: It was funny because a few weeks later someone asked her brother, Tom, why his sister looked as she did? and Tom said: "Oh, she's just quite poorly, and that white mark is God's thumb-print when he gave Freya to my Mum and Dad to look after", and I thought 'Wow! He's three years old, where did that come from?!'

So once Freya was out of intensive care and you were both back on a ward, what did the doctor tell you?

The doctor explained that Freya had Sturge Weber Syndrome which is a rare disorder that shows itself first of all with a port-wine mark on the face. This might be the only symptom, but it was obvious to Steve and I that some babies with this syndrome also have abnormally large heads.

I asked the doctor if I could feed her and the doctor said: "Well, I don't think she'll take to the breast because brain-damaged children rarely do..."

Whaaat?! He just came right out and said that?!

That was the first thing he said...

But at that point it could have been a purely cosmetic thing – You didn't know then that she might have additional needs?!

I know! Steve start crying again, and I said: "What do you mean, brain-damaged?" The doctor explained that everything you see on the outside was also going on on the inside, so there were additional layers of blood vessels just under the skin which were dilated.

Anyway, she did breastfeed, but then the doctor said: 'The only advice I can give you is to take her home and enjoy her while she's here because she's not going be here for very long. She will never have a birthday'.

We later learnt that some babies suffer from seizures, problems with sight and hearing and have developmental delay, but we didn't know any of that then, and he was clearly just assuming that this was Freya: she had the 'full set' in his opinion. As it turned out he was right, but we had no idea at that time what the future held for her.

How on earth did you even begin to process everything?

So, you know me, I decided it was time to exit the hospital! Freya was stable and the only thing stopping me from leaving was my catheter, so I just drank for England, weed for England, got that catheter out, and I was gone!

And did you light candles and put music on as soon as you got home?

Yes I did. I wanted Freya to never be in the dark: I wanted her to always be surrounded by light. So we put fairy lights up everywhere, we lit candles, and we played lots of music. I thought to myself: 'I haven't got this little one for long: I've been told she will never have a birthday, so we're going to make the most of our time together and make her little life count'.

So how and when were you introduced to the idea of Helen House in Oxford? (the first children's hospice in the UK)

It was during one of our many visits to the JR (John Radcliffe Hospital, Oxford) when Freya was poorly, and she had gone to theatre to have a shunt fitted to drain the fluid from her brain. A lady just came onto the ward and introduced herself: 'You don't know me, but my name's Halina. I'm from Helen House'. (Halina was the Head of Care). I said: 'Helen House? What's that?'

'It's a hospice she replied', and I said: 'Why are you here? Why do I need a visit from someone who works at a hospice?'

She said she had come to visit Freya and offer some support to us. Our consultant had mentioned Helen House, but I was confused because to be honest I didn't really even know what a hospice was or what it could offer us, so I just said: Thanks, but no thanks – we'll be fine'.

But little by little we began to trust her, and she often came to visit, and she would sit by the cot so that Steve and I could go for a coffee. 'I will stay here with Freya; I promise you, I won't move', she said. And it felt safe to go off knowing that there was someone there watching Freya.

Unfortunately, we had to have a stint at GOSH (Great Ormond Street Hospital, London) but – I couldn't believe it – Halina was waiting for us when we got back to Oxford! She explained that the doctors didn't want Freya to go home straightaway, but would we consider going to Helen House as a kind of half-way step to going back home?

I wasn't convinced, so she said: 'Just come and have a look around and see what you think'.

So, we did go and within minutes Tom was off and away into the toy cupboard and came out dressed as a clown! And that's when we thought, 'This is going to be good for all of us, especially Tom, because he can spend time with the siblings' workers and get some support from them and also meet other siblings in the same situation'.

Music Therapy for Freya

So what were your thoughts around the idea of music therapy for Freya?

Well, to be honest I didn't think Freya would get much from it, because she had so many issues. Up until that point I knew she could hear to a degree, and she was definitely aware when Steve, Tom or I were with her, but she couldn't see very well.

*I knew her hands were very important to her – She was very tactile – but it never occurred to me that she would get anything out of making music. I knew that **I** liked music, but I never realised just how magical it would be for **her** and how it would bring **her** alive and, as a knock-on effect, bring **me** alive too! It was a revelation when I did eventually latch on!*

And that's what makes music therapy so special to me because it focuses on what someone *can* do rather than what they *can't* do, even when they are very poorly.

Completely… So even when Freya was really ill towards the end, we had music on all night and if the music stopped then I would get up and put it on again because I felt it helped her stay relaxed.

What was it that helped you realise that this was something worth pursuing with Freya?

Well, I knew you had had some lovely moments with Freya and you had told me how responsive Freya had been with you, but I'm not sure I really latched on to what you were saying to start with…

So what was the tipping point for you, do you think?

Well, it was Tom's fault, because it was after one of his drumming sessions with you that he 'snitched' on me and told you I played the saxophone! So, when you came out with Tom you said: 'I hear you play the saxophone?'

'Oh, I used to', I said, 'but it's gathering dust under the bed now', and I remember you saying to me: 'Well, you might just like to get it out and have a go at playing it again?'

Yes, I remember saying to you: 'just imagine, if Freya loves lights, then she will love the look of it because it's so sparkly, and she might love the sound of it too; it might be something nice that you can enjoy together…' And you still weren't sure. 'Well, maybe…' you said!

I really was very reluctant, wasn't I?!

And I didn't let it drop – I think I challenged you a bit?

You did, yes!

'Next time you come', I said, 'why don't you just bring it with you?'

Then, when I got home, I thought about it a bit more and decided that if Tom, Steve and you were all nagging me then I'd better get it out and dust it down!

So I polished it up, and then the next time Freya was a bit miserable I thought, 'I'm going to try and just see what happens'. I remember first of all I just laid it on the carpet next to her, and straightaway she reached out and touched it. She loved the feel of it because it was cold, and she liked things that were cold…

Yes, she always loved the feel of the metal windchimes...

*That's right! She did! Then I picked it up and blew very gently, and she just sat there staring at it and staring at me, and I thought, 'Oh, she's actually stopped crying – She's smiling. Wow! OH WOW! Ceridwen was right, she **does** like it!'*

So, tell me about how it felt to know that *your* music and *your* playing had had that effect on her?

It was incredibly special, because in that moment it was just me and her, and I thought, 'How blessed am I that I can play this and that she loves it?' Life was so busy with looking after Freya and I just didn't think I had the time to play anymore, and it never even occurred to me that she would take to it.

So, when was the last time you had played the sax?

I occasionally picked it up when Tom was little, but I put it away when Freya was born... Then, with your encouragement, I started playing at the Helen House carol service, with Tom as your drummer, and I played carols round the tree in the village too.

Then school started asking if I would take it in and play for Freya's class, and they all really enjoyed seeing and hearing it and touching it. It felt so good to be making a difference to the children.

And what was it like to raise the bar and play for the Helen and Douglas House Anniversary services at Christ Church Cathedral in Oxford? They were high-profile events!

They really were, yes!

There were about eighty musicians and singers altogether: parents, siblings, care team, doctors, fundraisers and my daughter Bethan's local village school choir.

I loved it, because it gave me such a boost to know that you thought I could do something like that. It was also something for me, that gave me my own identity, rather than just being Tom and Freya's Mum. I absolutely love that don't get me wrong, but it gave me another dimension to my character and added to my capabilities I suppose...

You always made it fun as well! So much of my life was so serious, living on a knife-edge, not knowing when the next blue-light trip to hospital was going to happen. When I was playing the sax, I could leave all my fears behind for a while and get lost in making music. It gave me something to aim for too after Freya died; it gave me a reason to keep playing.

It gave you a lot then...

It really did. It gave me a sense of belonging too, because many of the performers were Helen House parents as well and the sense of camaraderie was wonderful, when so much of my life was taken up with being on my own with Freya and feeling very isolated at times.

That whole experience made me feel – well, it was like a giant hug – we were all in it together and we all understood each other. It just made me feel safe and 'held'...

Freya's last weeks

Things become really serious in November 2004. Tell me how it all unfolded...

She came home from school on 5 November, and she was not well, so we rang Helen House and they said we could take her there for assessment.

After a few nights she wasn't improving and so we decided to go home again, and then she stopped eating...

It was a very stressful few weeks, and I do remember one night just needing to go for a run. Then a friend turned up with chocolate cake, and she offered to sit with Freya so I could go running. I remember just putting my headphones on and turning the volume up and running hard and fast. It was exactly what I needed, and it did me a lot of good.

Music is in there again...

Yes, I hadn't thought of that...

And the chocolate cake?!

That was good for me too!

What happened with lights and candles in those last weeks?

I remember one night when the brilliant Shirley (community nurse) came and slept on the sofa, but she didn't like being away from Freya, so she said: 'Why don't we bring Freya into the sitting room?' We rearranged the sitting room, brought Freya's mattress in and we laid her here in front of the fire.

And Shirley decorated it with Freya's fairy lights from her room, we lit the fire and some candles, and we had music on constantly.

By this point we were having to face the fact that Freya was not going to live much longer, and after a long discussion, we decided that we would keep her here at home.

And that was...?

That was 13th December 2004: She was five-and-a-half...

Five-and-a-half?! She defied that doctor who said she wouldn't even have one birthday then!

Completely! And the next day, the 14th, Halina came to visit us, and one of the first things she said was: 'So where's the Christmas tree SJ?', I said, 'No tree, I don't want a Christmas tree'.

But actually, it was lovely; Tom and Halina's daughter, also called Freya, got the tree out and decorated it and it looked beautiful with all the lights...

Ah, those lights again...

That's true – I hadn't thought of that...

It was a very special afternoon, because we had Christmas music on really loud, the tree lights, Freya's fairy lights, firelight and candlelight. Tom was laughing and chatting with Halina's Freya, and my Freya was nice and relaxed...

And then, a few hours later, she just took one gentle last breath and quietly slipped away...

Halina went round and very calmly turned all the machines off and took Freya's tubes out so that we could have some time with her without all that 'stuff', and she went to turn the music off, and I said: 'No, leave the music, I want the music on still'.

Lights and music surrounded her at the end as well then; that must have been reassuring?

Yes, it was as good as it could be really: She was surrounded by light, music and by those who loved her most...

Freya's song

Take me now to your preparations for Freya's funeral? Why did you choose candles?

Well, I've already said I never wanted Freya to be in the dark. Her room was always well-lit, not bright, just warm and welcoming. Freya was my light too you know: She lit me up. I'm sure before, I wasn't a 'light' person as such – and she has candles down at her grave and lanterns as well, so she's never in the dark. Now I know as well as you do that those candles will go out as soon as I leave, but she has solar lights down there as well.

So above everything else, I knew I wanted candles at her service. I wanted everyone to come up and light a candle for Freya.

So that must be where I got the idea from to write a song for the candle lighting?

I guess so, but I don't quite remember how it all came together...

I think I just found myself offering to sing something, because our musical relationship had been so strong, and I wanted to do all I could to support you. That's I think one of the most powerful things about music; it doesn't stop when someone dies. Music makes memories and so their story continues, and I suppose I just wanted help fulfil that for you as best I could...

That's a lovely description, I like that. I definitely remember thinking I wanted you there, either singing or playing. I remember saying to Steve: "Ceridwen needs to be part of this funeral, because music has been so significant in my life and in

Freya's life and I want music to be part of her service too," but how you wrote it in such a short time I don't know, because she was buried on 20th December...

Six days?!

Yes! She died on the 14th, and she was buried on the 20th. Her service was on 20th December.

Well, I distinctly remember sitting at my piano at home and looking through all my music to find something suitable and not finding anything that felt 'right'... So I decided to write a song – in six days though?!

Amazing!

I must have sent you the lyrics, but I wouldn't have had time to play it to you. You must have had complete trust in me to give you the right song. The first time you heard it then was at Freya's service?

It must have been...

And it was printed on a separate sheet as well because there wasn't time for the lyrics to go into the order of service.

Yes you're right, it was, because I still have that sheet with my music folder with all of the music you wrote out for me...

It was perfect; and the words are so powerful, the way it goes through lighting a candle at every point in the day, and then lighting a candle in the midnight hour when there is no-one to turn to and everybody's asleep. That's such a strong thought and one that has kept me going on many nights since Freya died.

'Freya's Light'

*Verse 1 When you wake up in the morning,
And you're feeling all alone,
When your day seems kind of endless,
And all your hope is gone,
Light a candle in that morning hour,
Let it shine upon the dawn,
Candle in the morning hour,
Candle in the dawn.*

*Refrain: That candlelight will guide you,
Safely on your way,
Through the stormy waters,
To another day,
Shining in the darkness,
Bright for all to see,
Shining out so clear and strong,
For all eternity.*

Verse 2 When the midday sun is glowing,
And your heart has lost its song,
When you're feeling tired and weary,
And everything seems wrong,
Light a candle in that mid-day hour,
Let it shine upon the sun,
Candle in the mid-day hour,
Candle in the sun.

Refrain:
Verse 3 When the sun sets on the horizon,
And a cold chill fills the air,
When the shadows start to lengthen,
And you think that no-one is there,
Light a candle in that sunset hour,
Let it shine upon the eve,
Candle in the sunset hour,
Candle in the eve.

Refrain:
Verse 4 When the midnight hour's upon you,
And there's sleep across the land,
When you need someone to talk to,
And you need a helping hand,
Light a candle in that midnight hour,
Let it shine upon the dark,
Candle in the midnight hour,
Candle in the dark.

Refrain:

I've sung 'Freya's Light' many times since, at other candle ceremonies, and people always say what a beautiful song it is. Do you remember the candle lighting ceremonies we had at Helen House on our Remembering Days? That was the central part of the services there too.

Yes, and you sang 'Freya's Light' sometimes, but you always warned me when you were going to sing it! Just think Ceridwen, of all the funerals you have played and sung for, and all those remembering days? I don't know how you do it...

It's a big ask, but you know, I just tell myself it's a million miles away from what you as a family are going through, and I think writing a personal song really illustrates the power of music to offer something tangible and concrete at a time when I guess a lot of people must think to themselves: 'I feel so useless, I can't do anything to help this family…'

That's very true – well it was certainly a huge comfort to us to have such a personal song for Freya.

'Freyabeya'

Ok, so tell me a bit about the charity, how did that come about?

After Freya died, I remember thinking I wanted to do something to commemorate her life... I wanted to keep Freya's name alive, and with the music link and playing the sax for Freya at home and at school, something musical just seemed the obvious choice.

And did 'Freyabeya' give you something positive to focus on?

Yes, it was really important to have a positive focus in what were the toughest of times, and I wanted other children like Freya to experience the joy of music. I had learnt from you just how important music is, and I knew what it had done for me and for Freya and just wanted to give something back.

So, I spoke to Freya's school and asked if they would be interested in using any money raised to fund musical input for the children and of course they said 'yes!' So 'Freyabeya' funded visiting musicians; it provided money for them to buy musical instruments; we also supported a boy who had additional needs in Tom's mainstream primary school with some music sessions.

I did talks for the Women's Institute and the Church and other local groups to raise money. The Defence Academy here in Shrivenham became big supporters of ours too, and our local pub, The Prince of Wales, put on Quiz nights for us.

You also played sax at the charity concert!

Yes, that was very special, and Rosie's Rainbow Fund choir sang 'Freya's Light' for us. That's another amazing music charity that grew out of the loss of Carolyn Mayling's beautiful and talented daughter, Rosie. You suggested them I think, didn't you, because you did music therapy for RRF at the Oxford Children's Hospital?

That's right. It was a great collaboration, and I remember suggesting you might like to accompany them!

Well – you cajoled and badgered me, in the nicest possible way!

And I remember asking how you felt about playing the song on the night?

And I said: 'I really don't know...'

So I suggested that you just have the saxophone there and decide on the night whether you wanted to play or not – and you did play!

We both sat on-stage to play, but I remember we hid behind the choir, because I said: 'If I'm going to do it, I don't want to be seen!'

But how amazing that you played?!

It was a good night, wasn't it?

It really was...

So how did you make the difficult decision to wind up the charity?

Well, it happened organically really, because when Covid hit the playing just stopped. So there was that natural break. Then I found out that I was going to be a grandmother: I was also about to hit sixty and I began to wonder if 'Freyabeya' had served its purpose.

I remember going to Freya's grave one day, as I often do, and I had a chat with her, and the next morning I woke up and said to myself: 'Freya's ok with it, it's time...'

Freya's gift

So, thinking a bit now about why you thought of me as someone who might be able to use the remaining money; How often would you say we were in touch over these last 17 years?

Not that often I don't think, maybe twice a year? But it was only a brief message usually, just family updates really...

So how did I come up in conversation when you were thinking about what to do with the money?

Steve and I were chatting with a trustee about it one night over a drink and I said: 'Well, if Ceridwen was still at Helen house, it would be a no-brainer – I'd give the money to her, but she's down in Devon now'. How long have you been at CHSW (Children's Hospice South West) for now?

So, when you messaged me in February 2022, it would have been eight-and-a-half years...

Gosh, that long?! Anyway, Steve then piped up: 'Well it doesn't matter that she's not at Helen House, we can still give it to her: She's doing the same work, and it would still make a huge impact on families like us... Let's just see if Ceridwen wants it'.

And I just couldn't think of anything better: You were there at the beginning, you've been there all the way through, you've helped me with getting me playing again, you gave me some magical music times with Freya, and you've helped me with all the concerts, so to wind up the charity by giving you the money was just perfect.

So that's when you messaged and asked if we could chat...and the timing was unbelievable, because my old MacBook that CHSW had kindly bought for me when I began working there in 2013 was on the way out.

And I use it every single day: I write all my reports on it and do all my admin on it; I edit photos and videos of children in music to give to families – only yesterday I was showing a Mum some videos of her son in music. He had died a little while ago, but she said it was so wonderful to see the videos again and I sent them to her so that she could share them with her Mum.

That's so precious...

It really is, and I compose songs on it for the staff choir to sing on our remembering days, and I make up songs with the children and siblings and sometimes parents – I've even recorded a Mum singing a song which was then played at her son's funeral.

It really is the most amazing piece of musical kit, isn't it?

Completely! The hospice fundraisers were working hard to find the funds for a new one for me. Eddie Farwell, (co-founder of Children's Hospice SouthWest with his wife, Jill) who knew Helen House well from the times when they used to travel up to Helen House for respite stays was also very supportive of my bid for a new laptop. As father to Katie and Tom, who both had life-limiting illnesses, he witnessed how music helped his children settle when they were in distress.

Really, is that right?

Yes, he used to sing to them, particularly the songs of Purcell. He found real comfort in being able to do that, just as you did when you played your sax for Freya.

Ah, that's really lovely to know...

Yes, it's a really nice link… Then, at almost exactly the moment my old MacBook literally stopped working, Freya stepped in and shed her light onto the whole situation!

And your reaction was amazing! I remember thinking, 'Wow! This really means a lot to her...'

I burst into tears when you told me: I was absolutely staggered that you thought to reach out to me after all that time. I know that the music story of a child lives on in the hearts of parents, but this was beyond anything I had imagined. It means that the musical experiences that we shared back at Helen House are still so meaningful for you, even now, nineteen years on from when Freya died, and twenty-four years on from when we first met!

So important still, yes, of course they are... I was thinking only the other day how I would just mention a song I wanted to learn and then a few days later it would land on my doormat. I still have all the songs you gave me: Christmas Carols, 'Lean on Me', and of course 'Freya's Light'...

Do you remember that we always had this joke that it couldn't be anything less than 5 sharps?!

Yes, that was hilarious!

And sometimes even now I'll look through the music and you've written all over it, '5 sharps SJ, you can do it!!' And: 'This one's only got 2 sharps, so you won't want to bother with it – far too simple for you!'

You used to say to me: 'I don't do anything less than 4 sharps – Darling!!'

You know, sometimes when I look back, I think to myself how lucky I am, and I do feel so blessed. Even though we don't have Freya anymore, we have met such kind, generous, creative people, who I would never have met if Freya hadn't been so poorly.

I had that because of Freya...

Wow – that's an amazing thing to say...

Final thoughts

So how does it feel to know that her light shines on?

It's fantastic! It's come full circle, hasn't it? I know 'Freyabeya' doesn't exist as a charity now, but it and Freya are still working their magic; it's just wonderful to know that there are going to be hundreds of children and families who feel Freya's love and light.

Well, for me, it goes back to Bob's quote at the very beginning: Freya's song has captured her story, and it is secured for generations to come, partly thanks to this chapter, because others will now read all about her…

Yes, as you say, her story lives on – amazing!

It really is…

And, of course, this chapter is going to be typed on my MacBook…

Fabulous! So – Shall we have pudding now?!

References

Heath, B. (2021). *'Songs from a window'*. AntPress.org. Printed by Amazon.

Chapter 5

The Power of Connection: Family-Centred Virtual Music Therapy Groups

Tom Grey and Victoria Swan

Parent and Therapist Collaboration

The perspectives in this chapter are provided by Victoria, who is a Music Therapist and Creative Therapies Lead at Demelza (Hospice Care for Children), and by Tom, who attends the groups with his adopted daughter, who we will refer to as 'Milly'.

Victoria approached Tom (who is widowed) about working on this chapter because he has such a powerful story to tell of his experiences of music therapy with his daughter Milly and can bring the under-represented perspective of a father of a child with a life-limiting condition (Fisher et al., 2023). This chapter has been written in collaboration over a number of joint working sessions. Some of the material has been emotionally difficult for Tom, and so time was taken to talk these things through. As well as contributing his own perspective and experiences, Tom has provided a 'layperson's view' of the material, to ensure it is as accessible as possible.

Overview

There is no clear definition of music therapy in paediatric palliative care (Overå, 2023), and in an increasingly online world, there is a convincing argument for offering music therapy virtually. However, delivering this emerging practice with existing technology can feel awkward or even unworkable. To demonstrate the range of outcomes made possible by delivering music therapy groups virtually, we will explore the development and provision of such groups, offered three times a week, by Demelza. Demelza delivers care and support to children who are facing serious or life-limiting conditions living in Kent, South-East London and East Sussex in the UK.

Background and Context

The groups are offered via the secure online video conferencing platform Zoom, and are open, meaning participants can attend (or not attend) without needing to inform anyone of their intention to do so. Many participating families are vulnerable to social isolation (Collins et al., 2016), and the groups offer a connection to

DOI: 10.4324/9781032664378-6

The Power of Connection: Family-Centred Virtual Music Therapy Groups

Figure 5.1 "The Power of Connection", a non-verbal explanation of the groups, produced by Tom Grey, inspired by his reflections during the creation of this chapter.

Demelza, but also into the homes of other families with children receiving palliative care.

As well as Victoria and Tom's perspectives, Sam, mum to Lucy, who has complex medical needs and accesses the virtual music therapy groups, will contribute her reflections throughout this chapter. Sam shared with the authors:

'Opportunities for families like ours to feel connected to, deeply involved with and equally participating in an activity with other people are very hard to find. There are also the practicalities of getting ready and out of the house on time which are just harder, so being able to be part of a group from the comfort of your own living room makes it accessible and doable'.

How the groups started (therapist's perspective)

These music therapy groups were established during the COVID-19 pandemic, when the face-to-face delivery of music therapy was not possible. In May 2020 I was informed by Demelza that families were asking for online music groups to support their emotional well-being and decrease isolation. I had initial hesitations about running virtual groups. I had not offered therapeutic services virtually before.

What equipment would be needed? How could music therapy – an intervention that was so reliant on listening to one another, subtle sounds, gestures and eye contact – be effective through an online platform? How was I going to offer a reciprocal music intervention without families having musical instruments at home? How would I find the confidence to provide an intervention that would need an element of performance to large numbers of people? The need to offer the groups, and the fact that families had specifically asked for them, gave me the incentive to find solutions to these problems.

How I became involved in the groups (father's perspective)

My daughter, Milly, lives with a life-limiting condition, and initially attended the music groups with her mum, who heard about them during a well-being call from Demelza in the summer of 2020. Milly attended the groups on a weekly basis with her mum thereafter. In March 2022 Milly's mum was diagnosed with Lymphoma, but continued to attend the groups. I occasionally stood in for her when she was too ill to attend. Sadly, in October 2022, my wife, Milly's mum, died. I gave up work to care for Milly and her brother while we struggled with our grief. Giving up work was definitely the right decision, but it changed my life overnight, as I was thrown from being a senior manager in tech (albeit one who tried to be as involved with the kids as possible), to being a full-time parent/carer. In the upheaval immediately following my wife's death, Milly's attendance at the groups lapsed, but Milly said within a few weeks that she wished to attend again, and I contacted Victoria to be added to the mailing list in my wife's place. Attending the groups again, without her mum, was very hard for Milly and me, but Milly has continued to attend the groups every week since.

The lifecycle of group sessions

Session planning

Group music therapy at Demelza has historically been facilitated by a music therapist together with a co-therapist, but these online groups are facilitated by only a music therapist alone. This decision was made initially as the team was small and stretched, and while there is now a team of music therapists, it was agreed that the groups work well as they are.

Each session is themed to narrow down the endless musical possibilities, to give participants an idea about the type of music to expect and to support the social element of the groups. Themes recognise celebrations (such as Christmas, Diwali, Halloween, Chinese/Lunar New Year), important days (such as Earth Day, World Day of Languages, World Book Day) or sensory opportunities (including Weather, Animals and Wild West). Accessible learning opportunities are provided with Weird Science, Colours and also *Horrible Histories*, which Milly was empowered to suggest herself in the hope that we would sing songs from Six the Musical, which of course we did!

With the reduced possibilities for interaction in the virtual session, continuingly playing music live could feel like a concert, with the therapist pushed into the role of 'performer' and the participants of 'audience'. Using pre-recorded music avoids this dynamic and offers shared music making and interaction by freeing Victoria to join in with singing, playing, receptive music listening and showing the actions to songs. Pre-recorded music allows a range that could not be played by one music therapist alone, for instance choral and orchestral music. Victoria always includes songs that she sings herself to offer reflective music-listening, and also to provide theme-specific original lyrics to well-known tunes.

The children who participate in the groups have varied sensory needs and so sensory play is integral to Victoria's work as a music therapist, to support children's learning and development. There was no need to limit this in a virtual setting. Sensory items and resources are suggested before each group, such as spices to smell during Diwali and lights for stars during space-themed sessions. These items are also gathered by Victoria, contributing to a shared reciprocal activity – highlighting the similarities between child and therapist, rather than differences.

Preparing to run the group (therapist's perspective)

I initially hosted the groups from the hospice; but it proved more practical to hold the sessions from home as it was quieter, and there was a more stable internet connection. However, my home was now visible, which felt in conflict with my psychodynamically informed training and practice. I tried using virtual backgrounds, but these blurred out my hands or instruments, so I now hang theme-specific photography backdrops behind me. These are often commented upon by children and families as they 'zoom in' to sessions.

I send reminders by email to regular participants myself, as an opportunity to communicate with families if they have not attended the group the previous week, and to share whether the child has encountered difficulties, such as being worried about upcoming medical treatment.

It feels important to complete emotional preparation before a session. Given the open, dynamic nature of the group, I never know with certainty which participants will attend. I read through the clinical notes for any children who have been unwell or are known to be in-patient in hospital, which offers insight into how a child is going to present in the session. As is the nature of children's palliative care, there have been times when a child has appeared well one week, only to join the group from an Intensive Care Unit the following week. The shock of seeing this needs some level of preparation.

Additional emotional processing is needed when a regular participant dies. These groups have been running for nearly five years, so this has sadly happened multiple times. Part of this process is removing the child's name from the attendance sheet – the finality of this is always painful. The absence of sending the reminder email is also poignantly felt and acknowledged. Bereaved families will often speak with me following the death of their child. If they are not resident at the hospice in a Bereavement Suite, I send a card to the family or call them. I often see them again at a bereavement service where I sing and play, and we share memories of the groups.

I do not announce in the group when a child has died – some families might have known the child outside of the group, but others will not know them, and it could be quite distressing to encounter. However, I will say after the final song, that if anybody would like to stay behind and talk, they are welcome to.

I felt a painful loss following Milly's mother's death. This was the first death of a parent I knew well, and I struggled with the loss. It felt somehow 'closer to home' than the death of a child, which is perhaps a little more anticipated. I was very fond of Milly's mum and wondered often how Milly and Tom were coping without her. Milly was understandably visibly upset in the first group back without her Mum, and I could see her pointing out the other mums in the group and seeing Tom support her with this felt difficult. I considered it was important to not openly acknowledge her sadness as I didn't want to draw attention to it in a group situation, but I did describe how some music feels sadder than others, and that's okay. I also wondered how Tom felt, being the often sole father in the group, but also poignantly the only person who was widowed, navigating being a parent in this medical world alone while grieving deeply. I would always refer to the adults in the group as 'grown-ups', so as not to draw unnecessary attention to his gender. I took a walk after these sessions, to process my thoughts and feelings around wanting to do more to support the family. For possibly the first time, these groups did not feel 'good enough' to support Milly.

Getting Milly ready for the group (father's perspective)

In the hour or so before the session, Milly will hunt down the sensory items suggested by Victoria. For Milly, finding and collecting these items is an important part of her experience of the session, but also a shared experience between Milly and myself to find items in the house that match the suggestions. This is bittersweet, since it's often a chance to remember together how her mum would do it, and the funny things she sometimes said or did. Milly will also collect her music bag, which contains simple musical instruments, plus a few sensory items, that Milly brings to each session. This bag is dedicated to music sessions, and Milly will rarely touch it at any other time.

In the aftermath of her mum's death, Milly found themes around Valentine's Day and Geology difficult, the first because she used to buy her mum a gift from school, and the second because it was the subject of her mum's degree, and a group theme they had enjoyed together previously. Having the information in advance, allowed me to prepare Milly, explore her emotions and decide whether to attend or not. For me, in the first difficult weeks after my wife's death, Victoria's emails were a simple and human way to communicate with Demelza as an organisation, as well as to get information on the help they could provide, without finding an anonymous email address on a webpage. I found it hard to ask for help, perhaps because I was afraid people would think I was unable to cope as the primary carer, but having a level of existing trust with Victoria made her support seem much less of a threat.

Emotional preparation is equally important to Milly and I. I need to support Milly to be calm and receptive to participate, and to prepare to entertain, support and encourage her as much as possible, even if it means a lot of dad-dancing! I typically set up first, and Milly will join me about five minutes before and settle herself. About two minutes before, I will connect to the Zoom session, allow Milly to enter her name and join. Milly likes to control joining the session herself and to choose a 'name' to enter into Zoom, which is often intended to be funny, and which she uses as a talking point with Victoria. Being adopted, names are important to Milly, and she is maybe 'testing' that Victoria values her enough to still know who she is, despite some quite exotic name choices! The attachment Milly has built up towards Victoria over years of weekly groups is important to her, and I wonder if she is testing that it is equally valued by Victoria. Milly sees Victoria more often than she sees most of her extended family.

Running the session (therapist's perspective)

Unlike the boundaries of face-to-face sessions, I join the Zoom session 30 minutes before the start, to set up sound and video settings, and to be there to welcome families should they log in early. It also supports children with their uncertainties about the session, offering a chance to ask questions, such as whether we will be singing a particular song that day.

One of the most demanding yet interesting aspects of these groups is the diversity of the participants. They vary greatly in age, culture and (dis)ability, and it's important that I facilitate a meaningful musical experience for all. These groups are open to Demelza's full caseload of babies, children and young people up to their twenty-fifth birthday. The ages of caregivers range from young parent/carers to elderly grandparents, and these inter-generational differences need to be taken into consideration.

I create a flexible session plan to enable adaptations by selecting music intuitively, based on the engagement in the session. While this process requires additional preparation, it feels essential.

The groups have a secure framework, starting with tuning the guitar, which offers an auditory cue to the participants that the session is about to begin. I sing the greeting song accompanied by guitar and then begin the themed music, starting with a gentle piece at a low sound level, gradually increasing in volume and intensity throughout the session, interspersed with music which allows for quieter reflection. There is often an action song. I explain that if participants 'like' actions they can join in, that they 'might need help from your grown-up' to do the actions or that 'if it's not comfortable today, you can listen'. This approach allows for inclusivity at all physical levels.

Children have learned numerous cognitive skills through regular attendance at these groups, including: learning to clap; holding beaters/shakers; developing vocal sounds; learning Makaton signs; and concepts such as stop, go, loud, quiet, up and down.

Thoughts from Sam

Sharing that 45 minutes with other families who understand your life, accept you as you are and celebrate when your child bangs a drum or waves a shaker is golden time for us. I feel a solidarity with the other parents on the screen, many of whom I haven't met in 'real life' but who I feel safe being myself with Lucy in that session. Victoria has created this safe space, and I am eternally grateful for that.

Can you dance like nobody's watching? (father's perspective)

As the parent of a child who can mobilise independently, I sometimes wonder how other children and caregivers might feel seeing Milly 'dancing like nobody's watching', while their child can perhaps make few voluntary movements, especially since Milly's history means that she will often 'show off' to try to get a disproportionate share of Victoria's attention. I therefore rely on Victoria to maintain a fair and inclusive space and take direction from her lead, trusting her to judge how much attention to give Milly and how to balance that with the needs of children who cannot interact, but who must often want just as much to be included.

Ending the session (therapist's perspective)

The ending of the group is carefully considered. The session ends with a well-known upbeat song that matches the theme. I clearly signpost the fact that this is the 'last song before we sing goodbye', which helps caregivers prepare themselves and their children, especially if saying 'Goodbye' is hard. I share the theme of the next group, acknowledge any breaks and mention any upcoming family events that I will be attending, where I might see the children.

A See You Next Time Song is then sung. Most families unmute themselves and say 'goodbye'. Tom tells me that for Milly, unmuting, speaking to me and hanging up is a meaningful ritual, and it is important to her that she controls this transition, with Tom supervising. Some children struggle with transition, so I offer plenty of time allowing space to leave in their own time or wait for their adult to do this for them.

Beyond the session (father's perspective)

For Milly, the anticipation that Victoria will be present at in-person events can be reassuring, providing a friendly well-known face among an often vast number of unknown people. Milly also values the link between the virtual space she shares with Victoria and the physical space of the event – it reinforces that Victoria is a 'real' person, who knows, respects and cares about her, unlike a TV or YouTube presenter. In the immediate aftermath of her mother's death, it was Victoria that Milly asked to see when she visited Demelza, and Victoria is still the first person she seeks out at events.

Thoughts from Sam

'It's wonderful to see the other families on the screen, people logging in from their homes, from the hospice and sometimes from hospital. You can see the impact the music session and Victoria has on them, but also as a participant, you can feel the shared positive impact you are all having on each other. It is a very special, secret shared space, and I feel privileged to be a part of it. These online music sessions on a Saturday morning start our weekend off for us, they are something to look forward to and prepare for and a moment that Lucy and I can be part of a club together, which is very valuable to us'.

Practical considerations

Physical and virtual boundaries

Virtual music therapy groups are notoriously difficult to organise (McLeod & Starr, 2021) and the development of therapeutic rapport via video-conferencing platforms has been identified as a significant challenge (Fuller & McLeod, 2019). A virtual space brings together several physical spaces, some of which might be shared with people who are not participating in the session. Given the nature of the shared space, it is realistic to understand that risk needs to be assessed dynamically during the groups (Latchford, 2020). This need is exacerbated by there being no co-therapist. While no serious safeguarding issues have arisen during these groups, there have been incidents where behaviour has needed to be managed by Victoria and boundaries put in place before a more serious incident arises.

The main tool for managing the shared space confidentially is the Zoom 'chat' function. Victoria can message caregivers directly if something is occurring on-screen that might be concerning. In very rare extremes, if the caregiver isn't present, or isn't responding, Victoria can remove participants from the session.

It is expected that children and families are fully clothed for these groups. Victoria does however permit participants to attend in their pyjamas. It is important to remember that any music therapist entering a family home, whether virtually or in person, is doing so as a guest as well as a practitioner, and each family home has a very different set of values around what is acceptable (Forrest, 2014). On the few occasions when children have been unclothed, Victoria has used the chat function to send a direct message to the caregiver to ask that they please turn their camera off until the child is clothed. One of the benefits of these groups is that medical and personal care can continue while still experiencing the group, but there is a ground rule to respect everyone's privacy and dignity.

Overall, families attend these groups to engage in a shared music-based experience with their children, and the need to manage behaviour and put firm boundaries in place has been very infrequent.

Managing mute (therapist's perspective)

After numerous attempts to find ways to have sessions unmuted, I now mute participants once we have said our 'hellos', to accommodate the asynchronous nature of Zoom audio (Thompson & Khalil-Salib, 2021). While this way of working feels routine now, it was something I really struggled with initially. I feel the foundation of music therapy is shared music making of an improvisatory nature, and to be unable to hear the participants felt unnatural, awkward, and I felt a sense of embarrassment that I was the only one who could be heard. Over time, I now feel the muting of participants enables equity of access, which feels important when some children are non/pre-verbal and others communicate verbally. Muting also allows family life to carry on as needed at home, minimising disturbance to other participants. Some families play and sing along very loudly, while others simply observe, depending on what they need from the session. I've also found my lip-reading skills have significantly improved!

Possibly the most disruptive occurrence in the group is one young person who finds it funny to unmute and scream loudly when I'm singing. The first time they did this, I really jumped, and then laughed. This was difficult to manage as I authentically invite and encourage humour in my therapy. However, it was not possible to provide a space for this expression as many children attending have an exaggerated startle reflex, which can cause huge upset and potentially induce seizures. I attempted to address this boundary, taking time to explain this to the young person and asked their caregivers to support this. However this continued to occur, so I took the difficult decision to adjust the settings, so participants are unable to unmute once the session has begun, when this young person attends or when similar experiences occur.

Being muted (father's perspective)

As participants, being on mute is one of the more challenging aspects of the sessions. While it allows Milly and I to participate as loudly as we like (often 'very'!), and for me to speak freely to Milly when she's struggling emotionally, it also creates a more 'isolated' environment, where there is little interaction between the participants in the session, especially since Milly chooses to 'pin' Victoria's camera to the screen. The other participants can feel 'present' but 'not present', creating an experience that is more 'shared' than 'group'. As a man, I am always hesitant to speak during groups, and I wonder how other participants will feel about hearing a male voice in a predominantly female space, and if that will make them feel they have to behave differently. I am conscious too that men might dominate such spaces in a crass way – in my experience, any space with even one male in it, somehow becomes a male space.

Cultural and social considerations for music and themes (therapist's perspective)

It is essential for music therapists to take a broader view around cultural elements of children's palliative care. There should be an emphasis on skilful and compassionate communication with the families we support, and the professionals we work alongside, to value, promote and enable cultural difference. There have been clinical considerations around the themes of these groups. One family expressed their disappointment in the themes of Halloween and Diwali, feeling their Christian faith meant they were unable to participate. I sensitively acknowledged the family's disappointment, while still providing these themes which families had directly requested and can contribute towards spiritual needs and cultural responsiveness. The themes aim to represent the broad range of cultures/faiths of Demelza families who attend the groups, and I regularly seek requests to ensure these needs are being met.

Songs that match the theme can include lyrics some participants would find inappropriate, mostly owing to explicit language, but sometimes as a result of links with death/dying which could be upsetting to participants who are all experiencing anticipatory grief. I review lyrics to identify potential issues in advance, allowing me to make adaptations if needed.

On being 'the' dad (father's perspective)

It's clear that I am often the only father in the group. As a male single parent in a world which can feel like it is stereotyped around female caregiving, it's often common to feel like 'the only man in the room'. For instance, at review meetings at school, I will usually be the only man in a room of six to eight women. I often find I am treated specially and highly praised for things that would go unremarked if done by a female caregiver. However, I can also feel that there is a tinge of patronising and strange assumptions about what I can and can't do to care for Milly, for instance carers offering to brush Milly's hair for me, or quibbling about her bedtime routine. As a man there seems to be a subconscious assumption that I can't be the primary caregiver, and that I can't therefore have the definitive view of such matters – there is an unspoken assumption that I might have it 'wrong'. Such an environment can be beguiling too – a mother might feel shamed for forgetting her child's date-of-birth, when I forget mine, I just laugh slightly awkwardly, and all is forgiven. In the music groups, Victoria maintains an inclusive and equal environment, and they are one of the few places where being a father feels valued equally with being a mother, or indeed, any of the other wealth of different care relationships that enrich the special needs community.

Authentic human connection (therapist's perspective)

The nature of children's palliative care means these groups are attended by some of the most medically fragile children in the UK. They require personal care and medical intervention which is visible on screen. They might experience seizures, vomit, require suctioning or medication administration via various routes and chest physiotherapy; the list feels endless. In a face-to-face group situation, these medical needs and events are obvious, but this is not necessarily so in a virtual setting. Some families turn their screen off in such events, but others choose not to, perhaps as they feel they are among people who understand. Noticing and offering empathy during these medical events feels important but is not always appropriate to talk about in detail. I will say subtle phrases like 'I hope you're feeling better now [Child's name]', once a seizure ends and might say something at the end of the group to acknowledge the child's difficult time.

Technical issues are a rare occurrence now but will happen in virtual settings. As a practitioner, and indeed a human, I can feel a sense of needing to be 'perfect', but virtual communication is not perfect. Internet connections can falter, laptops can decide to update just before a session, and webcams can refuse to connect. When these rare but frustrating technical issues occur, I focus on the therapeutic relationship and the human connection, explaining the difficulty. It feels important to name the 'problem', explain why it is happening, offer reassurance that I care, and I will take action to fix it rather than allow it to continue. In essence, it shows respect and empathy to the children and families.

Thoughts from Sam

'Being able to connect with other families taking part in music therapy has been a lifeline. The sessions really helped tackle the feeling of isolation as we were connected as a group'.

Final thoughts on the groups

Delivering music therapy online is not always the family or therapist's preferred mode of engaging with children and young people (McLeod & Statt, 2021), but in this chapter we have described how family-centred virtual music therapy groups can thrive. These sessions originally began to reduce isolation among medically vulnerable families during lockdown. The intention was always to end the groups once face-to-face sessions could resume. However, participants have been vocal in voicing their desire for them to continue.

These groups deliver a broad range of positive outcomes:

- **Family autonomy:** Participants can decide when they attend without having to register or cancel attendance. They can participate on the best or worst of days, from home or hospital, and be late or leave early without disturbing the experience of others. Unlike most aspects of their treatment, the children and families are empowered to engage, or not, on their own terms.
- **Encouraging music-making and play:** Supporting families with the therapeutic potential of music, a resource readily available in their homes, as a way of

reaching authentic creativity (Winnicott, 1971), ensuring appropriate access to music and play.
- **Keeping in touch with the hospice:** Providing a regular, consistent and convenient way for families to touch base with a practitioner, and for the organisation to have awareness of people struggling to access the support they need. For many, Victoria is the only practitioner that is readily available on a weekly basis for children and families, at the click of a button, and with this comes a professional responsibility to share necessary information between families and the organisation.
- **Opportunities for increasing key performance indicators:** There is an increased pressure on our music therapists to provide statistics for session numbers in order to support funding. These groups enabled a sharp increase in children and families receiving music therapy and allowed increased attendance without the restrictions of a physical space, increasing the amount of reach there can be as there is not a cap on numbers for virtual groups. Music therapists providing community sessions at Demelza can spend up to 40 per cent of their working hours travelling. Virtual music therapy eliminates this unproductive use of valuable time.
- **Awareness of the wider Psychotherapeutic Services Team:** These groups could be considered a 'light touch' therapeutic service. They can offer a stepping stone towards more intensive individual or family therapy, or a step-down from this type of therapy after referred sessions have ended.
- **Focus on enhancing the quality of life:** Facilitate opportunities for fun as a family, fostering positive experiences and providing a chance for the caregivers to take a much-needed break from the potential monotony of their caring role, which families often report can improve the mood of the family home for the rest of the day and facilitate bonding.
- **Therapy which involves extended family:** Face-to-face music therapy sessions and groups usually only accommodate immediate family members, owing to space restrictions, however these virtual groups can allow wider family including grandparents, cousins, aunts, uncles and even pets to be involved when appropriate, and enable the therapist to be immersed in the culture of the family.
- **Flexible and dynamic approach to music therapy:** Children attending these groups do so at all ages, all abilities, all musical cultures and all stages of their illness and life trajectory, requiring a skilled professional to meet their multifaceted needs to ensure the service is appropriate and accessible.
- **Skill acquisition:** Benefits of skill development for children and young people, and psychoeducation for caregivers.
- **The Power of Connection:** Online groups provide a valuable, community-building service by increasing accessibility, offering isolated children and families a feeling of connection and enrichment through music with other families experiencing similar struggles.

Final thoughts from Sam

'There's a sweet spot in jamming together – which we now find as a family when we all play – where everything comes into a rhythm or harmony, almost by accident but it feels like destiny too. For a few moments, our souls join outside of our bodies in the music we have collectively created without following a script. It kind of guides itself and carries you along with it. That's where the therapy happens in music therapy and where all "voices" are equal'.

Is this music therapy?

Preparing and running these groups takes significant time, and it is reasonable to wonder if someone other than a music therapist could run them. Some aspects of the group could be prepared and delivered by any professional with experience of music-making with children. However, we would argue that many of the more subtle aspects of the groups require a highly experienced music therapist with responsiveness and flexibility to deliver safely. There are many concepts at play beneath the surface of these groups. The therapist needs to be able to bear when seemingly uncontainable feelings are brought by the participants and allow them to be expressed. The therapist needs to accept and accompany them in their experience without being swept along (De Backer, 1993). Regular participants in the groups refer to them as 'Music with Victoria', 'Music Club' (suggesting a sense of belonging) or simply 'Victoria'. This leads us to consider the context around the therapeutic relationships which have developed, for some over the past five years, and the boundaries of this intense therapeutic rapport could only be managed by a therapist with the awareness of the significance of music to different participants, the ability to manage the unexpected, and the skills to choose, review, adapt and perform pieces of music that are going to communicate, move, excite and enhance the lives of the people who participate. In short, a music therapist.

Conclusion

It is clear that these groups deliver a broad range of benefits and are demonstrated to be a successful modality for music therapy. Like many aspects of children's palliative care, it is hard to measure their impact, nor is it possible or perhaps appropriate to even try to apply quantitative measures. Providing vulnerable children and their families with a better quality of life, and a better quality of death, is not something the authors feel should be measured by anyone outside of the therapeutic relationship. It is clear that for the families supported by Demelza, the groups represent an invaluable connection in an often uncertain world, a connection that is accessible, easy, genuine, caring, human and fun, and what could be more 'powerful' than that?

References

Adjusting your video layout during a virtual meeting. (n.d.). *Zoom Support*. https://support.zoom.com/hc/en/article?id=zm_kb&sysparm_article=KB0063672.

Collins, A., Hennessy-Anderson, N., Hosking, S., Hynson, J., Remedios, C. & Thomas, K. (2016). Lived experiences of parents caring for a child with a life-limiting condition in Australia: A qualitative study. *Palliative Medicine, 30*(10), 950–959. https://doi.org/10.1177/0269216316634245.

DCP Digital Healthcare Sub-Committee, Latchford, G., Pote, H., Moulton-Perkins, A., Griffith, E., Raczka, R., Cavanagh, K., Papadopoulou, E., Richardson, G., Thew, G., Priest, P., Newman, C., Sinclair, H., Saunders, T., Rides, G. & Reed, R. (2020). Effective therapy via video: Top tips. *Clinical Psychology Forum, 1*(329), 37–39. https://doi.org/10.53841/bpscpf.2020.1.329.37.

De Backer, J. (1993). Containment in Music Therapy. In M. Heal, T. Wigram, *British Society for Music Therapy, & Association of Professional Music Therapists (Great Britain)* (Eds). (2005). *Music Therapy in Health and Education*. J. Kingsley.

Fisher, V., Fraser, L. & Taylor, J. (2023). Experiences of fathers of children with a life-limiting condition: A systematic review and qualitative synthesis. *BMJ Supportive & Palliative Care, 13*(1), 15–26. https://doi.org/10.1136/bmjspcare-2021-003019.

Forrest, L. (2014). Your song, my song, our song: Developing music therapy programs for a culturally diverse community in home-based paediatric palliative care. *Australian Journal of Music Therapy, 25*, 14–26. Gale Academic OneFile.

McLeod, R. & Fuller, A. (2019). *The Connected Music Therapy Teleintervention Approach (CoMTTA) and its application to family-centred programs for young children with hearing loss. 10*, 12–30.

McLeod, R. G. & Starr, V. J. (2021). Interdisciplinary music therapy and child life therapy telehealth in paediatric palliative care: Therapists' reflections on an evolving form of service delivery. *Australian Journal of Music Therapy, 32*(1), 25–41.

Overå, M. (2023). Music therapy in paediatric palliative care: A scoping review. *British Journal of Music Therapy, 37*(2), 58–70. https://doi.org/10.1177/13594575231196406.

Thompson, Z. & Khalil-Salib, L. (2021). Online Music Therapy Groups During COVID-19: Perspectives from NDIS Participants and Caregivers. *Australian Journal of Music Therapy, 32*(1), 53–63.

Winnicott, D. W. (1971). *Playing and reality*. Tavistock Publications.

Chapter 6

'Alive, brave and free. That's what music means to me': Celebrating the Diverse Voices of a Children's Hospice Community through Collaborative Songwriting

Rachel Drury, Polly Harris and Janet McLachlan

With thanks to: Anita, Iain and Lily Wilson, Lauren Adger, Louise Murray, Beatrice Clark, Ellie McConnell, Donna Nicoll, Eilidh Grant, Annabel Howell and all those in the CHAS community who contributed to the *Music & Me* project.

> 'We are extremely proud to be a part of Music & Me. We enjoyed every minute, and now we have a beautiful and meaningful piece of music to enjoy and to share with others'.
>
> Lauren (parent)

Introduction

This chapter will explore the notion of 'collaborative voice' through a songwriting project called *Music & Me*. The project involved babies, children and young people (ages 0–21) and their families, bereaved families, staff and volunteers at Children's Hospices Across Scotland (CHAS) writing, recording and filming an original song and music video. We collaborated with a total of 175 individuals in *Music & Me,* all of whom brought their unique stories and identities, while being ultimately united through the children's hospice. To best represent the project, we will focus on how equality, diversity, inclusion and belonging were central to our practice and explore how the 'voices of CHAS' were heard and celebrated within the collaborative songwriting process.

To honour this ethos, we will not exclusively explore the experience of one family or individual in this chapter. Instead, we offered all 175 collaborators the opportunity to be represented in some way and will draw on a range of quotes from discussions both during and after the project. We will consider what we have learned from the families, about cross-disciplinary work between music therapy and community music and how the project might contribute to the wider knowledge around musical care in the hospice context. We invite you to watch the *Music & Me* song on YouTube (www.youtube.com/watch?v=NRp0ZW0ragY) and offer it as a standalone representation of collaborative voice through music. While the

DOI: 10.4324/9781032664378-7

final song can be viewed as a whole entity, we will use this chapter to explore the component parts, each of which become representative of how the family and practitioner voice have shaped the experience.

Music & Me lyrics

When I'm missing someone
And I just can't find the words
When I'm feeling overwhelmed
I feel trapped and lost and hurt
Sometimes I feel fearful
And I just want to be held
Music helps me remember
To breathe

When my voice gets lost
I'll express myself in my own way
Music gives me the freedom
To let you know what I need to say
Soothes away my problems
I can face the next day
Music helps me remember
To breathe

BRIDGE
When everything feels too big and I feel too small
Music makes me feel better in no time at all
It helps my troubles melt away
I feel free to have a good day

CHORUS
I join with other people, connect to the world
Music makes me feel heard
Alive, brave and free
That's what music means to me

As soon as music starts
It fills my heart and makes me smile
Music makes me shake my shoulders!
Or gives me peace for a while
Energy and power
Together we can dance
Music helps me remember
To be me

Defining our terms

Before we explore the project in depth, it is important to provide a definition of some key terms and how we understand them in relation to *Music & Me*.

The term 'voice' is problematic as it is often attributed to spoken language. Views are predominantly sought from those capable of articulating their thoughts, feelings and experiences through words, which excludes many of the babies, children and young people we work with. We use the term 'voice' in this chapter to encompass a wide range of communications including, but not limited to, verbal sounds (with or without semantic qualities), movements, gestures and expressions. We also consider musical sounds to be a form of communicative expression. In doing so, we recognise all the contributions made to this project as equal, irrespective of what individual 'voices' sound or look like.

Collaboration in the *Music & Me* project is multidimensional. On a participatory level, it includes babies, children and young people, families, staff and volunteers. On a professional level, it includes collaborative practice between two professional arts-based approaches: Music Therapy (Polly and Janet) and Community Music (Rachel). We recognise everyone who contributed to this project as collaborators.

While we recognise the traditional definitions of 'family' (perhaps associated with birth parents and siblings), we understand the term as being much broader and reflecting all those involved in the care and support responsibilities of babies, children and young people with life-shortening conditions. This can include, but is not necessarily limited to biological, foster, adoptive and blended families, close family friends and, of course, the babies, children and young people themselves. In this way, 'family voice' cannot be seen as one singular entity, but a term that describes a range of different voices and perspectives.

Setting the context

Children's Hospices Across Scotland (CHAS) offer a full family support service for babies, children and young people with life-shortening conditions throughout Scotland. This includes family respite and support, as well as palliative care, through their two hospices (Rachel House and Robin House), homecare services and hospital presence. Our collective work as music therapists (Polly and Janet) and community musician (Rachel) encompasses in-person services in both Houses in addition to online sessions, which reach families in hospital and at home.

As a continuation and development of the support we offer through sessions with individuals, *Music & Me* was designed as a means of connection and creative expression for the whole CHAS community. Through songwriting, we hoped to provide entire family units, staff and volunteers the opportunity to express their individual and collective voices through music. We also aimed to achieve a greater understanding and appreciation of our different creative approaches at a time when our work felt especially disparate, owing in part to the COVID-19 global pandemic which provides an important contextual backdrop to the project.

Arts-based approaches evolve to represent the ever-changing social, cultural and political landscapes and must do so to remain relevant to the communities they serve. An obvious, and rather dramatic example of this was seen during the COVID-19 pandemic where evolution of approach, resources and creativity were required almost overnight and continued through the transition towards post-pandemic practice. *Music & Me* happened during 2022 and is situated in the transitional period 'back' to the 'new normal'. The project aimed to re-establish a sense of community at CHAS, one that was challenged by the pandemic, and celebrate the role of music in doing so.

Framing the project

Music & Me was a project in and of its time. In this section we explore how the timing of the project, the differences in our respective roles in CHAS, and our approaches framed the way it was designed and the decisions made along the way.

Positionality of the project

The post-pandemic context provided a strong rationale to collaborate between the hospices and (re)build a sense of community across CHAS. *Music & Me* used a blended approach of online and in-person collaboration beginning in March 2022 before culminating in October of the same year. Owing to the well-established online approach (both therapeutic and logistic) cultivated during the pandemic, the hospice community was familiar with the format and comfortable with the facilitators. This was an important part of ensuring *Music & Me* was inclusive of all who wanted to be part of it.

Positionality of the practitioners

Rachel is a community musician at Rachel House Children's Hospice in the East of Scotland, and Janet is the music therapist at Robin House Children's Hospice in the West. Polly's work as a music therapist involves the facilitation of online music therapy sessions across the whole of CHAS as part of their virtual hospice service and in-person sessions at one of the local children's hospitals. Initially, online work was set up in direct response to the COVID-19 pandemic but has since continued, ensuring that families in geographically disparate communities across the Scottish mainland and islands can access virtual music therapy without travelling to one of the hospices.

Our collective roles involve working with babies, children and young people and their families through one-to-one and group sessions, at home [online], during respite stays, at end of life and through bereavement. This work often includes CHAS staff and volunteers in addition to the families. All our respective work moved online during the pandemic and the collective experience in online and hybrid working, as well the relationships forged through this virtual support, was vital to the overall logistics, management and success of *Music & Me*.

The combination of music therapy and community music adds an interdisciplinary angle that is not often found in research literature (Tsiris et al., 2022). Although Community Music and Music Therapy are distinct approaches, we also recognise the similarities, particularly in relation to their social and cultural underpinnings (see Pavlicevic & Ansdell, 2004). It is important to state that both have, as Wood and Ansdell (2018) suggest, a 'shared broad agenda' with music at their core. Another useful framing from Wood and Ansdell (ibid) is that the two approaches can operate both 'jointly and severally' which respects the individuality of both approaches while harnessing the often complementary common ground, ensuring that both remain genuine to the values and ethics they are founded on.

Rights-based approach

A central tenet that unites our work is a rights-based approach. Through a Human Rights framing, we regard access to and participation in the arts as being a fundamental human right as set out by article 31 of the United Nations Convention on the Rights of the Child (UNCRC) and Article 27 of the UN Universal Declaration of Human Rights (UN General Assembly, 1948, 1989). Furthermore, we consider the arts a vehicle through which other participatory human rights can be realised, for example, the right for children to express their views freely on all matters that affect them and have those views given due weight, and their right to freedom of expression (Articles 12 and 13 UNCRC respectively). In other words, and of particular relevance to this book, the arts play a role in giving people 'voice'.

It is also important to situate this project in Scotland: the UNCRC has been incorporated into Scots law (2024), the first country in the UK to do so. Within our professional practices, we recognise our responsibility to ensure the babies, children and young people we work with, many of whom have complex needs alongside life-shortening conditions, can realise their rights in the same way as others. This framing has underpinned many of the decisions made in the design of *Music & Me,* particularly around inclusion and meaningful collaboration.

Music & Me

Music & Me, both in its process and product, represents a collaborative, creative, and musical conversation between the 175 contributors, in response to the question, 'what does music mean to you?' (see Figure 6.1). In welcoming a diverse range of collaborators, it was important to offer equally diverse means of taking part to ensure that every individual was heard, valued and had influence within the creative process.

In contrast with traditional models of participation in music therapy, where a therapist generally works with an individual child, family or small group, *Music & Me* adopted a multidimensional model that focussed not only on the relationship between facilitator (therapist) and client, but on supporting a connection between collaborators, the two hospices, and our professional creative approaches. Through a community-based approach (perhaps more commonly associated with Community Music), myriad contributions, ranging in size, style and content, influenced the process and development of the song and video. Participation was designed to be inclusive and non-hierarchical, the commitments to which can be seen throughout the structure of the project and the creative process.

Process

The collaborative process included a questionnaire; online songwriting workshops to write lyrics and to generate ideas around style and genre; and audio and/or visual recordings (in homes, hospices, hospitals and recording studios). Some of these happened within sessions (in-person and online) facilitated by us, while others were self-generated and sent in by the collaborators. It's important to note that this was not necessarily a linear process, rather contributions from all three stages had influence over the others.

Questionnaire

In the initial stage of the project, a questionnaire was sent out via email to the hospice community, asking people to reflect on and complete the following three phrases:

- 'music makes me feel...'
- 'music helps me when...'
- 'my favourite music is...'

We designed the questionnaire to be short and simple with the results generating broad themes and ideas to focus on, as well as specific words and phrases that ultimately became lyrics during the next phase.

Figure 6.1 Music Makes Me Feel Word Cloud.
Design created by authors.

Online songwriting workshops

In the second phase of the project, we invited people to join online songwriting workshops, facilitated by us, to discuss musical and stylistic decisions and form coherent lyrics from key words and phrases gathered through the questionnaires. Although we facilitated the workshops, they were purposefully designed to be led by the collaborators, offering them agency during the creative discussions and influence over the emerging song. The sessions were varied in format and content depending on who was attending: we included music-making activities and moments of playfulness alongside more structured conversations and practical decision-making.

> 'We all seemed to just gel, [...] we just talked and came up with suggestions all the way through, it was really, really good [...]. It was so nice to see the kids happy and even though it was all done on video, it kind of brought us all together [...] it felt like we were back in one of the hospices'.
>
> Ellie (volunteer)

It's important to recognise that the first two phases of the project (questionnaire and online workshops) were reliant on individuals who could communicate through written and spoken language to contribute their own thoughts and, where applicable, the ideas of others they advocate for. An example of how a non-speaking young person, Beatrice, was supported in this process was captured during an online session, when a carer described Beatrice's responses to hearing the first draft of the song.

Carer: *'She's very happy- she's really enjoying it,* [to Beatrice] *aren't you?'*

Beatrice: Smiles and raises her arm/elbow up towards her face. She vocalises, *'ha'* at an Eb pitch, followed by a longer and louder *'ha',* which slides downwards from an F to an Eb. Her phrase is finished with a softer, shorter sound at an F pitch.

Carer: *'She was really expressive during the song, she was, like, throwing herself forward and, like, you could tell she was enjoying it'.*

Beatrice: Continues to smile as her arm moves up and down. She vocalises *'ha',* louder again and with more force. Her pitch slides from a G to an F.

Carer: *'[...] As if she was trying to get out of her chair to, like, get up and start dancing'.*

Other areas of the project, for example the video and audio recordings, were designed to gather the voices directly of those who use different means of communication, without the need for an advocate. These different opportunities, open to collaborators across a number of months, increased the inclusivity and allowed people to participate in a way, and on a timescale, that suited them. Staff members from both hospices commented on the importance of this:

Eilidh: *'It was nice to see staff, volunteers, parents, bereaved parents and all the kids being involved – it was so inclusive!'*

Donna: *'Yeah, music was such an obvious highlight for CHAS children and families during the pandemic, so to be able to capture this in the Music & Me project has been brilliant'.* (CHAS staff)

Audio/visual recordings

Collaborators were invited to make audio and/or visual recordings of themselves singing and playing instruments or responding to the song (for example through movement or dance) in its developing form. Individuals recorded their offerings during music (therapy) sessions both online and in the two hospices. In addition, they were given the resources and guidance to record themselves at home, where possible. As facilitators, we supported collaborators in exploring their own creativity, making musical decisions and expressing themselves freely. Examples of audio/visual recordings include:

- vocalisations from non-verbal children and young people
- vocal harmonies from family members, staff and volunteers
- instrumental and percussion sounds from a range of individuals
- video footage of physical responses to hearing the song

Polly also facilitated a session at a recording studio that was donated by the studio owners, with siblings and parents from four different families. This offered the opportunity for families across both hospices to meet and connect through their shared experience.

> *'The recording session was really fun. I was the only one from Rachel House, there was, like, all other people from Robin House but it was really nice to meet other people who care for other little people'.*
>
> Lily (sibling)

From this professional recording to the recordings made at home and in the hospices, every contribution (visual and/or audio) was included in and helped shape the final song. This resulted in representation of all who contributed, irrespective of whether their voice was expressed through sound, movement or gesture.

Exploring the collaborative voice

Having considered the various platforms through which 'voice' was gathered during the project, we now turn our attention to what that voice looked and sounded like, and the influence it had on both the process and the final product. In presenting *Music & Me* as an artistic representation of collaborative family and practitioner voice, we can explore the different ways in which 'voice' emerged through the song. We will look at three key ways in which voice is represented: the lyrics and musical style, audio contributions and visual contributions.

Lyrics and musical style

The notion of 'voice' in relation to the *Music & Me* project, as outlined in our definition, is multifaceted. In songwriting, the spoken voice is demonstrated through the lyrics, however, the musical voice is also evident in the choices around genre, style, instrumentation and how the lyrics are set. The developing lyrics suggested that families wanted to use the song to share their genuine stories. While celebrating the happy times, the collaborators reflected on some of the more difficult experiences and realities of being part of a children's hospice community, as well as how music can provide support and solace.

> *'When I heard about the Music & Me project, I instantly knew I would love for my family to be involved. Music has always been important to me, and when my daughter Fearne died, playing piano and writing songs was an emotional outlet for me, it was where I turned when I couldn't face anything, or anyone, else. When we heard about Music & Me, my daughters Iris and Suzi were aged three and one, and I wondered if they were too young to get involved, but of course CHAS welcomed us with open arms as usual. The song-writing session was really fun, I love being creative with words and it was exhilarating to be collaborating with other CHAS families and the music therapists. I think we all enjoyed pitching in with suggestions and thinking of words that rhyme'.*
>
> Lauren (parent)

In expressing difficult emotions, for example, feeling *'trapped and lost and hurt'*, the collaborators seemed to feel comfortable within the process of songwriting to show this vulnerability. The themes explored throughout *Music & Me* perhaps speak to the artistic platform as being one that felt safe, responsive to the needs of the families, and ultimately representative of what they had to say.

When considering (spoken) 'voice', it is interesting that the notion of not being able to *'find the words'* is one of the first sentiments expressed in the opening lyrics. Similarly, the idea that voice *'gets lost'* is front and centre in the second verse. Finding alternative means of expression when words fail, or when words are simply not in reach, feels important. Music, which does not necessarily involve language, seems to offer a way of expressing what words sometimes cannot. A further validation of this is seen in verse 2, where music is defined as a vehicle for collaborators *'to let you know what [they] need to say'*. Here, music is represented as a platform to reach out and make meaningful connections with others: to *'join with other people, connect to the world'*.

This notion is reflected in how the process of creating the song forged connections between the collaborators, and how the product – the song in its finished form – forged connections with those who have since listened to it. In this way, music offers a means for collaborative 'voice' to be heard on a scale that moves beyond the hospice walls to the local, national and even global communities.

The lyrics also explore the concept of music providing space, and perhaps permission, whether metaphorically or literally *'to breathe'* or simply *'to be me'*. Similarly, there are references to using music as a distraction: to transcend reality, even for a short time, in its ability to *'give [one] peace for a while'*. Music can be a powerful tool in giving people a safe space to be themselves and perhaps speaks to the inclusivity that music affords. Rickard and Chin (2017) suggest that there is both musicianship in production (performing or producing music) and musicianship in listening (appreciation) which is representative of the ways in which music can break down barriers and not only become an alternative means of expression, but respect and validate the different ways in which individuals interact with it.

Iain (father): *'Bee watched the [Music & Me] video and heehawed and laughed away! And I think that was the important thing for her. She has music on all the time. Because of her visual impairment, music's really how she communicates'.*

Anita (mother): *'Yeah, Bee is very vocal with music, and you can see the happiness in her face and in her body – she gets so excited!'*

Anita and Iain (parents)

Finally, the lyrics explore the concept of music being an empowering force that makes people feel *'alive, brave and free'*, despite their challenges, and something that can act as a support: *'When everything feels too big and I feel too small'*. This idea is further reflected in the anthemic style of music, which was influenced by the interests and preferences of the collaborators, as expressed during the online songwriting sessions. Anthems are generally strong and emotive with key lyrics being repeated. The collaborators' choice of style is not only an expression of 'voice' in its own right, but one that enables the 'voice(s)' within the lyrics to be continually and repeatedly reinforced. As a community of people united by a children's hospice context, the song represents their collective group identity and provides a vehicle for their collective voice to be heard.

Audio recordings

In addition to the written lyrics, the *Music & Me* song comprised of audio recordings (singing, vocalisations, instrumental sections and harmonies) which enabled diverse communication styles to be represented within the project. For example, vocalisations from a young person (and a father responding) can be heard within the music (see video @4mins, 2 secs), and instrumental recordings (such as the shaking of bells) were embedded into the backing track throughout.

The audio recordings gave the collaborators an opportunity to be heard in the song and influence decisions within the creative process of songwriting. Individuals were able to communicate their relationship with music through joyful vocalisations (using words or sounds) and interactions with instruments irrespective of their individual means of communication or how they themselves perceived their own musicality.

As the different vocal parts were distributed among collaborators to record in isolation, a sense of anticipation was generated around what the final song would sound like. This ultimately added to the general atmosphere around the project and the sense of achievement experienced at the end.

Anita: *'We only got certain parts of the song, so we were, like, dying to know what the full song was ...'*

Iain: *'Yeah, like how it would all be put together ...'*

Anita: *'I kept saying "I want to know the whole song!", and they're like, "you can only get your bits of the song". And so, when it did all come together, we were like "oh my god, that's amazing!"'.*

Anita and Iain (parents)

The video

The music video allowed collaborators to express their 'voice' in a visual way during the creative process. They were asked to record themselves responding to the *Music & Me* song to capture and illustrate the meaning of the lyrics, perhaps the most relevant and all-encompassing being *'that's what music means to me'*. We also encouraged the use of Makaton sign language in the chorus section, to increase accessibility and represent this important visual means of communication, as well as reinforce the key message of the song.

While others were able to shape the project through more traditional (verbal) means of songwriting, the video offered non-speaking collaborators the opportunity to show what music means to them, rather than describe it. The responses to the song (and songwriting process) of these individuals were rich, varied and important to celebrate within the project.

> *'My daughter is profoundly cognitively impaired: non-verbal, unable to control any part of her body, and generally entirely shut in. The effect that music therapy has had on her has been miraculous. Watching her take part in the Music & Me project was like watching new batteries being put in! Nothing else has engaged or energised her to anything like the same extent. It's just been a joy to watch and, more importantly, a significant addition to Beatrice's quality of life'.*
>
> Louise (parent)

Through video, 'voices' were represented and had creative influence over the final product. An example of this can be seen when a child shakes his shoulders during an online music therapy session (see video @2 mins, 44 secs). This unique and joyful response to music was captured through film and included in *Music & Me* to visually represent that child's 'voice' and celebrate his experience of music. Furthermore, this contribution had influence over the lyric-writing, as it inspired other collaborators to write '*music makes me shake my shoulders*' in verse 3. This example speaks to the very heart of what *Music & Me* set out to do: uphold and celebrate the diverse voices and, through artistic means, reflect their relevance, importance and influence on the world.

Further examples of collaborators responding visually to music can be witnessed throughout the video: dancing (@2 mins, 56 secs), interacting with instruments (@1 min, 33 secs), playful gestures (@3mins, 30s secs) and images that represent the words of the song (@1 min, 2 secs), all influenced the creative output. As with other stages of the project, some of these moments of self-expression and creative freedom were encouraged and supported during highly specialised musical interactions with us as facilitators, and some were organic arising from family-led interactions.

Reflections

Reflecting on this project, particularly in relation to collaborative voice, has enabled us to examine what we have learned about our own individual practices as well as how they intersect. The influence of our collaborators – the families, staff and volunteers at CHAS – has been central to this.

We have been humbled by the willingness of our collaborators at every stage of this project. The openness through which they have contributed, and their sensitivity in doing so, has enabled the creation of a song that has both personal and collective meaning for all those who took part, including the three of us. We have been reminded of the importance of fostering relationships across the wider CHAS community and, at times, the need to look beyond our professional comfort zones and open ourselves up to new ways of working. We are also mindful of the important use of music as a form of advocacy to communicate beyond CHAS and champion the need for wider discourse around hospice work. We could not do any of this without the input of the families, staff and volunteers we have worked with on *Music & Me*.

Our own experiences of the project have highlighted the rich potential for future interdisciplinary practice between music therapy and community music and we are encouraged by the conversations that are already happening in this area (for example, see Kammin, 2019). We hope that *Music & Me* can contribute to the developing practice and methodology within musical care (as described by Spiro & Sanfilippo, 2022) from an interdisciplinary perspective, one that historically has been lacking (Tsiris et al., 2022).

> *'Many of the children at CHAS love music. Their faces light up and, to me, music is as much a part of the care and support that CHAS provides as anything else. Having seen the impact, musical care should be available to all'.*
> Annabel Howell (Medical Director, CHAS)

While we acknowledge the different and distinct lenses through which music therapy and community music operate, there are many ways in which the two approaches overlap and complement one another. *Music & Me* represents a collaboration between community music and music therapy where both the similarities and differences in professional approaches enriched the experience for us as co-facilitators. We all gained a more nuanced understanding of each other's practice, wealth of experience and skill, and endeavoured to use this in ensuring a meaningful and inclusive experience for those taking part. The responsibility of handling the creative offerings of the collaborators, taking them through an artistic process and presenting the material back in a way that provided them with a sense of genuine ownership can be quite overwhelming. The shared responsibility between us added a sense of quality, and indeed ethical, assurance to the process.

Throughout *Music & Me*, this collaborative approach felt instinctive and organic, both in how we professionally partnered with one another and how we designed the project to centre the diverse voices of the hospice community. We responded to the needs of the CHAS community, rather than defining our collective practice within a theoretical framework. When retrospectively reflecting on this process through the lens of music therapy, however, the literature in the field of community music therapy has been useful in framing our thinking and understanding the position of the project within the wider music therapy and community music spheres. The collaboration between the facilitators and the over-arching aims of the project created an approach to music therapy that both looked inwards towards the impact on individuals, as well as outwards towards connecting with others in the community, as described by Ansdell (2002). We suggest that *Music & Me* can be viewed as a project that celebrated the similarities between community music and community music therapy, in which both the music therapists and musician 'have expertise and facilitate as a member of and within the institutional community' (Powell, 2004, p. 182), in this case, a children's hospice.

Conclusions

With the central aim of cultural democracy (as described by Bartleet & Higgins, 2018), community music and community music therapy can be seen as a driver for social change. Within a children's hospice setting, this approach can be a way of championing the voices of babies, children and young people, and their families, who often find themselves existing at the very fringes of society. The inclusive approach adopted allows *Music & Me* to be framed as a means of artistic advocacy with potential to link the inner world of hospice and palliative care with the outside. It was important to us, therefore, that the song was representative of all voices in CHAS and illustrated the diverse realities of children's palliative care.

Furthermore, the scope of the project enabled a community to come together, in this case 178 individuals (175 collaborators plus the 3 of us), to collaborate on an artistic endeavour. The project allowed the many and varied offerings of the collaborators to be respected and valued and to have a tangible influence over what *Music & Me* looked and sounded like in its final form.

Many arts-based practices (therapeutic or otherwise) will argue the importance of the process over the final product with the view that it's the journey, not the destination, that counts. While this might be true for certain settings, we would argue that the product also has particular significance in the context of a children's hospice, as it creates a tangible legacy for babies, children and young people and their families.

> *'It was one of those things where you were pleased to be a part of it ... and part of that, I think, was about the quality of the recording and the quality of the end product, you know – it was probably more than the sum of the parts'.*
>
> Iain (parent)

The legacy of the *Music & Me* project has played out in several different ways so far, including the song being shared with family and friends and on social media, played at significant events (for example, funerals of those who participated), used at CHAS fundraising events and shared with you, the reader. We invite you to view the *Music & Me* song and video as collaborative family and practitioner voice in action, the shared legacy and strength of which lies in its many and varied contributions.

> *'The song is absolutely beautiful, and the video brilliantly conveys the loving and supportive environment at CHAS, as well as the immeasurable benefits of music'.*
>
> Lauren (parent)

Acknowledgements

We would like to thank Annabel Howell and Sue Hogg at CHAS for supporting us in writing this chapter.

References

Ansdell, G. (2002). Community Music Therapy & The Winds of Change. *Voices: A World Forum for Music Therapy*, *2*(2). https://doi.org/10.15845/voices.v2i2.83.

Bartleet, B. L. & Higgins, L. (Eds). (2018). *The Oxford Handbook of Community Music*. Oxford University Press. https://books.google.co.uk/books?id=Ru9IDwAAQBAJ.

Kammin, V. (2019). Performing, Sharing and Celebrating Life: An exploration of the value of performance in a joint music therapy and community music project in a children's hospice. In A. Ludwig (Ed.), *Music therapy in children and young people's palliative care*. Jessica Kingsley Publishers.

Pavlicevic, M. & Ansdell, G. (Eds). (2004). *Community music therapy*. Jessica Kingsley Publishers.

Powell, H. (2004). A Dream Wedding: From Community Music to Music Therapy with a Community. In M. Pavlicevic & G. Ansdell (Eds), *Community music therapy*. Jessica Kingsley Publishers, pp. 167–185.

Rickard, N. & Chin, T. (2017). Defining the Musical Identity of 'Non-Musicians'. In R. MacDonald, D. Hargreaves & D. Miell (Eds), *Handbook of Musical Identities* (1st edition). Oxford University Press.

Spiro, N. & Sanfilippo, K. R. M. (Eds). (2022). *Collaborative insights: Interdisciplinary perspectives on musical care throughout the life course*. Oxford University Press.

Tsiris, G., Hockley, J. & Dives, T. (2022). Musical care at the end of life: Palliative care perspectives and emerging practices. In N. Spiro & K. R. Sanfilippo (Eds), *Collaborative insights: Interdisciplinary perspectives on musical care throughout the life course*. Oxford University Press, pp. 119–145.

UN General Assembly (1948). *Universal Declaration of Human Rights*. United Nations. www.un.org/en/about-us/universal-declaration-of-human-rights.

UN General Assembly (1989). *United Nations Convention on the Rights of the Child*. *1577*.

Wood, S. & Ansdell, G. (2018). Community Music and Music Therapy: Jointly and Severally. In B. L. Bartleet & L. Higgins (Eds), *The Oxford Handbook of Community Music*. Oxford University Press. https://books.google.co.uk/books?id=Ru9IDwAAQBAJ.

Chapter 7

Music Therapy in Paediatric Palliative Care: A Link between the Hospice and Hospital

Cathy Ibberson, Music Therapist, with a reflection by Joanna Chambers

Introduction

This chapter explores the developing role of music therapy in providing a link between Martin House Children's Hospice (2024) and a local children's hospital, whose children are referred and receiving Paediatric Palliative Care (PPC). Through a collaboration between myself, Cathy, as music therapist and Joanna, the mother of William, we look back to 2022, when William received music therapy while an inpatient in the hospital. With William's story at the centre, we explore why the music therapy link between the hospice and the hospital, is pertinent, in offering a fresh perspective in the specialised field of PPC. When I suggested we write about their experience, Joanna felt keen to share her thoughts in representing the voices of families who have lived experience of music therapy in PPC. Joanna chose to express herself in a written reflection, based on a question-and-answer format. I have provided support throughout this process.

Within the chapter, as the facilitating music therapist, and also as a mother, I explore the sessions William, Joanna and myself have spent together, focussing on the integral bond between mother and son as a dyad. I also consider my role, in being part of a multi-disciplinary team (MDT), employed by the hospice and discuss related studies which emphasise the position of music therapy alongside our involvement with families, in the unique area of PPC. A quote from, Together for Short Lives (2023), reflects the ethos at Martin House, which remains at the heart of our holistic model:

> 'Palliative care for children and young people is an active and total approach to care, from the point of diagnosis or recognition, throughout the child's life, death and beyond. It embraces physical, emotional, social, and spiritual elements and focuses on the enhancement of quality of life for the child or young person and support for the whole family'.

During the time I spent with William and his family at the children's hospital, I was coincidentally studying to convert my Music Therapy qualification, into an MA at The University of West England (UWE). I chose their story and the link between the hospice and hospital, to evidence my practice. Thus, I reference myself as including in part, and expanding on the module, 'Evidence Work Based Learning' (Ibberson, 2023.) Joanna and William, for the purposes of this chapter have given further permission, with a preference to use their real names.

Development of the music therapy role

As a well-established children's hospice for over 30 years, Martin House has offered holistic care to young people and their families both in the hospice itself and in a variety of outreach settings. The hospice presently offers PPC, to the families of young people up to the ages of 25 years old and more recently includes antenatal referrals. Being a music therapist, employed there part-time since 1994, I have been involved both in-house and in community-based sessions, (Ibberson & Gilroy, 2019).

In 2017 several new referrals were receiving care in hospital. Our hospice medical team, who also work within the hospital, requested music therapy on the Paediatric Intensive Care Unit (PICU) for these children. The initial aim was for families showing an interest in music to be offered creative time for memory-making and to make a link with the hospice. Alongside hospital play leaders and teaching staff who offer creative and therapeutic support, music therapy introduced a different experience within holistic care.

I arrived for my first session at the hospital, with a bag of small percussion, my nylon strung guitar (which I feel is softer for shared strumming) and plenty of children's songs under my belt. I had trained and worked as a paediatric nurse between the 1980s–90s, so I was not a stranger to this setting. When I initially entered PICU, the sound and sight of bleeping machines attached to young children reminded me how overwhelming this space can feel. Seeing a camp bed for one parent in a tiny space, I felt immediate empathy for a young mum and baby beside me. Dindoyal, in her insightful study into mothers as music therapists, remarks on the concept of empathy as allowing therapists to 'appreciate, being with their clients in the moment' (Dindoyal, 2018, p. 108). Any anxieties I held swiftly diminished and were replaced with a sense of value and wonder. Not only was a tangible sense of well-being offered within the dyads of parents, children and me, but other families and staff in the unit were supportive and interested. Discussing, the wider perspective of music in PPC, Kammin states (2019, p. 137):

'Shoemark (2009) explored the impact that positive aesthetic experiences have on the general atmosphere or to distract, relax and energise patients, families, and staff in a hospital setting'.

I heard comments of how parents and staff enjoyed hearing live music from our little corner of PICU or in a side room. Within a few months, I received several more referrals across a variety of wards. These were children not able to access the hospice, owing to the need for surgery or symptom control. Some of the families had requested music therapy for their baby or child at the end of life. These might have been families I have met previously, who are appreciative of a familiar face, others were new referrals and glad of the creative and holistic approach.

One mum on PICU was concerned about the word 'hospice', for her newly diagnosed baby. Three years later, I met this mum and child at the hospice. Here she recalled with appreciation our early sessions, where an organic link was made. This mum explained the music therapy that she experienced opened or demystified her image of the hospice as a medical model. Knowing this, she could discuss their future visits for respite or emergency care at the hospice with more confidence.

The present wider role

As my hospital music sessions progressed, fortnightly visits were deemed appropriate. Time restraints and in-house hospice commitments were taken into consideration. The sessions reflect our way of working with flexibility and fluidity in the hospice. It is not always possible to meet for a set number of sessions, as the position of the child is ever-changing. Some sessions are ongoing and others spontaneous. In reflecting on the music therapist in hospital role, Edwards (2015, p. 62) describes the challenges that I too have found myself facing:

> 'Writing about the service was always more logical and organised than the day-to-day reality of delivering in a complex and busy environment'.

During music therapy sessions, the hospital clinical and play staff have at times stood back to watch and listen. Some have commented on the interaction or relaxation of the child and family they are caring for. Others have felt able to join the music sessions also singing or playing alongside children with chosen instruments. We collectively experience the ambiguity for the children sharing music in PPC. They might be losing the early motor or cognitive skills they had developed, while sound continues to be a fundamental way to communicate.

Evaluation of the service

Having experienced the benefits of parental involvement in music therapy, I conducted a short evaluation in November 2022 to assess the hospital's link to the hospice. The feedback from eight families and six members of medical staff, comments on:

- Increased bond between parents with their child
- Fun elements of music therapy
- Value of seeing a familiar face from the hospice
- Non-medical intervention
- One of few ways to see their child communicating, while being the focus of attention
- Poignancy recognised in particular for non-verbal children, who are able to respond with vocal sounds, changes in breathing or eye-contact

- 'Gentle' way to introduce children and families to palliative care. Parents often 'opening up' to the music team
- Viewed as holistic care. Recognition that it is not just the children who benefit, parent and carers often commenting on how much they appreciate seeing their child enjoy the music sessions in what is otherwise a clinical setting
- Challenges around timings, some preferring the afternoon as opposed to the morning session currently provided. Consistent and regular weekly offer suggested

Evaluation (Ibberson, 2023)

William's story

One of the young people I visited frequently is William, who was 12 years old, when we began our hospital sessions. As an ex-premature baby William developed a virus at four months old and suffered anoxia which resulted in visual impairment, epilepsy and developmental delay. William is tube-fed, requires suction for his respiratory challenges and is prescribed regular anti-convulsant medication. He has received treatment most of his life for recurrent severe chest infections, which have had repercussions on his quality of life. These factors consequently lead to William requiring 24-hour care.

William was initially referred at the age of six years old to Martin House for respite care, where I had briefly met the family, during an open group music session. However, my first one to one interaction with him, was in the spring of 2022 at the hospital. Here, William, became an in-patient for nine months. Joanna, William's mum, had mentioned to the doctors that music therapy was an experience they had enjoyed remotely during the pandemic. The palliative care medical team, linked to our hospice, responded by referring William for my Friday sessions at the local hospital.

During those months, there were times within the hospital environment when scheduled visits required flexibility, owing to William's treatment or cares. Also, my being at the hospital only fortnightly meant gaps in meetings naturally occurred. However, I recorded twelve full music therapy sessions.

The music therapy sessions

Initial sessions

During our first meeting on a busy open ward, I was struck by William's winning smile. His head of unruly curls and sturdy frame were bent over a wheelchair tray, as he manipulated a sensory toy with his busy hands. I soon realised that when singing our 'Hello', song, William was keen to vocalise and responded with enthusiasm, lifting his head to the sound of my piano accordion. 'Hello to William, x2 Hello to William on a Friday morning. Hello to Joanna…'. I used chords to accompany this: C/Am/F/G.

I recall an early session when Joanna asked if I could join her singing, 'A puppet on a string' (Shaw, 1967). William moved his head towards his mum and smiled, vocalising with loud and tuneful 'Aaahs', while simultaneously tapping his large tambourine. He played with a strong rhythmical beat using his chair-tray to support the percussion. I sang along and played guitar, enjoying the interaction and witnessing the strong bond between mother and son. As the music progressed, I spent time observing and waiting to be led by their direction. Oldfield (2011, p. 72), in discussing working in partnership with parents, comments:

> 'Perhaps my role with parents is a little like the musical improvisations that draw us together. We have to be sensitive to each other's contributions while at the same time allowing the musical exchanges to flow, be unexpected and creative'.

There were occasional Friday mornings, when William was tired after a restless night or post- seizure. Hence, I took the stance of sitting at the bedside and would wait to follow Joanna's lead, such as in her chosen, 'Scarborough Fair Canticle'. At times, we would drift into a free exchange of hums and non-verbal melodies. William, gradually waking, would move his head towards me and reach for the guitar to pluck gently with his fingers. Another favoured instrument was the ocean drum, which William would often choose to share a rhythm with Joanna at the opposite side of the bed.

I am reminded of my music therapy training, where the focus of our twelve-week observations of a mother and infant, began our personal development for future therapeutic relationships:

> The central truth observing the development of a mother/infant relationship, is directly applicable to the analytical couple. It is more painful to wait, to remain receptive and not cut off, to bear the pain that is being projected, including the pain of one's uncertainty, than it is to have recourse to precipitate action designed to evacuate that pain and to gain relief that one is doing something.
>
> Bick (1962, p. 23)

This quote from Esther Bick feels significant in describing my sessions with William and Joanna. The fundamentals of being in the moment and allowing the pace of mother and son to be my lead are skills I continue to develop and explore as a music therapist.

Middle sessions

As my relationship with the dyad progressed, I offer a vignette where William having recovered from a chest infection, was sat in his chair, with Joanna at his side. I am reminded of the many children I meet in my work who are non-speaking, but have a wonderful voice:

> *'As I strum playing an open 'D' tuning (DADGAD, A useful and relaxing technique on the guitar), William lifts his head, laughing. Within a song I have*

created to include his name, he joins with his voice. Making use of dynamics and changes in tempo, William swoops up and down with glorious inflections. Joanna watches with a smile and listens, as I leave the words to vocalise freely with her son. As we take turns in our musical conversation, William is animated and moves his body from side to side'.

Flower comments on her study into Music Therapy Trios, (2014, p. 843):

'The analysis suggests that the music therapy trio of child, parent, and therapist is experienced by the parent and therapist as a fluid, dynamic web of musical and interpersonal relationships, rather than a fixed entity. Within this emergent network, individuals, pairs, and the triad assume greater or lesser significance at different points.

Similarly, now an established trio, I feel Joanna, William and I have developed a relationship that he is able to recognise. I have followed William from being alongside him with his mother. Joanna in turn chooses at times to relax, while observing and trusting the interaction between her son and myself as the therapist.

Later sessions

One week, William was sat up on his hospital bed and his parents were taking a much-needed break. There was a new nurse, who was interested in learning about William and music therapy. Having discovered her ukulele skills, we explored songs which the nurse could share with William and other children during her twelve-hour shifts. During this session we played a song I had adapted for William, by OSIBISA (1975). This moves away from nursery rhymes and into more age-appropriate music, with a strong rhythm, reflecting the movements and engagement of William.

'Everybody, do what you're doing, your smile will bring a sunshine Day'. Playing in Am/Dm/E7, on the guitar, I insert, 'Hey William, do...'.

On this occasion we were joined by the play leader, housekeeper and ward clerk. Here, William vocalised with excitement, gathering his companions and communicating, through the exchanges of music. During our morning together, the nurse and I witnessed the tenacity from William. We discussed that despite him having little sight or clear verbal ability, he was the driving force for our musical conversations, where his authentic self-shone through. I recall Winnicott, in discussing the search for the self:

'It is in playing...that the individual child or adult is able to be creative and to use the whole personality, and it is only in being creative that the individual discovers the self'.

Winnicott (1971, pp. 72–73)

Before William was able to return home in January 2023, the need to continue exploring his love of vocalising was a concern for his family. Thus, a speaker valve for his tracheostomy was provided. We have since continued to enjoy occasional live music therapy sessions, both at home as outreach and during respite in the hospice setting.

Joanna's response as mother

I met with Joanna on the hospital ward in November 2022, at a time convenient for her to sit and write her thoughts. Sensitivity and flexibility in timings obviously played a large part, when the hospital environment can be stressful and tiring.

Question 1: How would you describe the link to Martin House?

> 'COVID made stays at the hospice much more difficult. Williams acute stays in hospital had often been in South Yorkshire, so we were limited in Martin House outreach. Having regular visits with Cathy the music therapist, has now strengthened that connection. It feels much more like a joined-up service, which supports us while we have been resident in hospital. Cathy, the Martin House doctors, the MH community nurse, have also been in touch and so very supportive'.

Question 2: Can you comment on how William seems after the music therapy sessions?

> 'William is generally much more relaxed and happier after a music therapy session. He usually lights up and participates physically and verbally with gusto and adores the variety of musical instruments. We will often continue singing or playing music after the session. It is certainly a mood lifter for him as he has more than once been upset from a procedure and much happier and settled after. It definitely strengthens our bond to sing together'.

William was given a tracheostomy, in July 2022 with the hope of improving his quality of life, and I met with him and his parents post-operatively. This was a memorable music therapy session both for the family and for me as the therapist.

Question 3: We had a music therapy session with William in PICU soon after his tracheostomy. How did this feel for you, and can you comment on the responses from William?

> 'The first tracheostomy change that I and William's dad did was very traumatic and upsetting for both William and us. Cathy arrived just after the procedure and asked if she could still do the session even though he was distressed. She played the guitar, and I sang along with her. William quietened and even started

to reach out to strum the guitar – it turned a very upsetting experience into a magical moment and relaxed everyone in the room.

That experience has encouraged his dad to start learning the banjo and myself the ukulele as it was so impactful for William.

We have done a lot of music therapy sessions online and he has had sessions at school, but the difference live music made when he was so very upset had a huge impact on us all'.

I am aware my role is as a therapist in sessions such as this. I am there to hold a space for the child and family and support what is brought to that space. Music therapy sessions can be joyous and lively; others can be more challenging or sad.

Question 4: What benefits has music therapy provided to your child?

'It has given us distraction after upsetting procedures, social interaction in a format William can access and enjoy. Also, an opportunity to have some fun while in hospital, with a friendly face who isn't in a uniform!'.

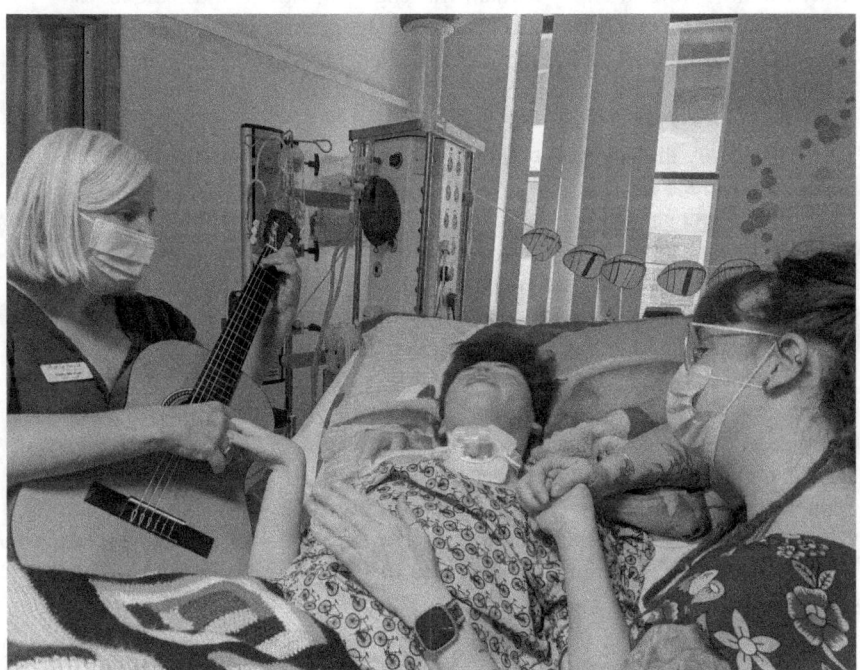

Figure 7.1 Photo of William, mum and Cathy during their music therapy on PICU. Photo taken by William's father.

Question 5: Would you like to make any further comments regarding music therapy your child has accessed at the hospital?

'It has been a lifesaver at times when William really needed some normality. An amazing service and very responsive to his level of need and ability'.

William's family, always appreciative and involved in the music sessions, commented, prior to leaving the hospital in January 2023:

'Music therapy is one of the best things we have shared while being in Hospital'.

My response as music therapist:

The dyad

The majority of the sessions for William have been and continue to be alongside Joanna, his mother. The dyad with me the facilitating therapist also being a mother, has presented an interesting and profound dynamic. At times we have made music together as a trio, and at other times I have been the accompaniment for mother and son. There have been moments where me and William have interacted, with mum present and listening. I also write of one occasion when Joanna was having a break away from the ward, trusting William was engaged with the music he loves.

Many music therapists are parents, I have again drawn upon Dindoyal (2018), who in discussing the feelings that can arise in being a music therapist and mother, states, (p. 105) 'I'd been able to banish all thoughts of my own child in order to be with someone else's'. I recall the challenge of being a newly qualified therapist, immersed in my therapy with children, yet missing part of my own children's day while they were at childcare or school. In exploring the dyad with Joanna and William, I have recognised that the therapy role has developed with me, as a mature therapist and my sons now young adults. I have more mental space, where once guilt and anxiety at times prevailed. Perhaps this is parallel to where my empathy has evolved. I can sit and be beside with a different sense of self.

I have found looking back through the years of my own profession, that if the age of a child I am working alongside has been parallel to that of my own, it has presented an extra challenge emotionally. This is a natural response I believe but does require considered boundaries from the therapist and exploration of the counter transference through supervision.

In considering my role alongside William and Joanna, the combined experience I bring with me of being a former paediatric nurse, a music therapist working in PPC, and also being a mother, feels of particular significance. Our role within a Dyad is thus unique for each therapist.

Boundaries

Boundaries are important to discuss here in relation to working alongside families via the hospice and in hospital. There is a need to provide privacy and confidentiality as far as is possible in a hospital setting. In addition, it is important that my role is explained with sensitivity and clarity. The Friday music therapy sessions are for referrals through Martin House, and the criteria for these are carefully considered by the hospice panel. Naturally, other children resident in the hospital or visiting, are in earshot to listen to the music or may be included, if the family and child choose. Equally, on occasions, staff may ask or be invited to be involved in sessions. During a later hospital session with William, I recall how appropriate it became for the staff on the ward to witness and enjoy being part of the music.

The therapeutic space

Having the creative flexibility of time and the protected quiet music room space being a given in the hospice, I recognise the difference on hospital wards. Setting up a bedside space with the instruments between sessions and having enough privacy for the child and family, requires communication and creativity. This may include using a ward playroom if possible, pulling up a chair to sit with a child in a quiet corner, or drawing a curtain around the bedside. Kammin describes a useful continuum between the private and public in the context of hospital music therapy (2019, p. 36):

> 'At times the private may intersect with the public and in turn provide the additional benefit of insight gained into the work (for example, a nurse being present or the therapeutic space becoming the child's bed'.)

Wilson, in considering how we as a profession work in a variety of settings, adopts, a 'matter of fact music therapy approach' (2018, p. 6).

> 'It is about starting with a stance that is welcoming and open to any possibility, but also consistent with a boundaried approach, which is flexible but has a clear limitation of parameters'.

The wider team

As Allied Health Professionals involved in educating each other, we continue to discuss the value of boundaries and the ongoing challenges these present, especially in the hospital setting. During a recent workshop for the 'Paediatric Palliative Care Registrar Module', in conjunction with families recording music sessions for their own special memories we were able to share consented music therapy footage and explore boundaries within the MDT. We discussed the dilemma of when a medical conversation may coincide with a music therapy session, and the possibilities of respectfully negotiating, the use of protected time and space as a team. One suggestion made, was to move a necessary conversation in speaking with parents, outside the child's room, in preference to speaking over the family and the therapy in progress. One doctor, appreciating the workshop, later joined me during his day at the hospital. On witnessing a music therapy session for a young girl, under his care, he commented:

> 'this is the first time; I have seen her so alert and heard her respond vocally'.

We have also had requests from members of the hospice care team, who wish to accompany or shadow music therapy at the hospital, to further experience the value of these sessions and the flexibility of boundaries required. Consequently, this has encouraged a model for further outreach, such as in visits to other regional hospitals from our family support team, thus increasing the links between the MDTs across different sites and the services offered via the hospice.

Perspectives

Parental

Being alongside and witnessing the enhancement of communication between children and their parents, is one of the benefits I find most rewarding as a music therapist. Annesley et al. (2020) led a research paper on a thematic synthesis of qualitative literature, drawing on the parental views when included in their child's music therapy sessions. Though not exclusively reporting on PPC, these are positive and important findings across a broad spectrum of therapy settings. Lindenfelser (2012, p. 223), similarly conducted a study of music therapy in family-centred care, stating:

> 'the promotion of physical comfort through the calming effects of music may provide physical relief for the child and thus emotional relief for the family'.

The calming effect of music emerged in the session I recorded with William and his parents, post-tracheostomy on PICU.

The multi-disciplinary team

In exploring further studies on the perception of parents sharing music therapy and those of the MDT, it seems the two are understandably interlinked. A recent study (Cousin et al., 2022) examining both the parental and staff perceptions on PICU in the Geneva University Hospital, offers progressive feedback for those children engaged in music therapy. The authors state, (2022, p. 3):

> 'The society of critical care medicine strongly recommended music therapy as part of a multicomponent intervention, aimed at reducing analgesic use'.

To report on the physiological benefits of finding a reduction in pain and anxiety during music therapy, is an important recommendation. As a music therapist in the context of a hospital setting, it can feel that you are on the edges of, rather than a central component in the MDT. For example, we may often not be included in MDT meetings, where decisions are made, as to the future direction for a given child.

Cousin et al. (2022, p. 2) continuing to report on music therapy as helping to promote communication between staff and families and thus parents feeling less isolation in PICU, is heart-warming and aligns with my own findings. In my experience, both on PICU and on the variety of wards, the nurses and the whole MDT will often join the families celebrating how the music has lifted everyone's mood or relaxed a child.

The MDT at the hospital have remarked on the poignancy of music therapy at the End of Life, as requested by certain families. This has led to a further link between the hospital and the hospice, as in a recent experience with one family. Choosing to transfer their child from PICU to use the hospice cool room, post death, the family became resident at Martin House and were thus supported within the hospice team, for the recommended five days. During these transition days they were given opportunities for further memory-making, such as with our artist in residence and creating music alongside myself for their child's funeral. As the music therapist known to them at the hospital, I was able to offer additional emotional and therapeutic support to the family, in continuing the relationships we had fostered during the music sessions with their child.

Support for the therapist

Clinical supervision and peer support from both my line manager, and my music therapy colleagues at Martin House (Ibberson & Gilroy, 2019), remains an essential part of being supported in the area of PPC. Opportunities to exchange peer experience and resources through the British Association of Music Therapy and the charity Jessie's Fund have provided immense support from the beginnings and throughout my music therapy career (Ibberson, 2005).

In the context of the hospital, much as I feel appreciated and engaged with staff on the wards, in my aim to see three or more children on a Friday morning it can feel isolating to move around a sprawling building while simultaneously harbouring emotions for each child and family and being creatively spontaneous in the music. Returning to the hospice on a Friday afternoon to liaise and share feedback with my colleagues, feels of great benefit.

Conclusion

In 1994 Martin House was the first children's hospice in the UK to include music therapy in their offer of holistic care. I feel fortunate to have been part of the developments in this role and celebrate most recently how the music therapy has evolved to include the link between our hospice and the hospital. The value of these links is evidenced through receiving qualitative feedback from families, medical staff and in particular, through my collaboration with William's family.

We reflect on the benefits of music therapy for creativity, memory-making, self-expression and in providing a grounding experience for the children and their families. It is valued highly by the staff who care for them, embedded in the holistic model of care we offer in PPC. Joanna, William's mum, has described their music therapy sessions as being, 'fun' and providing a sense of 'normality'. The families receiving music therapy have had an opportunity to voice their opinions and report on what is important to them in the care of their children. This feels fundamental when so much choice and control is taken away from the lives of these children and families. Importantly, we have found since 2017, that music therapy has in part provided a bridge for families referred to Martin House, in demystifying the perception of a children's hospice being a predominantly medical model.

Throughout this chapter, with William and Joanna at the centre, there appears to have been a ripple effect in the hospital and hospice, with the sharing of feedback from our evaluation in 2023 and the ongoing education and discussions within the MDT. Parallel with current research these have led to an increased understanding and appreciation as to the benefits of music therapy in these settings. I acknowledge the work of many music therapy services, now providing and initiating research across hospitals in the UK. (Wood et al., 2016) in their article discussing developments at Chelsea and Westminster hospital, echo much of our findings. The authors (2016, p. 41) cite: Fearne and O'Conner (2003, p. 74):

> 'The need to support parents while their children receive music therapy has been found to be crucial. When they feel supported, emotionally, and practically they are in a much stronger position to support their child's therapy'.

If we are to continue being responsive, across PPC, in achieving the correct balance within a holistic model of care, there is evidence here, that the families are seeking regular and continued therapeutic support to sit alongside the necessary and vital medical interventions for their children. William and Joanna have provided us with a lived experience of music therapy, which highlights the pertinent role of music therapy in enhancing communication, not only between the children's hospital and Martin House hospice, but for the families and the multi-disciplinary teams working together, across paediatric palliative care.

Acknowledgements

The author wishes to thank Joanna and William, for sharing their story. You, along with the many brave families I meet in my music therapy role throughout PPC, are the inspiration for our developing profession.

Huge thanks to the editors Vicky and Julie for the opportunity to be part of this unique book and to Helen Copeland, for your wisdom in proof-reading.

I would also like to thank; my academic supervisor at UWE: Adam Kishtainy, my work mentor at Martin House: Doctor Debbie Box, Olivia Fallon and Mike Gilroy as proof-readers. Thank you all for your valuable part in the EWBL, 2023.

References

Annesley, L., McKeown, E. & Curtis-Tyler, K. (2020). Parents perspectives on their children's music therapy: A synthesis of qualitative literature. *British Journal of Music Therapy, 34*(1), 39–52.

Bick, E. (1962). *The Contribution of mother-infant interaction and development to the equipment of a psychoanalyst or psychoanalytical psychotherapist.* In M. Harris (Ed.), Collected Papers of Martha Harris and Esther Bick. Clunie Press (on behalf of the Rowland Harris Trust).

Cousin, V. L., Colau, H., Barcos-Munoz, F., Rimensberger, P. C., & Polito, A. (2022). Parents' Views with Music Therapy in the Paediatric Intensive Care Unit: A Retrospective Cohort Study. *MDPI* [online]. Children, 9(7), 958. [Accessed 21 November 2022].

Dindoyal, L. (2018). 'In the therapist's head and heart': An investigation into the profound impact that motherhood has on the work of a music therapist. *British Journal of Music Therapy*, 32(2), 105–110.

Edwards, J. & Kennelly, J. (2015). Music Therapy for Hospitalised Children. *The Oxford Handbook of Music Therapy* [online]. 1st ed. Oxford: Oxford University Press, pp 53–65.

Flower, C. (2014). Music therapy trios with child, parent, and therapist: A preliminary qualitative single case study. *Psychology of Music*, 42(6), 839–845.

Ibberson, C. (2005). The beginnings of music therapy in our hospice. In M. Pavlicevic (Ed.), *Music Therapy in Children's Hospices-Jessie's Fund in Action*. London: JKP, pp. 37–47.

Ibberson, C. (2023). *Music therapy in Paediatric Palliative Care-A link between the Hospice and Hospital. Evidence Work Based Learning. MA module*. [Unpublished manuscript]. Faculty of Health and Social Wellbeing. University of the West of England.

Ibberson, C. & Gilroy, M. (2019). Music Therapy at Martin House Children's Hospice: The developing role in a Multidisciplinary team. *Music Therapy in Children and Young People's Palliative Care*. In A. Ludwig (Ed.). London: JKP, pp. 127–144.

Jessie's Fund. (2023). jessiesfund.org.uk.

Kammin, V. (2019). 'Performing, Sharing and Celebrating Life': An Exploration of the Value of Performance in a Joint Music Therapy and Community Music Project in a Children's Hospice. In A. Ludwig (Ed.), *Music Therapy in Children and Young People's Palliative Care*. London: JKP, pp. 127–144.

Lindenfelser, K.J., Hence, C. & McFerran, K. (2012). Music Therapy in Paediatric Palliative Care: Family-Centred Care to Enhance Quality of Life. *American Journal of Hospice and Palliative Medicine*, 29(3), 219–226. http://ajhpm.sagepub.com DOI:10.117/1049909111429327.

Martin House. (2024). www.martinhouse.org.uk.

Oldfield, A. (2011). Working in partnership with parents. Ch 4, in J. Edwards. *Music Therapy and Parent-infant Bonding*. Oxford University Press, pp. 58–72

OSIBISA (1975). *Sunshine Day* [Song]. *On Welcome Home* [Album]. Bronze Label BRO 20 UK.

Shaw, S. (1967). *Puppet on a string* [Song]. Pye label. UK.

Together for Short Lives (2023). *Changing lives: speaking up for children and families*. www.togetherforshortlives.org.uk/changinglives/supporting-care-professionals/introduction-childrens-palliative-care.

Wilson, S. (2018). Considering the ways music therapists are working in 2018 and beyond. *British Journal of Music Therapy*, 32(1), 4–7.

Winnicott, D. W. (1971.) *Playing and Reality. ed:* Routledge Classics (2005.) London and New York: Routledge.

Wood, J., Sandford, S. & Bailey, E. (2016). 'The Whole is Greater'. Developing music therapy services in the National Health Service: A case study revisited. *British Journal of Music Therapy*, 30(1), 36–46.

Chapter 8

'Things change, and that's the way it is': Therapeutic Songwriting with Young Adults Transitioning from Paediatric Palliative Care

Giorgos Tsiris and Daphne Rickson

Moving on...

Moving on from children to adult palliative care services can be paralleled as moving 'from the pond into the sea' (Care Quality Commission, 2014). The complexity of this transition is underpinned by concurrent, multiple and multidimensional life transitions young adults experience (Jindal-Snape et al., 2019). In addition to adapting to their changing health needs, young adults experience developmental and other transitions, including education and employment, future planning, independence, sexuality and relationships (Earle & Blackburn, 2021; Johnston, 2016).

The transition from children to adult services is commonly a stressful time for young people with a life-shortening condition and for their families and carers. When transitional care is weakly managed – which can still be the case even in countries where hospice care is well established – young adults fall into a gap in services with negative implications not only for their medical care, but also for their psychosocial, educational and vocational needs (Campbell et al., 2016). A survey of British hospices highlighted a lack of adult respite provisions and the need for developmentally appropriate services, a skilled and confident workforce in adult hospices for young adults with complex life-shortening conditions, and more integrated provision between children and adult hospices (Knighting et al., 2018).

A key recommendation of the Hospice UK transition programme (Shouls, 2023) highlights the need to put young people at the heart of the transition process by providing them with a platform to influence change, in partnership with care providers and key stakeholders. Providing safe spaces for asking young people what is important to them without being afraid of the answer is at the heart of such initiatives. We argue that music can be a catalyst to this end.

...with music

Music is not just 'entertainment' for adolescents and young people. Research shows that music can play a crucial role in influencing and supporting the developmental and psychological needs that are fundamental to their personal and social identity formation, their emotional developmental and self-regulation, and their sense of wellbeing (McFerran et al., 2019; Saarikallio & McFerran, 2022).

Music's function as a promoter of health, however, is not something given or universal. It depends on how young people use music, and indeed, there is an increased body of knowledge documenting healthy and unhealthy uses of music. The latter include using music to intensify negative emotional states through rumination and isolation (McFerran & Saarikallio, 2013; Saarikallio et al., 2015). As a result, there is a need for informed and intentional engagement with music especially within and around one's care environment. The work of music therapists – as an integral part of the multidisciplinary care team – can be particularly helpful to this end, supporting individuals and their families as they navigate different palliative care contexts and continua of musical care practices (Tsiris et al., 2022). Such musical care practices can range from private music therapy provisions to musical engagements in public contexts and to everyday uses of music as a form of self-care. Keeping the young person at the heart of their work, music therapists also support the family and pay attention to the wider ecology of care (Kammin, 2019a; Pavlicevic, 2005). They nurture and enrich the care environment and seek opportunities for community engagement and raising awareness of death and dying to the public. Collaborative projects with orchestras (Kammin, 2019b) and public sharing of children's and families' music work (Drury et al., 2025) are examples of such public-facing collaborative initiatives.

Across these continua of palliative care music therapy, songwriting is widely practised as a creative and powerful form of self-exploration and expression (Giordano et al., 2022; Heath & Lings, 2012). Through the creation of songs, young people can make sense of their developing identity, they can give form to their feelings, their thoughts and questions. Songs in music therapy can be created in diverse ways (e.g., impromptu creation as part of improvisation, or planned process with an output in mind) and can serve different functions across a private-public continuum, including legacy and advocacy work, as well as intergenerational initiatives for raising awareness of loss, change and grief (Tsiris, 2024; Tsiris et al., 2011).

As a creative and non-invasive medium of expression, music can provide 'words' to young people's experiences (Saarikallio & McFerran, 2022) without necessarily depending on their ability for verbal communication. Technology-aided songwriting can also offer unique possibilities and offer an age-appropriate medium of expression. Experimenting with modifying, layering and mixing sounds as they create their song, young adults can also explore different and new possibilities and resources within themselves (Viega, 2013). In this context, the acoustic, material and interpersonal qualities of songwriting can afford a sonic environment where the young person can experience, relate and listen back to themselves differently. These considerations were at the heart of the 'Moving on With Music' project.

The project

The 'Moving on With Music' project was developed by Nordoff Robbins Scotland (NRS)[1] in collaboration with the Transitions Team of Children's Hospices Across Scotland (CHAS), responding to young people's wish to continue accessing music therapy as they were moving on to adult services.

Taking place between 2017 and 2019, the overall project included ten short-term individual or group music therapy projects, all facilitated by music therapist Joanne Edgar. In consultation with the young people, the project focused on technology-aided songwriting. In addition to a huge range of built-in sounds and drum loops, the use of music software and its digital interface offered the capacity to use microphones and record acoustically and, importantly, the possibility to experiment with and manipulate recorded sounds using different effects. When working with small groups, the music therapist projected her computer screen on the wall to enhance accessibility and collaborative working.

Each songwriting project included two-hour weekly sessions and lasted between eight and 12 weeks. In total, 12 young adults took part with some of them participating in more than one project. The creative direction and focus of each songwriting project were shaped collaboratively between Joanne and the participants depending on their needs, wishes and interests, as detailed in a previous publication co-authored with the music therapist (Edgar et al., 2019).

Aiming to generate a sense of community between the participating young adults, a closed and private social media group was created where members could share their songs and connect with each other beyond their individual songwriting projects if and as they wished. The overall project culminated with a closing celebration event where the young people had the opportunity to share their creative work with their families and friends. In this event, the young people had the opportunity to perform their songs with a live band of musicians, or to have their songs performed for them.

The 'Moving on With Music' project held the potential to generate knowledge that could inform other similar initiatives in the field. To maximise its potential and, given the gaps in transitional care as outlined earlier, we co-designed the research study presented below.

Research aim

Our research aim was to explore how short-term therapeutic songwriting work can support young adults facing a life-shortening condition as they transition from children to adult palliative care services. We explored and documented the young adults' experiences of the songwriting process and its perceived impact on them and those around them. We also considered the nuanced music therapy practices and complexities embedded within this project, including the use of technology.

A note on method

In line with the practice-led nature of this study, we designed the data collection methods in close consultation with the music therapist while considering together the pragmatics and the ethics of the practice itself. As part of the co-designing process, Giorgos also observed a songwriting session and discussed with the young adults their ideas and suggestions for the direction of the research study.

After considering research ethics and resource allocation, our research design focused on three songwriting projects (one individual and two group projects). For each project, our data gathering involved three key components: i) an interview with the participating young adult(s); ii) an audio recording of the song and a copy of its lyrics; and iii) the music therapist's log reflecting on the songwriting process (Figure 8.1). We also conducted an online interview with the music therapist at the middle and at the end of the overall 'Moving on With Music' project, where she was able to reflect on her broader experience of the work beyond these three songwriting projects. Data collection took place between April 2018 and May 2019.

In total there were six research participants (one music therapist; five young adults) and our dataset included: five interviews, three sets of song recordings and lyrics, and three project logs. We also engaged with artefacts that emerged naturally from the work. Serving as supplementary materials, these artefacts included materials available to the public, such as press releases regarding the project as well as video recordings from the closing event.

We conducted the music therapist interviews jointly via online conferencing. The young adult interviews however were conducted face-to-face by Giorgos at the location where their songwriting sessions also took place. All

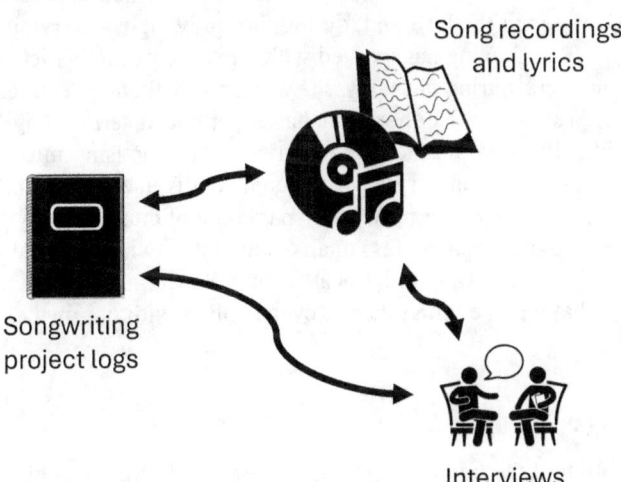

Figure 8.1 Key data components per songwriting project. Image created by authors.

interviews were semi-structured and audio-recorded. During their interviews, the young adults were invited to listen back to their song recording as a prompt for reflection.

Our analysis process involved multiple readings and listenings of the textual data (i.e., interview transcripts, project logs and lyrics) and auditory data (i.e., song recordings) respectively. Through our readings and listenings, we sought to explore and understand people's lived experiences of the project, its processes and its impact. Paying attention to people's narratives (Aldridge, 2008), we noted areas of common focus and organised these in thematic areas. Alongside our reflexive engagement with the musical qualities of the songs, young people's feedback on the meaning of their own music creations (O'Callaghan & Grocke, 2009) was instrumental to our understanding of the lyrics.

Ethics, quality and voice

Research ethics approval for the study was provided by Queen Margaret University. The NRS Research Advisory Group also reviewed the project and NRS provided host organisational approval. All young adults' names have been disguised.

Our engagement with the different data sources allowed a greater degree of contextualisation and triangulation of the findings. We also checked qualitative inter-rater reliability (O'Callaghan & Grocke, 2009) by discussing the different data components, cross-checking each other's analyses and refining the findings accordingly. Self-critique and reflexivity (Stige et al., 2009) were of essence, serving as guiding principles for our research stance and work.

Throughout the research process and while writing this chapter, we were reflexive towards our own positionalities. Giorgos has worked in several adult palliative care settings in the UK, and, during the study, he was serving as Head of Research for NRS. Daphne has worked with adolescents in a variety of contexts in New Zealand and, during the study, she was a music therapy lecturer at Victoria University of Wellington. Neither of us has experienced serious ongoing illness, nor do we identify as professional songwriters. As practising music therapists, however, we have used songwriting with people in diverse ways. While our work is framed within a predominantly Western paradigm of music therapy practice and research, we recognise that professionalisation comes with potential pitfalls and power issues. Listening was at the heart of our stance, and this includes listening to voices that may be unfamiliar or even conflict with our own experience or knowledge.

Three songs

Our presentation of the findings seeks to foreground the young adults' voices and lived experiences. As such, instead of 'reporting' research results, we draw on the three songwriting projects – 'Dark Light', 'Love is Everything' and 'Feel the Heat' – as our primary lens.

'Dark Light'

> We must find a way
> We can make it to the sunrise
> Light up the torches and wake up the king
>
> Fear the edge of the blade
> Run for your life with us
> Only god can judge us
> We are surviving the times
>
> The screams crashed into silence
> Paranoia clouding your judgement
> But things change and that's the way it is
> It's got us scared, scared of running on
> Paranoia clouding your judgement
> But things change, and that's the way it is
>
> My future seems like one big past
> I've waited last, my time's elapsed
> But the rain will kill us all
> My future seems like one big past
> I've waited last, my time's elapsed
> So scream while there's life left
> My future seems like one big past
> I've waited last, my time's elapsed
> One day the shadows will surround us
> So scream while there's life left

Dark Light was created by the self-named group *The DMDs*. The group was formed by John, Harry and Tom; three young men living with Duchenne muscular dystrophy (DMD), a degenerative neuromuscular and life-shortening condition.

Inspired by their favourite musicians and music videos, the group members created the lyrics through collaging and adapting pre-existing lyrics from artists such as 2Pac, Nas, Foo Fighters and Drake. The directness, energy and sense of defiance of the lyrics, channelled through powerful dub style drum, bass and other electronic sounds, seemed to address themes of anger and fear (e.g., 'Fear the edge of the blade'). John, Harry and Tom kept working and refining the lyrics into an order that made sense to them all. They spent considerable time changing the lyrics from 'me' to 'us', and from 'I' to 'we', reflecting perhaps their group identity and their shared experiences of living with a life-shortening condition (e.g., 'We are surviving the times' or 'I've waited last, my time's elapsed').[2]

Despite initial hesitation, all three young adults used their voices in the song. They took turns speaking different lines of the lyrics. Then they played with various sound effects, controlling and playing with the sound of their voice. Using echo, distortion and other effects, each young adult created their unique sound identity and coloured the overall feel of the song that they commonly described as 'dark'.

'Love is Everything'

> Love is us
> Love is James
> Love is Anna
> Love is me
> Love is you
>
> Love is family
> Love is friends
> Love is good times
> Love is football
> Love is Rangers
> Love is Celtic
> Love is powerful
> Love is sun
> Love is rain
>
> Love is everything! *[repeats]*
> Love, love, love *[repeats]*
>
> Love is trying
> Love is adventure
> Love is music
> Powerchair football
>
> Love is free
> Love is fun
> Love is happy
> Love is freedom
>
> Love is everything! *[repeats]*

The sound of a car engine starting, accompanied by mysterious synth melodies, forms the opening of this dance song. Fast cars passing by, sirens and spinning of tyres follow alongside the introduction of a strong beat. After building a sense of anticipation, the lyrics above start.

James and Anna, who were engaged as a couple, created this song over nine sessions. The lyrics, as James put it, were 'just what love is all about really'.

During the songwriting process, they explored and shared what they love, and what love means to them as individuals and as a couple. Adapting the duration and pace of each session according to James' and Anna's fluctuating health and energy, the songwriting process involved some guided listening. They listened to different songs and samples, and the music therapist invited them to focus on specific sounds, melodies and rhythms each time as prompts for generating their creative ideas.

The lyrics contain some perceived opposites, such as 'sun' and 'rain' and the Glasgow-based teams, 'Rangers' and 'Celtic'. The latter resonated with their love of football and perhaps the fact they had met each other through powerchair football. With a sense of humour, James and Anna were also pointing to the rivalry between these two teams and perhaps the connecting power of love. After several sessions where they freely explored sounds, feelings and words, James and Anna started creating the lyrics about 'trying' and their sense of 'adventure' and 'freedom'. The music therapist noticed a shift in their engagement during this time. They both seemed quieter, serious and focused.

'Feel the Heat'

> I feel heat, you feel cold *[repeats]*
> I want you closer, time is running out *[repeats]*
>
> The heat from my body is beginning to burn out
>
> Feel the heat within me
> Feel the heat (power) within me (power)
>
> Every day I see you, I want to get close to you
> Our bodies will evaporate when we touch
> I feel ok, feeling hotter than you *[repeats]*
>
> Feel the heat within me
> Feel the heat (power) within me (power) *[repeats]*
> Feel the heat within me

This song was composed by Brian; a man in his early 20s who was a keen ukelele player. Living with Brittle Bone disease, a genetic condition that causes bones to be weak and break easily, Brian used a powered wheelchair and had an active social life. His love of music-making fuelled his excitement to engage with the project and music technology more generally. In his song, using expansive synth sounds and harmonies, Brian created a rich musical landscape underpinned by a steady, relaxed rhythm. The music therapist felt that Brian relished the opportunity to share and explore his musical interests and ideas with another musician, and they planned for Ricky Ross, the lead singer from the rock band Deacon Blue, to visit and discuss creative ideas through a workshop.

The initial sessions focused on music composition and exploring the sentiment that Brian wanted to express. The lyrics convey some kind of differentiation of self and others and a wish to get closer to each other. There is also a sense of time and potential urgency denoted both in the lyrics (e.g., 'time is running out') and the opening ticking sound of the track. This sense of time, while being aware of Brian's life-shortening condition, could be understood in relation to one's experience of mortality as denoted also in the lyrics (e.g., 'The heat from my body is beginning to burn out'). This seems to expand later to a sense of connection and shared mortality (e.g., 'Our bodies will evaporate when we touch'). Brian recorded himself singing the lyrics and asked the music therapist to sing certain lyrics ('time is running' and 'power') as backing vocals. This duo resonated in-action with the song's meanings around self, other and connection.

Reflections

Through their interviews, the young adults were able to reflect on their experiences of the songwriting process, including the emerging meanings of their songs and the overall impact of the 'Moving on With Music' project. Through our engagement with their narratives, as well as the music therapist's interviews and logs, we identified four key thematic areas as developed below.

Improvisation and uncertainty

Improvisation was at the heart of the 'Moving on With Music' project and the therapeutic relationship between Joanne (music therapist), and the participants. Joanne's improvisational stance was underpinned by an intentional sense of openness and direction which impacted on her way of listening and engaging with the participants. Getting to know each young adult as a person, learning about their unique musical experiences and interests, and inviting them to reflect on what they would like to create and communicate through their song, were key. Owing partly to the short-term nature of each songwriting project, she tried to keep a balanced focus between process and product, between the explorative process of writing the lyrics and music, and the production of the final song recordings. In one case, a young adult worked purely on orchestrating one of his favourite video clips from Game of Thrones.

The generation of an open and safe improvisational space enabled the young adults to explore potentially strong emotions, and to express these through music by experimenting with sounds, melodies, effects and creative lyric writing. Inevitably, this improvisational space involved managing uncertainty and a sense of unknown. Listening to young people's favourite artists and songs, as well as experimenting with the existing sound banks of the software, were important in creating a secure base in the early steps of their songwriting 'adventure'.

For James and Anna, their experiences of 'adventure' (resembling the adventurous car chase sound of their song intro) was coupled with their sense of 'trying' with each other's company and support. Indeed, they both described a sense of becoming 'more adventurous' by meeting and being with each other. Trying out different words and sounds, they navigated a sense of uncertainty and had creative disagreements, negotiating to reach shared choices.

James: You don't know where the song was gonna go and what the final product was when we started at first [...] I think that we made way too many [lyrics], so we had to take a few out...

Anna: We didn't know what words we were gonna use.

James: We threw all the beats in there... it was good trying to do that as well... we listened to all different sounds... Now we like a sound and then... so it went and we both like it, then we both won't like it [...] we didn't know what we wanted in it or not.

Without a predefined idea about their final product, the young people, with Joanne's support, navigated this uncertainty together. This sense of navigating creative uncertainties during the songwriting process seemed to resonate with young people's capacity to manage uncertainties in other aspects of life and with regards to their transition from children services. The songwriting process created a microcosm within which the young adults could creatively exercise their capacity to engage with uncertainty, feeding their autonomy, their independence and their ability to make choices within other contexts of their lives too.

Autonomy, independence and making choices

On a basic level, the young people highly valued the opportunity that this project gave them to 'get out of the house' and to have 'something to concentrate on' and 'somewhere to go to be with friends'. Since their discharge from children's hospice care, some young adults had kept in touch with each other through online games and social media but would meet in person only occasionally. While building on their acquaintance with technology, 'Moving on With Music' – as a technology-aided songwriting project – offered a creative focus and reason for them to meet on a regular basis. Even though John, Harry and Tom knew each other prior to working on their songwriting project, Harry noted:

Harry: We've probably talked even more because of that [the songwriting project] because we were in here [...] we've seen each other more often. Because before that I don't think we'd spoken or seen each other in like a good couple of months.

Young people's enhanced social contact was accompanied by a sense of autonomy and independence. Anna, for example, was pleased that the songwriting project helped her to feel more confident and to work independently with James, without her support worker in the room. They both shared how they depended on other people for various aspects of their daily living. James' ability to drive his own car is perhaps one of the few experiences of freedom and independence they have.

During the songwriting sessions, they were also able to participate alone as a couple alongside the music therapist, and they felt that with music they could go wherever they wanted. As Anna put it, 'it's like with the car, you can go anywhere' (resembling perhaps the opening car sounds of their song). Overall, they both conveyed that the project process enabled them to feel 'more grown up' and empowered to do 'bigger and better' things.

The sense of achievement and pride was accompanied by a sense of learning new skills and their drive to, as Brian said, 'live life to the max':

Brian: I have got Brittle Bones [...] I don't know what my life expectancy is, but I like to live my life to the max [...] so I like to eh, keep myself busy, carry on with life, just like any other person.

Songwriting and meaning making

By generating lyrics and reflecting on the theme of their song, young adults had opportunities to reflect on what mattered to them, and what they wanted to communicate. The songwriting process offered opportunities to notice and consider their feelings, without judging or dismissing them and to express what they meant.

James: It's hard to describe what it means, it's not an easy sort of thing, but it's really good [...] expressing it in a song really. [We created the song] for each other; for each other, yeah. But probably what other people would feel as well.

The young adults were also able to express their musical identities and interests, such as the artists and genres that they liked:

Brian: [My song was] set in the 80s, sort of like an ET, conspiracy type of thing [...] I thought, there's so many sounds 80s has, like synthesizers, basses, funk – its smart. It's smart music, and it's cool [...] It's got quite a cool vibe – funky and also dark at the same time.

And the DMDs not only constructed their lyrics 'so it kind of told a story' but also agreed that the lyrics narrated aspects of their own stories. Both the group and the music therapist, Joanne, noted that the lyrics of their song, 'Dark Light', were 'dark'; 'aye, cos some of the words it's got in it like "fear", "judge" and "survive" and things like that' (Tom). The words 'we are surviving the time' and 'but things change, that's the way it is' resonated with their sense of survival as things keep changing.

John: I think maybe like how things have changed for us like the past, to now, to the future [...] I think probably because [...] our condition is progressive so I think maybe that's part of it because things will change for us. So, I think it's just how we cope with it, stuff like that, like good or bad.

Tom: Like muscles slowly get worse so like things that we used to be able to do we can't do any more.

John: Yeah, so we slowly get less movement. (We notice) but it is gradual so like it's not just all of a sudden.

Similarly, through his song, 'Feel the Heat', Brian expressed the physical impact of his illness. While he did not want anyone to feel sorry for him, he wanted to express through his song how he is different from others, particularly referring to the heat he commonly experienced when others felt cold. When he writes 'I feel heat, you feel cold', he is writing about the conflict that he experiences when he has difficulty getting the temperature right for him and others, and when he has trouble sleeping because he is too hot.

It is clear then that the playful songwriting process enabled young adults to share aspects of the self that might be difficult to do in other ways. The creative processes enabled them to represent their identities and their health/illness narratives by deviating from literal meaning to the employment of metaphorical representation, symbolic language and humour, which in turn allowed them to exaggerate and at times to provoke. As James and Anna agreed, 'it gives me freedom and us freedom… to go wherever we want' – an idea that was similarly expressed by Brian:

Brian: It's creative music, that's how song writers do it, they create; just create sound. […] It's like making yourself a stir fry, you can add whatever you want to it, that's what I like about music production, you can add whatever you want and just hope for the best. It tastes good, and it feels good.

For some participants, working alongside other young adults with the same condition was a catalyst for their meaning-making process in relation to their forming identities and their health/illness conditions.

Harry: I talk about it with friends who also have the same condition 'cos it's easier to talk to them about it because they like come from the same thing […] yeah there's quite a lot of us and we all talk to each other, and we all have that instant bond like 'cos we've all got the same condition, we are all going through the same thing.

This initial exploration and sharing within their own songwriting microcosm were a necessary step for then considering an audience with potential advocacy and legacy implications.

Being heard, advocacy and legacy

The recording of the songs served as a vehicle through which young people, their creativity and lyrics could be heard, witnessed and remembered. This seemed particularly important in the light of the ongoing impact of their life-shortening conditions.

Joanne: A young man created a piece of music that is energetic, full of life and attitude, strength, and masculinity. He's got Duchenne's muscular dystrophy, and his health is going to decline. Even within the ten weeks he was working on his project, he was starting to struggle with his swallowing. But his song remains. And he will have that up until the end and it will be a representation of the man that he is, and beyond that, for his family, for the man that he was.

Listening to young adults' voice, their interests and choices was at the heart of the project. This stance was evident in the relationship that the music therapist, Joanne, developed with each young person and the microcosm of each unique songwriting project. As the 'Moving on With Music' project kept developing, the young adults and Joanne explored how the produced songs could be shared with others with potential implications for legacy and advocacy.

The young people conveyed that sharing their songs with their families and friends was an important and potentially sensitive aspect of their experience. For example, James' and Anna's song helped them to communicate with their families how they love each other which was something that had been hard for them both to do. Moreover, they expressed pride in their achievements. James and Anna noted not only that listening back to their music was 'really good', 'enjoyable' and 'brilliant', but also that they were excited that family and friends loved their song too.

Brian reflected on how he learnt how to use musical elements to build anticipation and convey emotion through a song. As he developed new skills, his support workers also observed that he has 'quite a creative mind in music' and saw him under a different light. At the same time, Brian was reluctant to share his music with family and friends, at least initially. His two brothers did not know that he had composed a song. His dad had asked him a few times to share his song, but Brian kept 'pulling it back' saying 'yeah I'll show you later'.

Brian: I haven't shown any of my other friends. I've got a lot of friends, so I do, (but) I haven't even shown my dad [...] I don't know why, it's like: Do I want to show him? Do I want to let him hear me? Or maybe I could get [Joanne] just to send me the backing track and cut out my voice and then I could show him. Cause every time I hear my voice I feel, I feel a bit cringe worthy. [...] My voice didn't sound right and that, but it's like watching your own film [...] actors don't like looking back at the films – I don't like to hear my voice.

Brian seemed to be critical towards his voice and how it sounded in the recording. Yet, he conveyed confidence in his creativity and his auditory and technology skills. During the interview, when he listened back to his composition, he was excited about the 'amazing bass' he had created. Similarly, when Anna and James talked about sharing their song with their families, their excitement was palpable.

James: Cause our families are football fans…

Anna: Yeah

James: We all love football [and] we say that 'love is Celtic' and then so we say 'love is Rangers' [...] and they loved it.

Anna: They both loved it.

James: They were proud of us.

Anna: My family danced! [...] Yeah, everyone loved [our song].

James and Anna were excited about the planned closing event and keen to invite family and friends so people could hear their song and 'have a night out really'. They were keen to have the event videoed and shared online; and for their song to be widely distributed, 'to go around the world'. In contrast, Brian was nervous about public performance, having had a previous bad experience. Knowing he would not have to perform if he did not want to, and his eagerness to 'see the bands, hear what they'd be singing, because they know how it is', enabled him to not only attend and hear his work performed, but to do so together with his two brothers, their fiancés and his dad.

In addition to the closing event, the 'Moving on With Music' project involved opportunities for engaging with different famous or known figures. For example, famous musicians such as Ricky Ross and Horse McDonald visited a couple of the sessions and Horse recorded the last line in the 'Love is Everything' song. The music therapist also got one of the actors from Game of Thrones to send a message to the young adult who did the orchestration project and played it at the closing event. This connection to celebrities seemed to serve multiple purposes. Apart from potential fundraising implications and the excitement that brought to the young adults, there seemed to be another layer: by connecting with 'known' people, the project seemed to bring an 'unknown' or less spoken about issue to the surface, raise awareness and promote advocacy.

Moving on together

Songwriting can offer a medium for expressing the expert voices of young people with lived experiences of transitional care, and for communicating their voices and creativity to their families, carers and the wider public. Ensuring young adults with life-shortening conditions are heard carefully requires a safe space. This is a key suggestion from the Hospice UK transition programme (Shouls, 2023), and the 'Moving on With Music' project shows how therapeutic songwriting can play a key role to this end with potential implications for raising awareness, breaking down taboos and inviting people to listen. Music therapists can work more strategically in collaboration with other stakeholders to influence and input discussions with care providers and decision makers.

As shown in this project, songs can be a particularly creative and powerful vehicle for articulating one's voice and expressing their story with potential legacy and advocacy implications. Similarly, contemporary literature argues that illness narratives expressed through popular songs is an education resource for healthcare practitioners which has been largely untapped to date. Indeed, Childress and Lou (2023) argue that songs can be a rich source of insight into people's experiences of suffering, healing and coping with illness, disease and death. Songs can expand practitioners' perspective and their imagination, and as such enhance their communication with people. In addition to popular music, we argue that songs emerging from music therapy work with people with lived experience can be an equally valuable source of education, bringing to the surface the varieties of people's lived experiences of illness, disability, change, dying and loss. One's engagement with such songs requires exercising their capacity to listen carefully and expanding their metaphorical and imaginative thinking for understanding the multiple potential meanings and narratives contained in the lyrics.

As it transpired from the 'Moving on With Music' project, young adults' sense of *moving on* was not, strictly speaking, associated with their transition to adult palliative care services. Their experience was more broadly about continuing to live their lives to the fullest while coping with their ongoing health challenges, including their own losses in life:

Brian: [My mum] passed away. She had a big impact on the family [...] she was supportive towards everyone as well as me. Going to [the children hospice], she liked to come with me some weekends. She liked the fact that she could just leave me there and I'd be fine and especially my dad as well, he liked the fact that my mum and dad could have time together and I liked that as well but, it's a shame that my mum has gone, but eh, we have to do things ourselves, which I mean, you're supposed to do when you are an adult and mum brought me up to be like positive [...] don't be pessimistic all the time; be optimistic and life will make it. Make my life big as I can, So my mum left me a lot of tasks to do in my life, you know what I mean, go out and have fun, go do this, do that. I think about her every day. My dad does as well [...] we all know that you've got to move on, she always said that to us.

All young adults stressed their and their families' need for respite. This was an essential component of their care in children's hospices that allowed them, as Brian put it, to be 'away from their home for a couple of days, and so they can be themselves'. This support ceased after their discharge, and they feel that 'there's not really anything else that we can like go to for respite' (Tom).

Although the songwriting project did not offer respite in that sense, it offered a space where they could be creative without necessitating a focus on their palliative care needs. Brian explained that he was not accessing an adult hospice as it is 'for people who are seriously unwell'. Some of the young adults were receiving 24 hours support from support staff and spending significant part of their time at home. The 'Moving on With Music' project offered a welcome opportunity to get out of their home environment, meet and spend time with other people.

The project's connection to CHAS seemed to offer a sense of safety and continuity of care to participants. This connection informed the referral process to the project and held the potential to contribute to the overall care pathway of the young adults. At the same time, the young adults seemed to welcome the fact that the project was led by an external, non-palliative care provider, and that sessions took place at a fully equipped music room outside a hospice context. This non-clinical environment seemed to positively influence their creative engagement.

However, the lack of collaboration with an adult palliative care provider was a limitation of the project. Such a link could strengthen the sustainability of similar initiatives in the future. Some young adults wanted the project to last longer and/or to be engaged in multiple songwriting projects, but this was not possible, owing to its short-term nature and limited funding. The project did not carry on and, to our knowledge, no other similar project was delivered following this one. Since the 'Moving on With Music' project, provisions for young adults have not changed dramatically. Some promising initiatives and new services, however, have been developed such as the Young Adult Service of The Prince and Princess of Wales Hospice in Glasgow that includes the provision of a new specialist short break stay service for young adults with life-shortening conditions (Laidlaw & Wylie, 2023). In all cases, the need for an interdisciplinary approach has been highlighted, and we argue that music therapists can play an instrumental role across different continua of care, from specialist to everyday and from private to public contexts of musical care (Tsiris et al., 2022).

As the 'Moving on With Music' project shows, the role of the music therapist can foster synergies between different practitioners and providers such as performing musicians and healthcare providers. This is in line with other research perspectives (Kammin et al., 2024; Saarikallio & McFerran, 2022) pointing to the role that music therapy, and musical care practices more generally, can play in influencing and supporting national and international policy efforts for the wellbeing of the young generation. Indeed, the impact of the 'Moving on With Music' project resonates strongly with current youth strategic priorities internationally (The European Union Youth Strategy 2019-2027) by promoting opportunities for creative engagement, connection and a sense of empowerment for young people. The project points to the potential of therapeutic songwriting and wider musical care practices to provide pathways of engagement for young people, encourage them to be as independent as possible and create safe spaces for paying attention and listening carefully to their voices.

Acknowledgements

This project was only possible thanks to the participating young adults and the music therapist Joanne Edgar. We warmly thank them all for sharing their experiences and creativity. We also thank Elli Xypolitaki and Amy Hendon for their support as research interns. The project was funded by the Young Start Awards, and the dissemination of its findings was partly funded by Santander Universities.

Notes

1 NRS was a music therapy charity in Scotland. In 2018, it merged with its sister charity in England and Wales and is currently known as Nordoff and Robbins.
2 The songwriting process of Dark Light is detailed further in Edgar et al. (2019).

References

Aldridge, D. (2008). Therapeutic narrative analysis: A methodological proposal for the interpretation of musical traces. In P. Liamputtong & J. Rumbold (Eds), *Knowing differently: Arts-based and collaborative research methods*. Nova Publishers, pp. 205–227.

Campbell, F., Biggs, K., Aldiss, S. K., O'Neill, P. M., Clowes, M., McDonagh, J. ... & Gibson, F. (2016). Transition of care for adolescents from paediatric services to adult health services. *Cochrane Database of Systematic Reviews*, 4(4), CD009794.

Care Quality Commission (2014). *From the pond into the sea: Children's transition to adult health services*. CQC.

Drury et al. (2025). 'Alive, brave and free. That's what music means to me': Celebrating the Diverse Voices of a Children's Hospice Community through Collaborative Songwriting. In *Music Therapy in Children's Palliative Care*. Abingdon: Routledge.

Earle, S. & Blackburn, M. (2021). Young adults with life-limiting or life-threatening conditions: sexuality and relationships support. *BMJ Supportive & Palliative Care*, 11(2), 163–169.

Edgar, J., Tsiris, G. & Rickson, D. (2019). 'The screams crashed into silence': A therapeutic songwriting project for young adults with life-shortening illnesses. In A. Ludwig (Ed.), *Music therapy in children's palliative care*. Jessica Kingsley Publishers, pp. 159–173.

Giordano, F., Rutigliano, C., Baroni, M., Grassi, M., Muggeo, P. & Santoro, N. (2022). Music therapy and pediatric palliative care: Songwriting with children in the end-of-life. *World Journal of Pediatrics*, 18(10), 695–699.

Heath, B. & Lings, J. (2012). Creative songwriting in therapy at the end of life and in bereavement. *Mortality*, 17(2), 106–118.

Jindal-Snape, D., Johnston, B., Pringle, J., Kelly, T. B., Scott, R., Gold, L. & Dempsey, R. (2019). Multiple and multidimensional life transitions in the context of life-limiting health conditions: longitudinal study focussing on perspectives of young adults, families and professionals. *BMC Palliative Care*, 18, 1–12.

Johnston, B., Jindal-Snape, D. & Pringle, J. (2016). Life transitions of adolescents and young adults with life-limiting conditions. *International Journal of Palliative Nursing*, 22(12), 608–617.

Kammin, V. (2019a). Balancing the public and the private: Music therapy in a children's hospice. In A. Ludwig (Ed.), *Music therapy in children's palliative care*. Jessica Kingsley Publishers, pp. 31–46.

Kammin, V. (2019b). Performing, sharing and celebrating life: Music therapy in children and young people's palliative care. In A. Ludwig (Ed.), *Music therapy in children's palliative care*. Jessica Kingsley Publishers, pp. 127–144.

Kammin, V., Fraser, L., Flemming, K. & Hackett, J. (2024). Experiences of music therapy in paediatric palliative care from multiple stakeholder perspectives: A systematic review and qualitative evidence synthesis. *Palliative Medicine*, 02692163241230664.

Knighting, K., Bray, L., Downing, J., Kirkcaldy, A. J., Mitchell, T. K., O'Brien, M. R. ... & Jack, B. A. (2018). Meeting the needs of young adults with life-limiting conditions: A UK survey of current provision and future challenges for hospices. *Journal of Advanced Nursing*, 74(8), 1888–1898.

Laidlaw, S. & Wylie, F. (2023). *Alex's journey to respite: 'It's been six years since their last respite...'. A report on the innovative pilot trialling the provision of a new specialist short break stay service for young adults with life-limiting conditions, including the sharing of the pilot evaluation, learnings, and recommendations for the future*. The Prince and Princess of Wales Hospice.

McFerran, K., Derrington, P. & Saarikallio, S. (Eds). (2019). *Handbook of music, adolescents, and wellbeing*. Oxford University Press.

McFerran, K. & Saarikallio, S. (2013). Depending on music to feel better: Being conscious of responsibility when appropriating the power of music. *The Arts in Psychotherapy, 41*(1), 89–97.

O'Callaghan, C. & Grocke, D. (2009). Lyric analysis research in music therapy: Rationales, methods and representations. *The Arts in Psychotherapy, 36*(5), 320–328.

Pavlicevic, M. (Ed.). (2005). *Music therapy in children's hospices: Jessie's Fund in action.* Jessica Kingsley Publishers.

Saarikallio, S. & McFerran, K. (2022). Musical care in adolescence. In N. Spiro & K. R. Sanfilippo (Eds), *Collaborative insights: Interdisciplinary perspectives on musical care throughout the life course.* Oxford University Press, pp. 70–85.

Shouls, S. (2023). *Being curious and confident – Learning from the Hospice UK transition programme for young people with life-limiting conditions: Evaluation report.* Hospice UK.

Stige, B., Malterud, K. & Midtgarden, T. (2009). Toward an agenda for evaluation of qualitative research. *Qualitative Health Research, 19*(10), 1504–1516.

The European Union Youth Strategy 2019–2027 (https://eur-lex.europa.eu/legal-content/EN/TXT/?uri=OJ:C:2018:456:FULL).

Tsiris, G. (2024). 'GRESCO Agape' – An international songwriting project for hospice patients and school children. In C. Dileo & M. Baroni (Eds), *Music therapy at the end of life* (2nd ed., Chapter 51). Jeffrey Books.

Tsiris, G., Hockley, J. & Dives, T. (2022). Musical care at the end of life: Palliative care perspectives and emerging practices. In N. Spiro & K. R. Sanfilippo (Eds), *Collaborative insights: Interdisciplinary perspectives on musical care throughout the life course.* Oxford University Press, pp. 119–145.

Tsiris, G., Tasker, M., Lawson, V., Prince, G., Dives, T., Sands, M. & Ridley, A. (2011). Music and arts in health promotion and death education: The St Christopher's Schools Project. *Music and Arts in Action, 3*(2), 95–119.

Viega, M. (2013). *'Loving me and my butterfly wings': A study of hip-hop songs written by adolescents in music therapy.* [Doctoral dissertation, Temple University].

Chapter 9

The Gods of Music

Nicky Hale and Victoria Kammin, with contributions from Jocelyn Watkins, Jane Wood, Adam Gorb and Megan Steinberg

Co-authoring process

This chapter was collaboratively written by Nicky and Vicky, along with contributions from four other significant figures in Lucy's musical journey. Nicky initiated the process by sharing her perspectives and experiences, inviting those who had supported Lucy musically over the years to contribute. Many of the contributors gathered over lunch at a local theatre near the hospice where Lucy was supported, reminiscing about her and planning the chapter. These conversations greatly influenced the chapter's structure and further inspired the writing process. Vicky then added her own experiences, insights and supporting literature, and together, a chronological structure was decided upon. The draft was circulated via email among the contributors, with everyone eager for Lucy to have the final word in the chapter.

Nicky Hale, Lucy's mother

Music has so many gods and goddesses in every culture. Lucy's great Grandmother was Cerridwen. One of the names I had wanted for Lucy. In Celtic mythology she was the keeper of the cauldron of wisdom and prophecy, also known as a crone, symbolising the darker side of the goddess. Her son Taleisen was the greatest of Welsh poets. Both are associated with music and the Arthurian legends. Lucy always joked that she was an old crone at every birthday after twenty. She also had a dark side. Once asked, during a music viva, if she could not be a bit more cheerful, she responded, bemused, 'This is who I am'. As a teenager she went with black goth fashion, hair dyed blue, green, red and Dr Marten footwear. If she wasn't so sick of needles, owing to all the medical interventions, she'd have had a lot more piercings and tattoos.

It was never really clear what Lucy's diagnosis was. The first neurologist named her condition as Hereditary Motor and Sensory Neuropathy Type 3. It fell under the umbrella of Charcot Marie Tooth Syndrome. However genetic testing in later childhood did not confirm this and suggested a mutant gene, which caused us all some mirth. 'We always said you were a weirdo Lu'. The effect was a deteriorating

DOI: 10.4324/9781032664378-10

myelin sheath leading to decreasing muscle function. She was in a wheelchair from an early age and the disability impacted on her ability to eat and swallow and her respiratory system from her early teens onwards. She had approximately seven admissions to Paediatric Intensive care and in the final admission it was thought that she would be unlikely to survive. She needed long term non-invasive ventilation, tube feeding and speech aids. From early teens she needed full-time care.

Lucy's musical journey began young. There was always either music or Harry Potter on in the car. Her sister, Ellie, played the flute. The house was full of music. Lucy would sing along with all the Disney films she loved. She asked us for keyboard lessons and started with a school teacher, Mr Yelloff. He soon became Mr Yellhisheadoff. It wasn't a happy association and nearly put her off for life. One evening I found her at the keyboards in tears. He had given her some sheet music and asked her to practice but hadn't taught her to read music. I taught her the basics in about five minutes, and off she went. Keyboards became increasingly difficult as her motor skills diminished. So a friend offered singing lessons. Lucy loved these and really worked hard at them. Thwarted again by her failing vocal-chord muscles and the start of all the intensive care admissions she moved to drums and percussion in secondary school.

Treloars School and College was the breakthrough, a non-maintained residential and day special school and college for Disabled children and young people. Mainstream secondary school was able to meet her academic needs but not her physical ones. She spent whole days not going to the loo. The friendships she made did not work out leaving her lonely and isolated. A kindly physiotherapist spent the better part of two hours explaining why she needed an environment such as Treloars. There was nothing local that would meet her needs.

Lucy was described by her history teacher as 'That rare thing: a genuine intellectual. She has a very fine mind'. When she suffered repeated critical illnesses, it became crystal clear that she would be unable to access any mainstream education without a medical facility which would enable her to take time out without losing whole days if she felt unwell. Treloars was the only school close enough to us that offered physiotherapy, occupational therapy and an onsite health centre supported by the local GP practice. None of us, including, Lucy, wanted her to be so far away and in residential care but having visited Treloars we were all realistic enough to accept the necessity. The local borough accepted that need without any resistance; other families are not so fortunate.

Lucy turned to music in the absence of History GSCE, her preference, but not available to her at Treloars. Her teacher, Jocelyn Watkins, is passionate and committed to special education needs music. She sent Lucy's first piece of music home with a note to us, to have a look and a listen to this 'It's special'. Fanfare For A Battle, a piece that came to typify Lucy's love of the atonal, dark and difficult, conjured up, in the mind's eye of the listener, smoke drifting across the bloodied battlefield strewn with bodies. Gelert followed with a horrific musical fight between dog and wolf. The Selfish Giant was sparse and unsentimental. She had barely started and encouraged by Jocelyn the music was pouring out of her. Jocelyn collected her work and sent it to the Head of Composition at the Royal College of Music Junior Department (RCMJD), David Sutton Anderson. He offered her a place, knowing that she had potential and needed help to understand the difficulties faced by flautists if she didn't allow breathing space or pianists who didn't have finger spans the size of Rachmaninov's.

Jocelyn Watkins, Director of Music, Treloars School

Lucy was, and still is, one of the greatest influences in my career as a music teacher and I am immensely proud to have been her teacher and to have supported her on her musical journey.

Lucy was in one of my first classes when I started at Treloars in 2008. In the first autumn term she came to a couple of lessons and then was in Great Ormond Street Hospital for around seven weeks. When she got back, it was quickly apparent how keen she was to learn, her extraordinary intelligence as well as her wonderful sense of humour. Lucy did not choose to study music but, as we had such small class sizes, it was a majority decision. To me, Lucy was always very cool. Her hair was dyed a different colour each week and she had an eclectic taste in music. I was quite a traditionally trained music teacher and often felt quite untrendy and in awe in the face of her London vibe!

At this point the world of music and disability was still very new to me. My students had any number of physical and cognitive challenges to face and therefore everything that could be done to support them should be put in place. I had a year 11 Music GCSE group, and it was with this cohort that I was soon to discover the discrimination the students would face in taking part in formal music exams. Some of the students could perform at a level that matched their musical ability in the listening paper and composing section of the GCSE; most could not. The spasticity of their fingers (the term here used in a medical sense) could not play keyboards or guitars to a level needed, neither could most of them play any wind or brass instruments (many had difficulties with lip control as well as breath control). Some could sing but did not have the confidence to do so in public, and it is unlikely that the majority of their previous schools would have prioritised music for them or encouraged them to take part. The distance between their ability level and their physical limitations meant that I decided to approach the exam boards to see if the performance section of the Music GCSE could be exempted for these students. This was not an unreasonable request in order to allow my students to take part.

The response I received was not what I expected. One after another the exam boards said no, the *'integrity of the exam is more important'* (than Disabled students taking part). I phoned every exam board who did GCSE Music, and the result was the same. I suggested we could do extra sections, another listening paper or historical studies of music. I remember very clearly watching one of my students, who was in tears, trying to play the keyboard and to make their body do what they wanted without success. The lack of equity was to me truly shocking and heartbreaking. I could see how intelligent and hard-working my students were and they were effectively doomed to either fail or not have a seat at the music table; to be excluded from a whole world of music and opportunities that their peers could enjoy.

Are we only musicians if we can perform? Music is not just made up of performers; the majority of us are destined to be listeners, some to be composers, and the idea that you can exclude a whole tranche of society who have already suffered so much trauma is devastating.

Around the same time as I was phoning GCSE exam boards and trying to work out ways my students could perform, I had got to know Lucy better. Lucy had speech and language difficulties and significant restrictions with breath control, so using her voice to perform was not an option. Lucy could still play the drum kit with two hands at this point, if it was set up for her and didn't have a bass foot pedal. She managed to get to around Grade 2 in the drum syllabus, but it was not easy for her and took a lot of physical effort, however she did have something she could play for the exam.

At this time when we started to think about the composing part of the exam. Lucy could not eat and was fed via a gastrostomy, along with her having a quiet voice it meant lunchtimes in a noisy dining room with the other students was not much fun for her. I therefore arranged for Lucy to come to the music room at lunchtimes around three times a week. We had any number of discussions, mostly about music. Sometimes she would mention parts of her life which she had struggled with, giving up eating or missing the taste of strawberries. As I got to know her, I better appreciated the challenges that she faced and grew to understand her insecurities. Always present was her abundant humour.

The first time I showed Lucy Sibelius music software for her to use to compose, she was too nervous to put a note on the stave. Scared to fail at something new, or too daunted by the task in hope that this was something she could achieve, I don't know but she slowly found the courage to start. For her first piece, we had discussed a vague theme, and it was the one in which Lucy I think found her initial tonality. It ended up being a type of funeral march and I was so pleased that, after the initial qualms, Lucy loved composing. Over the next few months Lucy continued to compose most lunchtimes. It soon became apparent that Lucy would need a composition teacher who had far greater skills than I did to develop her burgeoning talent. It was also around this time that I found out that Lucy's disability was degenerative. I knew the name of Lucy's condition but, being quite new to it all, I did not realise what this meant for her future. I remember being devastated at the time and I think it was what spurred me on to the next step.

I had been at the RCMJD in my sixth form years and devised a 'cunning plan' to get in touch and see if they would accept Lucy. She had composed around four pieces by this time and I thought this would be enough to show off what she could do. I did not want Lucy to know in case it did not work out and got permission from Lucy's parents to send up her work. When I phoned, I was delighted that Gail, the administrator, was someone who remembered me from ten years earlier. Lucy's work was posted off. Once they had heard it, I had a meeting in London with a group of people from the RCMJD including the person who would become her composition teacher. The rest I suppose you could say, was history. Once Lucy was invited to go and meet the team at the RCMJD I knew that she would be accepted. I had also arranged for Lucy to have lessons with an old university friend of mine, a composer called Michael Jennings. He taught Lucy composition and theory in the summer holidays and this again supported her development. Once she was at the RCMJD I got in touch with the company Sibelius (now Avid) and they very kindly donated Lucy the Sibelius 7 software and laptop which meant that Lucy had the freedom to compose where and whenever she wanted to.

It was obvious that Lucy was going to want to do Music A-Level. Although she could manage some performance it was clear her physical disabilities were too severe to allow for a performance at the level of her musicality and required for A-Level. Over a period of six months I phoned the same person at the exam board our local sixth form college was doing every two weeks asking for an exemption for Lucy's performance in her A-Level. The fact that Lucy was studying composition at the RCMJD gave me ballast and I did finally manage to get the agreement that Lucy could do the Music A-Level without the performance section.

I kept in contact with Lucy's progress mainly through our head nurse, Jane, who would let me know how she was getting on. I commissioned Lucy to compose a piece for the Royal Marine Association Concert Band who were supporting us at our bi-annual Glaziers concert, and later I also commissioned a vocal piece set to Lewis Carroll's The Jabberwocky for my students to sing.

Lucy was the student who made me push every system to get what we needed; who opened my eyes to the unfairness of the systems we were in, and she was the one who spurred me on to do whatever I could for my students in the knowledge that success could be achieved. I have had other students go on to study A-Level music. I was able to show them that it had been done before. It was possible.

Lucy and the musical legacy she leaves behind are a testament to how persistence and tenacity can open the doors and enable talent to flourish. My mother asked me, not long ago, whether the Lucy Hale whose music was being performed as part of a concert at the Royal Northern College of Music, was 'your Lucy from Treloars'. And I replied, 'yes, yes, it is'.

Jane Wood (Lucy's nurse at Treloars and 'school mum')

I first met Lu when she commenced at Treloars School. It was clear from the outset that she had an interesting and unique way of expressing herself. Lu had the nurses dancing round the medical centre to the music that she enjoyed while she recuperated from a lengthy hospital stay. The music was an eclectic mix of bands but would always include The Killers. Lu later met the Killers and had a drum masterclass with them which gave her great joy. The meeting certainly helped to speed her recovery.

Lu moved on to Treloars College for her A-Level studies, by this time, she was following her passion and talent for composing. One of Lu's compositions at this time drew on her experience of the Intensive Care Unit and the sounds that were ever present within that setting. To help with this she would visit the College health centre to record and listen to as many of the medical devices that made a noise as she could.

When Lu moved on to the RNCM we would occasionally meet up, visiting exhibitions and the annual Proms. During her time at RNCM Lu matured into an amazing young lady. I once told her that she was very talented. This did not go down well; at some length and very eloquently she told me that I was glossing over the hard work that she put into her composing. We had to agree to differ, and I continue to believe that Lu had a rare talent and worked hard to build on that and to allow others to enjoy her music.

Nicky Hale, Lucy's mother

During Lucy's final admission to Great Ormond Street Paediatric Intensive Care Unit, the family had been referred to the children's hospice Christopher's in Guildford. All of us were reluctant in our own ways to follow this up as we didn't realise that the hospice offered respite to the whole family and the chance to be together without being responsible for caring. We could all go to bed when we liked and stay up playing games and watching movies. The hospice offered therapies for all the family and the chance for Ellie to meet with siblings who were facing similar issues to her in terms of anxiety and the pressures of being a young carer. None of us understood what music therapy entailed. Vicky explained that among other things the hospice held an annual three-day workshop in music composition during the summer. Although uncertain about this Lucy agreed to give it a whirl. The workshop was led by Jason, a charismatic workshop leader, Vicky and three other orchestral musicians from the Royal Philharmonic Orchestra Community and Education team. Lucy took to it like a duck to water and found herself invited back on a yearly basis, becoming much loved and respected by the musical team. Lucy loved to immerse herself in that world for these all too brief days.

Victoria Kammin, music therapist

Many of my first encounters with children and young people at the children's hospice I worked for many years were through a referral for individual music therapy, perhaps to provide an opportunity for emotional expression at the hospice, home or in the community. With Lucy, this was different, we first met at an annual music therapy project myself and my colleagues ran in conjunction with a workshop leader and musicians from leading London orchestras (Kammin, 2019). Lucy was a percussionist who was developing an interest in composition, this project provided the motivation for her and her family to cross the dauting threshold of a children's hospice for the first time.

'The Festival of Music' took place annually over three consecutive days, culminating in a performance in which families, the wider hospice and local community were invited. One aspect of this project was to provide young people with a particular musical interest or talent with the opportunity to create a collective composition or bring their previously composed music for masterclass style workshops. Lucy attended this project as a young composer every year for three days over the course of eight years.

Lucy was 13 when I first met her, a shy, trendy young person with shocks of blue in her dark hair and big green eyes full of perception and humour. It quickly became apparent that this project had the potential to provide Lucy with a safe, accessible space to showcase and develop her considerable musical talent and collaborate with others, free from many of the barriers frequently encountered by Disabled musicians. This was a space where Lucy had the potential to engage, develop and thrive despite her life-limiting condition (Amadoru & McFerran, 2007; Lindenfelser et al., 2008, 2012; Steinhardt et al., 2021; Kammin et al., 2024; Zuckerman, 2019).

Reflecting on the barriers to Lucy's musical development in comparison with the opportunities I had personally and professionally benefitted from provided a driving force for the work that lay ahead. Lucy was no longer able to sing or play the drums when I met her, she needed full time medical care and support with her physical needs and communication. She faced significant hurdles at every stage of her journey as a musician, including access to education, exams, performing and ensembles and had not experienced representation in the music industry (Bremmer, 2023). Lucy and her family had spent much of her life fighting systems and barriers, access to music had proven itself to be no different.

Arts Council England undertook a study (Cox & Kilshaw, 2021) which surveyed the classical music industry workforce and reported profound inequalities in access. The findings identified that 80 percent of classical musicians surveyed were from affluent areas with high proportions attending university, a quarter of female participants had faced financial barriers and half of LGBT+, Disabled and Black, Asian and other ethnically diverse participants reported significant barriers restricting their opportunities. A range of barriers, discrimination and harassment in training and work settings related to protected characteristics were cited.

I was very conscious that my intersectional identity of a white, middle-class, able-bodied, heterosexual, cisgender woman who had also benefitted from instrumental lessons, instrument loans and multiple ensemble opportunities provided by my local music service, (before austerity and cuts to the arts, Burland et al., 2020) had provided me with a contrasting, privileged access to musical life. Going some way to rectifying these inequalities lay at the heart of this project.

The hospice provision provided the foundations for attempting to remove some of these barriers, enabling Lucy and her family to stay comfortably with medical support, personal care, an accessible environment and skills and knowledge in the workforce to understand and support her communications. As I got to know Lucy and her family and built trusting relationships with them over the years, they provided me with insight and understanding into how she was, the highs and lows of the year and how best to support her at that particular time.

'The Festival of Music' enabled Lucy and her family to return to the hospice annually; they later shared with me that this was the only respite in their year they felt comfortable to access and it was clear how much they valued this as a family. The project provided a family-centred environment (Lindenfelser et al., 2008, 2012; Kammin et al., 2024), supporting their emotional and physical reprieve (Amadoru & McFerran 2007; Kammin et al., 2024; Steinhardt et al., 2021) and family wellbeing (Lindenfelser et al., 2008, 2012; Kammin et al., 2024; Streinhardt et al., 2021; Verberne, 2017). Not only was Lucy able to benefit from her musical experiences but her family were able to witness and find joy in their daughter's engagement (Lindenfelser et al., 2008; Steinhardt et al 2021, Zuckerman, 2019), creating significant memoires which would support their continuing bonds in the future (Amadoru & McFerran 2007; Lindenfelser et al., 2008, 2012; Zuckerman 2019). In turn, this allowed Lucy and her family to experience the wider benefits of a children's hospice and community.

'The festival transformed the hospice from a place that I associated with difficult feelings and memories, into somewhere that I actually enjoyed being' (Hale in Kammin, 2019).

Disability studies have challenged the music therapy profession to think critically about the relationship of power between the therapist and the person seeking therapy, moving from a position of trying to change individuals to supporting change in systems (Hadley, 2014). This project offered a profound sense of realigning power as Lucy increasingly took control in workshops; a talented young composer was emerging extending into a blossoming musical career outside of the hospice. A playful bonding platform between Lucy, myself and the orchestral musicians emerged as we tried to technically master and do justice to her ground breaking compositions. We had countless rehearsals playing these through and waiting with bated breath to see what Lucy's response was and her direction lay. This often resulted in hysterical laughter as we repeatedly struggled to play the complex notes on the stave, with Lucy teasing us that she would rewrite the parts to help us access them. Or sack us! There was an unspoken driving force from us all to wholeheartedly honour her compositions despite their technical challenges, acutely aware that Lucy's voice and music needed to be heard.

'The festival was my first opportunity to have my work played by professional musicians, and their feedback was a great confidence boost, without which I doubt I would have gone on to study at music college' (Hale in Kammin, 2019).

Central to my role as music therapist was providing a secure base (Bowlby, 1969) for Lucy and the orchestral musicians, facilitating an initial bridge between them. I hoped to convey through sensitive role modelling how fiercely intelligent and capable Lucy was, recognising how easy it might be to make assumptions when communication is challenging and the potential impact of this. Over time, they became increasingly confident communicating directly with one another using verbal communication, gestures and technology to support this. Without the experience, training and support professionals receive when working in paediatric palliative care, it was imperative to provide practical and emotional support for the orchestral musicians (Kammin, 2019). As relationships and mutual respect developed, they began to position themselves alongside one another, allowing me to step back. This progression aligns with one of our main aims as therapists: supporting therapeutic growth to support independence rather than dependence (Blatt et al., 2010).

Accessible performance space was an important aspect of the project, providing children and young people with the opportunity to perform, a sense of occasion and belonging and for families to take pride in their children's achievements providing lasting memories (Kammin, 2019). Lucy needed encouragement and support to take credit for her compositions by coming into the stage area for the applause after these were performed. While Lucy was humble about her accomplishments, this perhaps was also difficult for her to be 'seen' by others, which we worked hard on together over the years. I shared my own discomfort with performing and taking any applause and our playful relationship allowed us to use humour to explore our feelings here, enabling a shared space where we would gently challenge and support one another. Lucy's bravery in being seen and coming forwards after the performance of her work provided powerful representation for other Disabled young musicians in the project and their families which she seemed to increasingly recognise.

Over the years we witnessed Lucy's identity as a musician and confidence in her abilities grow year upon year. We began to be in touch by email before projects to discuss instrumentation and themes as she increasingly took control pre, during and post projects. Lucy's directions as a composer became clear, direct and confident; she was the expert, we were working for her and we wanted to get it right. In Lucy's final years on the project when she was longer supported by the hospice, owing to her age, she transitioned to a guest composer role supporting other young musicians on the project.

'Witnessing the enjoyment of the other young people participating in the festival gave me an interest in arts outreach and as a result I undertook a work placement with a charity bringing music to patients in a children's hospital and am currently working on a project with the Bournemouth Symphony Orchestra which will involve performances and workshops in schools as well as more traditional concerts' (Hale in Kammin, 2019).

Nicky Hale, Lucy's mother

Back at Treloars, Jocelyn was seeking out all the opportunities that she could to get Lu's work performed and with her persistent support, Lucy started at a local college studying Music, Philosophy and English Literature. Sixth form wasn't a happy period for Lu. Back in mainstream, although still resident at Treloars, she again felt lonely and isolated. She began self-harming. However, she loved the music and became fond of her tutors Martin and Pande, who found similar opportunities for her to have her work performed. They encouraged her to apply for the Hampshire Music Award. She was successful.

Weekends at home were spent studying and at the RCMJD. Lucy and I wandered around the old corridors in a happy, disbelieving haze. When asked by the college principal how we were finding it, I replied that we were both were still pinching themselves with disbelief and Lucy nodded in agreement. He looked a little taken aback and responded 'You should believe it Lucy. You absolutely deserve to be here'. After a time, we employed a young carer, Katie. She knew Lucy from Treloars and was also a musician. We hoped that with us out of the picture Lu would make friends more easily and would also prefer the company of Katie, a lively, caring young woman who was held in great affection by all of us. It was a loss for me as I loved to go with Lucy and immerse myself in orchestra rehearsal and some of the lessons. One of her tutors, Avril, subsequently commented that she had at times wondered who she was teaching, the mother or the daughter. Lucy threw herself into that world and seized every chance given to her to compose and have her music played. She entered the BBC Young Composer of the year but didn't hear back.

Supported by David and Avril she grew in confidence and came to believe that she could study composition at University. David and Avril believed that she would flourish and fly at the Royal Northern College of Music. Lucy was open to Universities and Conservatoires. She craved independence, knowing that it would not be easy to achieve, would take a great deal of effort and be of a more limited nature than her peers. With us, Lucy visited various universities and conservatoires, all were welcoming and offered her good advice. The visit to RNCM however was a turning point. Lucy and I visited together and immediately felt right at home. It was very accessible, and the city was flat. The Head of Composition, Adam made time for Lu and was gently encouraging. He asked her to send him a portfolio, which she did. She was too terrified to open the email and asked me to open it. It started 'You have an interesting imagination' and went on to encourage an application.

She was so very chuffed when she received an unconditional offer from the RNCM. She already had Philosophy A-Level so didn't need to do much else. This was a good thing as when her A-Level results came in, Music was disastrous. I went into her room on my way out to work and she was totally covered by duvet. Something was off so I asked if she was alright. The duvet shook its head, and I realised her results had come through. 'OMG, it's results day. How bad can it be??' An arm appeared with the phone. She had failed Music A-Level, specifically composition. I couldn't help myself and fell about laughing. 'Lu, RNCM doesn't give a flying fart about exam boards. Your offer is unconditional, so it doesn't matter. RNCM are only interested in talent and aptitude, and you have both in shedloads'. Obviously Lu couldn't see the funny side. She was mortified and thought that she would be a laughing stock. Whereas I thought she should wear it as a badge of honour, Lucy disagreed and wanted the results checked, the college appealed, and she got a D. Her RCMJD tutor David was appalled and disbelieving. We later found out that nobody at RNCM had ever been aware that she had failed, and nor did they care. The Principal, Linda Merrick commented that she could only imagine that the examiners had no idea what to do with Lu's composition.

Lucy accepted her place, and we went up with her during the summer to see what arrangements would be made. The welcome was exceptionally warm. We were walked round the college by 8 members of various departments to see what adaptations were needed and could be made, including in a ground floor room in halls set aside for her. We found an agency prepared to manage her care and she was all set. We helped with recruitment of carers, and she had the makings of a good caring team around her, all of whom also had an interest in music.

Lucy joined the RNCM as an undergraduate student in 2013. She loved her time there and did well, graduating with a distinction in her MMus. She made good relationships with her tutors and seized every learning opportunity that she could. She found some longstanding friends in her composition group. They bounced ideas off each other but were all true originals and very talented young women. She was accepted as a fully funded PhD student with a proposal that encompassed, music, disability and assistive technology.

Adam Gorb (principal tutor, Royal Northern College of Music)

I first met Lucy in 2012 when she auditioned for the undergraduate course in composition at the Royal Northern College of Music (RNCM). It didn't take long at all to realise that here was a very special talent – a young composer with something truly original and different to communicate. I was delighted she accepted the place and was one of her principal tutors during her four-year undergraduate course.

Lucy was a model student. She never missed a lesson or a seminar, made full use of the RNCM's resources, and most importantly of all wrote some truly fantastic music. Her compositional ambitions and range were evident from day one, from the jagged and challenging orchestral work 'Against the Tide', to the friendly accessibility, albeit with some unexpected melodic and harmonic surprises of 'Four Folk Tunes' for string quartet. Compositionally Lucy never stood still, always relishing a challenge. Above all, her music was always about something – the works really needed to be written and performed, and consequently there were many inspiring and exciting performances of her pieces.

During her weekly lessons she would communicate with me on an iPad, and sometimes things took a surprising, even bizarre twist. Once, on giving a suggestion about a particular passage in a work she wrote: ...I'll think about it then a pause: .... I've thought about it.... I don't like your suggestion. (We were still on speaking terms at the end of the lesson.) On another occasion, looking at a score of hers I enquired the identity of a particular instrument with the initial 'Wh' was, and she explained that the percussionist needed to hit and scrape the wheelchair (one of her spare ones).

After leaving the RNCM with a master's degree, Lucy started getting commissions from various sources including the Bournemouth Symphony Orchestra and the National Orchestra for all. She was due to return to the RNCM to start a PhD in 2021.

The last time I saw her was at a performance of Britten's 'The Turn of the Screw' at The Lowry theatre in Salford in February 2020. We had a lovely catch up before COVID-19 put a stop to most socialising for an indefinite period.

Lucy was a composer with a unique idiom, she was a very special and memorable person who touched the lives of everybody she met.

Nicky Hale, Lucy's mother

During Lucy's time at RNCM she began an association with Drake music that was to last for the rest of her life. They offered her a paid commission for a piece which premiered at the Institute for Contemporary Arts in London. Her piece, In the Wind was beautiful and haunting and a resounding success. She received a standing ovation, at exactly the moment her nephew Finley was born. Of course she dedicated it to him. Lu was always writing music to gift to others. Drake Music trained her as a music mentor, and she very much enjoyed the work. She was especially proud of the compositions she helped a group of neurodiverse teenage girls to put together and perform a song at the Imperial War Museum North. She took Stockhausen in to them, and these rap-loving girls all thought she was a bit bonkers but they respected her, and she them.

At about this time Lu was applying for commissions with various orchestras. She was appointed the inaugural young composer with Bournemouth Symphony Orchestra. She was the young composer in residence with Orchestras for all. Lucy was especially proud of this as it was an orchestra for children and young people of all abilities and backgrounds. She gained a place on the Royal Philharmonic Society's composers programme. She was both thrilled and disbelieving about this and tweeted her delight with an excited duck gif. Lucy continued to go to the hospice for the music project up until her 21st birthday, and Lucy's relationship with Vicky and the musicians deepened, there was considerable affection and mutual respect between them.

Lucy's death was sudden and shocking. She had been with us over Christmas, having been isolated because of the pandemic for most of 2020. She was unable to meet with friends and her sister and nephew because of the remaining restriction and her acute awareness of the risks to her of mixing with others. She struck me as increasingly frail but not at immediate risk. She was more upbeat than usual, and we spent a lovely Christmas bingeing on Disney. On her return to Manchester her carers also noticed how upbeat she was. She collapsed very suddenly and had stopped breathing when Kat, her carer, found her. Kat got her heart beating again and the ambulance came within eight minutes. However, in that time she had suffered catastrophic brain damage, and her consultant told me that he was very worried about her as she was fitting. This was nothing at all like previous admissions to intensive care.

Ellie came up but of course we were not allowed to visit. Lucy was the only patient on the ward who did not have COVID-19, so was in a separate room. After a week we were told that she was stable, though unresponsive. We took Ellie back to

London. Finley, then aged three, ran out to hug his mum and asked if Auntie Lucy was out of hospital. When Ellie said no, he replied 'Well what are you doing here then?'. We drove back to our London house and parked up, to be told that Lu had suddenly deteriorated, and her lungs were filling up. We headed back to Manchester and were allowed to be with her. It was very plain to us that she was not going to recover. There was no sense of her presence, and the monitors were showing worrying, deteriorating readings. We agreed to let her go and remained with her until her heart stopped. It was unreal. She was gone. There would be no more music, no more imaginary friends, no more hugs, strokes and pokes. No more bashed up doors and skirting boards. No more shopping for silly T-shirts and Dr. Martens. No more concerts, operas and proms with Lu.

The online response to Lucy's death blew us all away. We knew she'd worked hard both in terms of music composition and disability advocacy but had no idea how she was seen by the wider music world. A sad announcement by Professor Linda Merrick on behalf of the RNCM was followed by flowers, cards and online tributes from all the organisations with whom she had worked and on whom she had left an indelible impression. The National Orchestra For All created a memory book of her time with them and sent it to us. Requests began to come in from Orchestras for her music and the RNCM planned a memorial day, which was lovely. A Lucy Hale Day of Music, Technology and Disability followed a year later and has now become an annual week. Her impact on the RNCM has been profound and she was chosen as one of their 50 most influential Faces during their 50th anniversary celebrations.

Megan Steinberg (PhD student, Lucy Hale Doctoral Award, Royal Northern College of Music)

It has been a joy and an honour to continue Lucy's research through a PhD in Composition at Royal Northern College of Music, supported by AHRC, undertaking practice-based research which consists of a portfolio of works and documentation of compositional processes created in association with the charity Drake Music, with whom Lucy worked closely. I am exploring accessible musical instruments and experimental processes with professional musicians, placing accessibility first in the composition process. The research and portfolio interrogate and highlight the value of experimental music systems for d/Deaf, Disabled and/or neurodivergent musicians. The three primary aims of this portfolio, resulting performances and documentation are to: develop sustainable creative processes built on the social model of disability; create new works for accessible musical instruments; and explore the role and impact of artificial intelligence on Disabled, d/Deaf and neurodivergent people.

The output will include new scores, recordings, performances/installations, film and a accessible music-making guide, informed by rehearsals, shared documentation and research. Musical works will not look to adapt inherently inaccessible techniques, which can perpetuate a state of 'other' for Disabled musicians and reinforce the outdated ideal of a Disabled person adapting to conform with society. Instead, compositions will begin from conversations with performers about access requirements, and new notation styles and formats will be developed based on these conversations. Performers will be invited to explore their disabilities, Deafness and/or neurodivergences through music by highlighting their unique perspectives and abilities, rather than attempting to conform to an ableist expectation of how they must perform. Improvisation, alternative scores and formats will be key in developing these works. This is underpinned by the social and human rights models of disability, that state how people are Disabled by barriers in society and disability is a natural part of human diversity that must be respected and supported in all its forms.

This research will be looking to suggest a Universal Composition style, which could be used by composers and performers to create music in an accessible manner. Universal Design is 'the design and composition of an environment so that it can be accessed, understood and used to the greatest extent possible by all people regardless of their age, size, ability or disability' (Centre for Excellence in Universal Design). It has not yet been discussed widely in music, but we can introduce these principles into music-making through experimental composition, 'like a piece of sports equipment – a bicycle, say, or a sailboat. The design is very important, but all the experiences of bicycling or sailing can't be foreseen or controlled at the boatyard or factory, nor should they be' (Gross, 1997). These works and collaborations will further research into accessibility in new music and provide practical frameworks for future application. Compositions will use the social model of disability as a foundation: unique abilities of the musicians, 'cannot exist without the context and content of that interaction' (Radigue, 2017). It will produce repertoire for future performances that are accessible for both Disabled musicians, and musicians who do not identify as Disabled, while additionally more widely promoting accessible processes. This project will establish and promote a framework of accessible methods of music-making. In order to develop a Universal Composition process, research will need to explore performers' perspectives by asking questions about their preferences for formats; how they best learn information; how comfortable they feel with improvisation and what their access requirements are for rehearsals and performances.

The first piece in this portfolio, 'Outlier II' for Distractfold, Luke Moore, Elle Chante, Visuals and AI was developed with close collaboration with all performers, which culminated in six different scores being created for each performer. Their scores were highly personalised to their needs, preferences and access requirements. They included a graphic score, video score, audio score and a tactile score for bassist Luke Moore. An A5 card wrapped in a wide variety of textiles that moved (left to right) from soft to hard textures, which represented the timbral shift in the piece and was 'read' (felt) by the performer in performance.

The second piece, 'This is happening', for Kathryn Williams and Sonia Allori, is a duet that explores perception of sound through the lens of performers' and composer's health conditions. Kathryn was provided a text-graphic score to respond to and a pitch set to play with; Sonia, who has a hearing impairment, responds to this via creative captioning. Sonia does not see the initial text score, only the wonderfully written creative captions. There are many ways in which accessibility is driving this piece, as opposed to being an adjustment made afterwards: creative captions are a core part of the piece, in essence acting as a score for Sonia. The flute text score could be triggering for Sonia and so is not given to them but prompts a 'telephone' style re-interpretation. The flute part is recorded and arranged for playback as, for health reasons, Kathryn could not be present at the concert. It will also provide time for creative captioners to work on the captions and for the electronic wind instrument player to practice responding to the track. There is an emphasis on improvisation over notated rhythms and phrases, which could have been inaccessible to either players' respiratory condition or facial muscle weakness and improvisation allows comfort in playing what is possible. Finally, the piece will be composed alongside visual elements that react to and represent the sounds, making the piece accessible to an audience with sensory requirements.

For this project, music has also been written for and with Kris Halpin, Steve Varden, Clarence Adoo, CoMA London, International Contemporary Ensemble, Hebrides Ensemble, Morwenna Louttit-Vermaat, Liza Bec and Abigail Whitman. Their input has been invaluable and has helped us create a portfolio of accessible musical works.

Victoria Kammin, music therapist

Everyone contributing to this chapter has one thing in common; a young woman who profoundly inspired us personally and professionally and a sense of privilege in collaborating with her. Lucy championed us to recognise and understand barriers to accessing music and our collective responsibility in creating a musical culture which people of all abilities can take part and flourish (Murphy & McFerran, 2017). Megan Steinberg has profoundly illustrated the outdated notion of a Disabled person adapting to conform with society; instead listening to the voices and unique perspectives and abilities of Disabled people rather than attempting to conform to ableist expectations. This chapter has illustrated how Disabled people are limited by barriers to accessing music which society place in their way, reflecting a broader picture of society placing limits on a person rather than their disability (Union, 1976; Oliver, 2008).

The government national plan for music education (Department for Education, 2022) states that all children in mainstream and specialist education settings should have access to inclusive high-quality music education, naming the importance of adaptive instruments, representation and collaboration. However, there is much work to be undertaken to achieve this, with improved access and choice, increased representation in the workforce, research to inform policy and practice and knowledge and skills to better support Disabled musicians urgently called for (Drake Music, 2011; Youth Music, 2020). Working collaboratively with Disabled people, policymakers, educators, retailers, venues, promotors, labels, studios are recognised as central to change (Youth Music, 2020).

The music therapy profession is well positioned to support access to musical life through collaboration with service users, their families, communities and systems around them (Kammin, 2019; Kammin et al., 2024; Tsiris et al., 2022). In parallel, there is a responsibility to engage, collaborate and champion conversation around equity of access to music and its relationship with the music therapy profession to ensure a more diverse and inclusive workforce (Langford et al., 2020).

Lucy pushed countless boundaries and barriers to accessing music for Disabled musicians to create a vast musical and compositional legacy, the ripples of which continue to resonate for future generations of Disabled musicians. We leave the last words to Lucy from her blog after David Bowie's death. In your own words to Bowie Lucy, 'Rest in peace, the world is a much better place for having had you in it'.

Lucy Hale

David Bowie: an inspiration to activists as well as artists

I've never been into make-up, owing partly to just not having inherited the fashion victim gene and partly to an inability to see that looking obviously Disabled and being attractive can go hand in hand, so my attitude was always 'why bother trying?'.

Therefore, when my sister requested that I wear makeup to her 18th birthday party, I wasn't enamoured by the prospect of girlying up. My response? An 'Aladdin Sane' lightning bolt down my face, just like David Bowie. If I was going to wear makeup, I wanted to do it in a way that matched how I saw myself at the time; an outsider with a passion for music, not unlike David Bowie himself.

Rewind a few years to when I fell in love with alternative music, just before leaving junior school. Old school Bowie, thanks to my mum, was one of the first acts to draw my attention.

Following my first year or so at secondary school, I had an irreparable fallout with my friends. I was left feeling very alone in a place where I felt I didn't fit. 'Life on Mars?' came to feel like an anthem to me. The isolation it described really resonated with me but also the yearning to be somewhere else and to do something more.

Bowie's entire career epitomised this desire to explore, be adventurous and push boundaries. His music and image evolved constantly, he challenged our perceptions of gender, sexuality and what was acceptable. He also made great protest art, such as the song 'Changes', the video for 'Let's Dance' and his performance atop the Berlin Wall, where he could be heard by both East and West Germans. He's an inspiration to activists, as well as artists.

In my early teens, I began having frequent hospital admissions and music became an even more important part of my life. Listening to music was something I could do even in an intensive care bed with countless tubes and wires attached to me and it provided a solace.

So many artists and bands were important to me during those times, but none took me out of myself in quite the way Bowie did. The sense of adventure in songs such as 'Space Oddity', 'Starman' and 'The Man Who Sold the World' meant listening to them was like visiting another planet.

However, Bowie didn't just provide an escape from reality. Like all the best artists, he has taught me valuable lessons about reality. Bowie was the outsider who made being an outsider cool, and it's easy to feel like an outsider as a Disabled person. I'm currently studying at music college and, though my musical taste has expanded hugely, Bowie, along with certain others, will always feel special to me.

Physically Disabled classical musicians are few and far between and sometimes I feel slightly out of place. I've had to be exempt from a couple of assessments on my degree, as a result of my disability and things like that serve to remind me of my difference from my peers.

There's also always that one person at every concert where one of my pieces is performed (I'm a composer) who can't believe that a Disabled person can write music. That person's irritating.

But I'm happier with my outsider identity than I was in school, or even when I had my 'Aladdin Sane' makeup at my sister's birthday. I just think to myself 'If David Bowie can be an androgynous, cross dressing rockstar, I can be a Disabled composer'.

Thank you, Bowie, for enabling me to think like that. Rest in peace, the world is a much better place for having had you in it.

Lucy Hale, (2016) Muscular Dystrophy Trailblazers blog

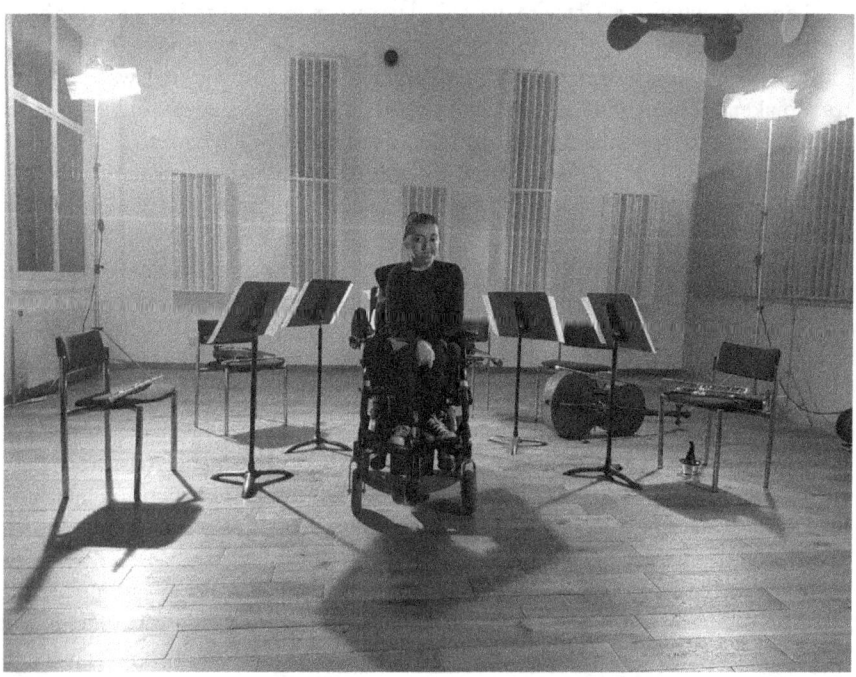

Figure 9.1 Lucy on stage before the performance of one of her compositions.
Photograph provided by parents.

References

A Blueprint for the Future | Youth Music. June 2020.

Amadoru, S. & McFerran, K. (2007). The role of music therapy in children's hospices. *Eur J Palliat Care, 14*(3), 124–127.

Anonymous, Centre for Excellence in Universal Design. (n.d.) 'What is Universal Design'. http://universaldesign.ie/What-is Universal-Design.

Blatt, S. J., Zuroff, D. C., Hawley, L. L. & Auerbach, J. S. (2010). Predictors of sustained therapeutic change. *Psychotherapy Research, 20*(1), 37–54.

Boehm, C. (2019). The End of a Golden Era of British Music?: Exploration of Educational Gaps in the Current UK Creative Industry Strategy. In *Innovation in Music*. Taylor & Francis.

Bowlby, J. (1969). *Attachment and loss: Vol. 1. Attachment*. Basic Books.

Bremmer, M. (2023). Encountering disability in music: Exploring perceptions on inclusive music education in higher music education. *Research Studies in Music Education, 45*(3), 512–524.

Burland, K. (2020). Music for all: Identifying, challenging and overcoming barriers. *Music & Science, 3*, 2059204320946950.

Cox, T. & Kilshaw, H. (2021). Creating a More Inclusive Classical Music. A Study of the English Orchestral Workforce and the Current Routes to Joining It. Executive Summary.

Department for Education (2022). The power of music to change lives: a national plan for music education. www.gov.uk/government/publications/the-power-of-music-to-change-lives-a-national-plan-for-music-education.

Gross, J. (1997). 'Behrman Interview by Jason Gross', Perfect Sound Forever, August 1997. http://universaldesign.ie/What-is-Universal-Design.

Hale, L. (2016). David Bowie: an inspiration to activities as well as artists, Muscular Dystrophy Trailblazers blog. www.drakemusic.org/experience/disabling-barriers-to-formal-music-education-consultation; www.gov.uk/government/publications/the-importance-of-music-a-national-plan-for-music-education; www.gov.uk/government/publications/the-power-of-music-to-change-lives-a-national-plan-for-music-education.

Kammin, V. (2019). Performing, Sharing and Celebrating Life. *Music Therapy in Children and Young People's Palliative Care*, pp. 127–144.

Kammin, V., Fraser, L., Flemming, K. & Hackett, J. (2024). Experiences of music therapy in paediatric palliative care from multiple stakeholder perspectives: A systematic review and qualitative evidence synthesis. *Palliative Medicine, 38*(3), 364–378.

Langford, A., Rizkallah, M. & Maddocks, C. (2020). British Association of Music Therapy diversity report.

Lindenfelser, K. J., Grocke, D. & McFerran, K. (2008). Bereaved Parents' Experiences of Music Therapy with their Terminally Ill Child. *Journal of Music Therapy, 45*(3), 330–348.

Lindenfelser, K. J., Hense, C. & McFerran, K. (2012). Music therapy in pediatric palliative care: Family-centered care to enhance quality of life. *American Journal of Hospice and Palliative Medicine®, 29*(3), 219–226.

Murphy, M. A. & McFerran, K. (2017). Exploring the literature on music participation and social connectedness for young people with intellectual disability: A critical interpretive synthesis. *Journal of Intellectual Disabilities, 21*(4), 297–314.

Oliver, M. (2008). The social model in action. *Disability, 1*, 396–409.

Radigue, E. (2007). 'Naldjorak I' in Agape: Miguel Abreu Gallery, June 3 – July 28, 2007, Alex Waterman (Ed.) (New York: Miguel Abreu Gallery) as cited by J. Gottschalk (2016), *Experimental Music Since 1970*. London: Bloomsbury.

Steinhardt, T. L., Mortvedt, S. & Trondalen, G. (2021). Music therapy in the hospital-at-home: A practice for children in palliative care. *British Journal of Music Therapy, 35*(2), 53–62.

Tsiris, G., Hockley, J. & Dives, T. (2022). Musical care at the end of life: Palliative care perspectives and emerging practices. In N. Spiro & K. R. Sanfilippo (Eds), *Collaborative insights: Interdisciplinary perspectives on musical care throughout the life course*. Oxford University Press, pp. 119–145.

Union of the Physically Impaired Against Segregation. 1976. *Fundamental principles of disability*. London: Union of the Physically Impaired Against Segregation.

Verberne, L. M., Kars, M. C., Schouten-van Meeteren, A. Y., Bosman, D. K., Colenbrander, D. A., Grootenhuis, M. A. & van Delden, J. J. (2017). Aims and tasks in parental caregiving for children receiving palliative care at home: a qualitative study. *European Journal of Pediatrics, 176*, 343–354.

Zuckerman, K. (2019). Parents' Experiences of Music Therapy with Paediatric Palliative Care Patients (Doctoral dissertation).

Index

Note: Locators in *italic* indicate figures.

5-stage grief model (Kubler-Ross) 50–51

Abendroth, M. 25
ableism 134–135, 144
accessible music portfolio 145–146
accessible musical instruments 144
accessible music-making guide 144–145
adaptations 18, 23, 77, 81, 114, 121, 142; *see also* flexibility; accessible
Adger, Lauren 86
Adoo, Clarence 146
adult services, moving to 114–129: 'Moving on With Music', songwriting project/research (*see* 'Moving on With Music' project and research (NRS)); music in children/adolescent development 114–115; music as health indicator 115; transitional care, needs and gas 114, 116, 127
advocacy 2–3, 4, 92, 97, 98, 115, 125–127, 144
Allied Health Professionals 5, 6, 109
Allori, Sonia 145–146
Anderson, David Sutton 134
Angelou, Maya 43
Annesley, L. 110
Ansdell, G. 90, 98
anxiety (parents, therapist) xi, 2, 14, 33–34, 45–46, 48, 49, 50, 110
Arts Council England 138
audio scores 145

Baines, S. 3
BAMT Diversity Survey and Diversity Report (2022) 4
BBC Young Composer 141

The Beatles 39
Bec, Liza 146
bereavement: post-bereavement coping and support 24–25, 42, 48, 51, 53, 65–69; 76; bereavement suite/room 25, 42, 43, 48, 76
Bick, Esther 104
boundaries: physical 15, 22, 77, 79–80; therapist–clients 7, 25, 84, 108–109
Bowie, David 147–148
Bowlby, J. 19
Bradt, J. 24
breathing, breath control 24, 44, 87, 135
British Association for Music Therapy (BAMT) 4–5
Brittle Bone disease 121, 124
burnout, therapist's 15, 23, 25
'Butterfly Suite,' Claire House Children's Hospice 42, 43, 48

candles, candle light 58, 60–61, 64–65, 66–67
care environment 8, 16, 24, 49, 81, 115, 129
Carroll, Lewis 136
Cerridwen 132
Chambers, Joanna 100–112
Chante, Elle 144
Charcot Marie Tooth Syndrome 132–133
Chelsea and Westminster Hospital, London 112
Children's Hospices Across Scotland (CHAS) 86–99, 116, 128; 'Moving on With Music' project and research (NRS) (*see under own heading*); *Music & Me* songwriting project (*see under own heading*); Rachel House Children's

Hospice, Kinross 88, 89, 93, 128; Robin House Children's Hospice, Balloch 88, 89, 93
Childress, Andrea 127–128
Chin, T. 94
Christopher's Children's Hospice CHASE, Guildford 12–27; Fraser (Julie and Ian Russell, client experience) (*see under own heading*); 'The Festival of Music' (CHASE) 137, 139–140
Claire House Children's Hospice 42–54; care provision types 42; family support approach 42; geographical area 42; music therapy service 42; post-bereavement support, 'Butterfly Suite' 42; Sophie (Nguyen family client experience) (*see under own heading*); team 42
Clark, Batrice 86
classical music industry and disability: ableist expectations 134–135, 144; inequalities report (Arts Council) 138; practice-based accessibility research and programme 144–146
client experience reports: Anna, Brian, Harry, James, John, Tom (young adults) 118–127; Fraser, Julie and Ian Russell 11–27, *11*; Freya and Sarah Jane Dawes 56–71, *57*; Lucy and Nicky Hale 132–148; Milly and Tom Grey, experience 74, 76–77, 78–79, 80, 81; Reiaan, Mariam Titus and Devang Ram Mohan 31–40; Sophie Nguyen family 42–54; William and Joanna Chambers 100–101, 103–109, *107*, 110, 111–112; *see also under their own headings*
client-centred approach 3, 17, 26
client–therapist relationship; *see* therapist–client relationship
clinical supervision 15, 25, 51, 111
co-authoring, collaborative writing/authorship 1, 6–9, 12, 31, 43, 56, 72, 100, 116, 132
collaborative voice, collaborative song creation 46–48, 49, 86–99, 116–129; *see also* 'Moving on With Music' project and research (NRS); *Music & Me* songwriting project (CHAS)
CoMA London 146
communication: Makaton system 78, 96; musical sound, songs 88, 95, 105, 115, 122, 126, 127–128; non-verbal 35, *36*, 95, 115; parent–child 34–36, 37, 110;

post-bereavement 38–39, 40; virtual, therapist–clients 75, 76, 82; visual 96; voice-based baby bonding 34–36, 37
communicative musicality as non-verbal experience sharing 13
community forming, connective energy 16–17, 22, 37, 83, 86–99, 116; *see also* Fraser (Julie and Ian Russell, client experience); *Music & Me* songwriting project (CHAS)
Community Music approach (Drury) 86, 88, 89–90, 97–98
compassion fatigue, therapist 25
composition, composing: music composition (*see* Lucy Hale, music education/industry and disability); song creation (*see* 'Moving on With Music' project and research (NRS))
connective power of music therapy 16–17, 73, 75–76, 76–77, 78, 81–82, 83
Contro, N. 23
countertransference 14, 25, 50, 108
Cousin, V. L. 110
COVID-19 pandemic 33, 69, 73, 88–89, 106, 143
cross- and multi-disciplinary approaches 16, 86, 88, 89–90, 97–98, 100, 115
cultural differences, adaptations xii, 3–4, 15–16, 37, 44, 52, 81, 98

dad(s), roles and perspectives 45–46, 49, 50, 74, 76–77, 78–79, 81, 95, 126, 128
'Dark Light' songwriting project 118, 119–120, 123, 124–125, 129n2
Dawes, Sarah Jane 56–71
de St Paer, Wendy 42–54
death, social awareness 15–16
death acceptance: avoidance culture 23, 51; language directness, clarity 50–52; parental anxiety, acknowledgment problems 45, 46, 48, 49
Demelza (Hospice Care for Children) *see* virtual music therapy groups (Demelza)
Dileo, C. 24
Dindoyal, L. 25, 101, 108
disability, social and human rights models 145
discrimination, instructional 134–135, 138
diversity 4–5, 77, 138
The DMDs group 119–120, 124
Drake Music 143, 144
Drury, Rachel 86–99

Dual Process Model of bereavement coping 51, 52
dual role (therapist-mother), therapy potential and support need as 13–15
Duchenne Muscular Dystrophy (DMD) 121–122
dyadic relationship 14, 100, 101, 104, 108
Dylan, Bob 34, 38, 39

Edgar, Joanne 116, 129
Edwards, J. 102
emotional needs, emotional processing: clients 18–19, 22, 23–24, 35, 47, 48–49, 53, 76–77, 94, 122; therapist 23–25, 50–51, 53, 75, 111 (*see also* self-care support)
end-of-life care 23–24; countertransference feelings 25; death avoidance culture 23; family experience 22–24; therapist (preparation, demands, self-care) 23, 25
environment: care environment 8, 16, 24, 49, 81, 115, 129; medicalised, hospital 32–33, 34, 36, 40, 103, 106; Universal Design principles 145
ethic, ethos 1, 13, 16, 22, 23, 117, 118
'Evidence Work Based Learning' (UWE) 101
experimenting with sounds 115, 116, 122, 144, 145
extended family xii, 13, 42, 61, 77, 83, 88, 93, 137

family, broad definition 88
Family Advisory Board (University of York) 3, 4
Family Integrated Care strategy 33
family support team 42
family-centred virtual music therapy groups; *see* virtual music therapy groups (Demelza)
Farwell, Eddie 70
father(s), roles and perspectives 45–46, 49, 50, 74, 76–77, 78–79, 81, 95, 126, 128
fear xi, 14, 15–16, 34, 38–39, 53, 63
Fearne 112
'Feel the Heat' songwriting project 118, 121–122, 124, 125, 126, 128
'fellow traveller' concept 7
'The Festival of Music' (CHASE) 137, 139–140
Flannery, J. 25

flexibility 83, 84, 102, 103, 106, 109–110; *see also* adaptations
Flower, C. 105
Fraser (Julie and Ian Russell, client experience) 11–27, *11*, *21*; Christopher's Children's Hospice CHASE 12, 16; community, belonging 16–17; experience and impact (Julie, mother) 17–18, 20–21, 22–23, 27 / (Vicky, therapist) 13, 19–20, 23, 24, 26; family sessions, end-of-life/post-bereavement 22–25; individual sessions, self-expression 17–18, 19–20; individual sessions, workshops, performance-based intervention 20–21, 22; medical condition, background 12; session planning 19
Freya's light (Freya and Sarah Jane Dawes, client experience) 56–71, *57*; Freyabeya charity 68–69, 71; Freya's light' song 65–67; Helen House hospice, Oxford 61; light/candles as metaphor and practical help 58, 60–61, 64–67, 70, 71; medical condition, impact 59–61; music, child–parent connecting 62–63; music in end-of-life care 64–65; music for parental self-expression, self-soothing 63; music in family history 58–59; music therapy, hospice 61; post-bereavement, coping and charitable work 65–69
Freyabeya charity 68–69, 71
'Freya's Light' song 58, 66–67, 68
funding, fundraising xii, 13–14, 21, 42, 68–69, 70, 71, 111, 129
funerals 23, 40, 48, 65–67, 70

Geneva University Hospital, Paediatric Intensive Care Unit (PICU) 110
Glasgow 121, 129
Gorb, Adam 142–143
Grant, Eilidh 86
graphic scores 145–146
Great Ormond Street Hospital (GOSH), London 31, 61, 134, 137
Grey, Milly and Tom, client experience 74, 76–77, 78–79, 80, 81; *see also* virtual music therapy groups (Demelza)
grief, grieving xi, 25, 37, 43, 46, 50–52; 5-stages model (Kubler-Ross) 50–51; Dual Process Model (Stroebe and Schut) 51, 52

group settings; *see* virtual family-centred music therapy groups

Hadley, S. 7
Hale, Lucy; *see* Lucy Hale, music education/industry and disability
Hale, Nicky 132–134, 137, 140–142, 143–144
Halpin, Kris 146
Hampshire Music Award 140
Harris, D. X. 6
Harris, Polly 86–99
Health and Care Professions Council registration 32
Heath, Bob 56
Hebrides Ensemble 146
Helen and Douglas House 63
Helen House Children's Hospice, Oxford 61, 63–64, 67, 69, 70; *see also* Freya's light (Freya and Sarah Jane Dawes, client experience)
Hendon, Amy 129
Hogg, Sue 99
holistic care approach 9, 17, 100, 101–102, 103, 111, 112
Hospice UK transition programme 114, 127
hospice–hospital link, music therapy linkage 100–112; boundaries 108–109; dyadic and triadic relationships (parent–child–therapist) 100, 101, 104–105, 108; holistic care ambition, multidisciplinary teams 97–98, 100, 101, 102; Martin House Children's Hospice, Boston Spa 100, 101; music therapy role development 101–102; perspectives, parental 110; service evaluation 102–103; therapeutic space 108–109; therapist support 111; William's story 100–101, 103–109, 110, 111–112 (*see also* William (Joanna Chambers, client experience))
hospices: Children's Hospices Across Scotland (CHAS) 86–99, 116, 128; Christopher's Children's Hospice CHASE, Guildford 12–27; Claire House Children's Hospice, Birkenhead 42; Helen House Children's Hospice, Oxford 61, 63–64, 67, 69, 70; Martin House Children's Hospice, Boston Spa xi, xii, 100–112; Rachel House Children's Hospice, Kinross 88, 89, 93, 128; Robin House Children's Hospice, Balloch 88, 89, 93; Shooting Star Children's Hospices, Guildford 12–27

hospitals: Chelsea and Westminster Hospital, London 112; Geneva University Hospital, Paediatric Intensive Care Unit (PICU) 110; Great Ormond Street Hospital (GOSH), London 31, 61, 134, 137; University College London Hospital (UCLH), Neonatal Intensive Care Unit (NICU) 31–40, 61
Howell, Annabel 86, 97, 99

Ibberson, Cathy 100–112
Imperial War Museum North 143
improvisation: as connection help and self-expression 24, 45; music therapy's improvisatory nature 80, 104, 145, 146; songwriting as improvisation, uncertainty, adventure 122–123
inclusivity 4–5
intuitional educational discrimination 134–135
intensive care units: Neonatal Intensive Care Unit (NICU), University College London Hospital (UCLH) 31–40, 101 (*see also* Reiaan (Mariam Titus, Devang Ram Mohan, client experience, neonatal care))
International Contemporary Ensemble 146
intersectional identities 4–5, 138
isolation 16, 33, 63, 72–73, 82, 83, 133, 147
'The Jabberwocky' (Carroll) 136

Jane, Kirsty 31–40
Jennings, Michael 136, 146
Jessie's Fund charity xii, 13–14, 111
John Radcliffe Hospital (JR), Oxford 61

Kammin, Victoria (Vicky) 1–9, 11–27, 132–148
Katz, R. S. 25
Kübler-Ross, E. 50–51

language directness vs euphemisms 50–52
legacy work, transactional objects 39, 49, 98–99, 125–126, 136
life-limiting conditions, prevalence 1
light as metaphor and practical help 58, 60–61, 64–67, 70, 71
lived experience: definition 2; in music therapy (practice, research) 2–3, 6; practice development focus 4
Loewy, J. V. 37
loneliness and isolation 16, 33, 63, 72–73, 82, 83, 133, 147
loss-oriented behaviours 51

Lou, Monica 127–128
Louttit-Vermaat, Morwenna 146
'Love is Everything' songwriting project 118, 120–121, 122–123, 124, 126–127
Lucy Hale, music education/industry and disability 132–148; classical music industry inequalities 138; composition studies, PhD (RCMJD, RNCM) 134, 135–136, 137, 141–143, 144; David Bowie 147–148; end-of-life care, post-bereavement response 143–144; family as musical environment 132–133; hospice care and opportunities (CHASE) 137, 138, 139–140; institutional discrimination experience (GCSE access) 134–135; legacy 144–146; mainstream education limits 133; medical condition, impact 132–133; reflections from Adam Gorb, RNVM tutor 142–143 / Jane Wood, school nurse 134–136 / Jocelyn Watkins, music teacher 134–136 / Nicky Hale, mother 132–134, 137, 140–142, 143–144 / Victoria Kammin, music therapist 137–140; Treloars School and College 133–134, 136–137, 140–141

MA Music Therapy 31–32, 100–101
Makaton 78, 96
Malloch, S. 13
Martin House Children's Hospice, Boston Spa xi, xii, 100–112
maternal elements, psychotherapy 13
McConnell, Ellie 86
McConnell, T. 24
McDonald, Horse 127
McLachlan, Janet 86–99
medicalised, hospital environment 32–33, 34, 36, 40, 103, 106
memory making 20, 20–22, 23, 25, 26, 32, 38, 65, 101, 111, 140, 144
Menuhin, Yehudi x–xi, xii
Merrick, Linda 141, 144
Milly and Tom Grey, experience 74, 76–77, 78–79, 80, 81; *see also* virtual music therapy groups (Demelza)
mindfulness 15
Mohan, Devang Ram 31–40
Moore, Luke 145
mother–therapist role intersection 13–14; maternal role/elements in therapeutic work 13–14; pregnancy, therapist's 14

mourning, grieving: death, loss xi, 25, 37, 43, 46, 50–52; unlived future xi, 42, 119
'Moving on With Music' project and research (NRS) 114–129; being heard, advocacy, legacy 125–127; 'Dark Light' (John, Harry, Tom) 118, 119–120, 123, 124–125, 129n2; experiences: autonomy, independence, choices 123–124; experiences: improvisation, uncertainty, adventure 122–123; 'Feel the Heat' (Brian) 121–122, 124, 125, 126, 128; 'Love is Everything' (James, Anna) 118, 120–121, 122–123, 124, 126–127; moving on experience 127–128; music in children/adolescent development 114–115; project reflections, young adults 122–127; project structure 116; research ethics 118; songwriting as meaning making 124–125; songwriting as self-exploration/expression 115; study aim and design 116–118, *117*; transition challenge (paediatric to adult care context) 114–115
multi- and cross-disciplinary teams 16, 86, 88, 89–90, 97–98, 100, 115
Murray, Louise 86
Music & Me songwriting project (CHAS) 86–99, *91*; audio and/or visual recordings 93, 95–96; collaboration levels 88; collaborative voice 86, 93, 97; context, CHAS work 88–89; cross-disciplinary arts-based approaches (Music Therapy, Community Music) 86, 88, 89–90, 97–98; individual impact, participants 92, 93, 94, 95, 96, 98, 99; lyrics, musical style 94–95; online songwriting workshops 92–93; positionality (project, practitioners) 89–90; project aim 89; questionnaire stage 91; rights-based approach 90; song lyrics ('Music and me') 87
music education, exam discrimination 134–135
music therapist, training requirements 4
music therapy: accessibility, adaptability 18; community forming, sense of belonging 17; cultural and religious method determinants 37; definition 2; diversity-sensitive approach 4–5, 77; Family Integrated Care (UCLH) model 33; group settings 72–84; as

holistic child and family support 9, 13, 18; performance-based interventions 22; self-expression, communicative focus 19–20, 34–36, 37, 44, 45; socio-economic barriers 4; 'Songs of Kin' intervention (Loewy) 37; virtual, online 72–84; and wider therapy team 109–110
Music Therapy approach (Harris and McLachlan) 86, 88, 89–90, 97–98
Music Therapy in Children and Young People's Palliative Care (Ludwig) 3
music therapy, potential and impact: ability and celebration vs loss focus transformation 19–20, 21, 22; anxiety, pain reduction 2; bereavement, mourning, grief dealing 24–25, 38–39; end-of-life care 23; individual sessions 17–18, 19–20; longevity, impact continuation 69–71; memory making 20–22, 23, 25, 26, 32, 38, 65, 101, 111, 144; parent–baby-communication enabling 34–36, 37; respite 18–19; roles and role ambiguity/multitude 42–43, 49; sense of normalcy provision 18
Music Therapy Trios 105

National Orchestra for All 142, 144
neonatal care, UK (NHS): Family Integrated Care (UCLH) model 33; medicalised environment, child–parent relationship impact 33, 35; music therapy, aims and accessibility 32, 33, 34; parental isolation 33; parental trauma and PTSD 35; parents' role and emotional reaction 32–33; tiers 33
Neonatal Intensive Care Unit (NICU), University College London Hospital (UCLH) 31–40
neonatal music therapy 31–40; accessibility 32, 33; aims 33; availability 32; cultural and religious method determinants 37; parent advisory group 32; parental identity forming 32, 34; parental self-efficacy, therapeutic growth 34–36; practice standards 31; 'Songs of Kin' intervention (Loewy) 37; training programmes 31–32; voice as tool for baby bonding, communication 34–36, 37; *see also* Reiaan (Mariam Titus, Devang Ram Mohan, client experience, neonatal care)
Nicoll, Donna 86

Nordoff Robbins Scotland (NRS) charity 116, 118, 129n1
normalcy need 18

O'Conner 112
Oldfield, A. 104
online music therapy; *see* virtual music therapy
'Outlier II' (Distractfold Ensemble, Luke Moore, Elle Chante 145
'Over the Rainbow,' TV programme 20
'Over The Rainbow,' TV programme 21

Paediatric Intensive Care Unit (PICU), Geneva University Hospital 101
paediatric palliative care (PPC): definition 1; family vs child support as target 16; music therapy potential 2; WHO goals 2
Paediatric Palliative Care Research Group, University of York 3, 4, 26
parental self-efficacy 34–36
parents/guardians, caregiving role demands 1
Parker, M. M. 14
performance: ability, GCSE exam access 134, 136; anxiety 127; performance space, opportunity access 20–22, 137–138, 139, 140, 142; performance-based interventions 20–21, 22, 47
Person-Centred Practice 17, 26
positionalities (project, practitioners) 89–90, 118
Post Traumatic Stress Disorder (PTSD) 35
post-bereavement coping and support 24–25, 42, 48, 51, 53, 65–69; 76
pregnancy, therapist's 14
prevalence of life-limiting conditions 1
The Prince and Princess of Wales Hospice, Glasgow 129
psychodynamic music therapy 13, 75

Queen Margaret University, Edinburgh 118

Rachel House Children's Hospice 88, 89, 93, 128
Rainbow Connection (Williams and Asher) 40
Rees, Ceridwen 56–71
Reiaan (Mariam Titus, Devang Ram Mohan, client experience, neonatal care) *36*; bereavement, mourning, grief dealing 38–39; experience and impact

(Kirsty, therapist) 34, 36, 37 / (Maria, Devang, parents) 33–34, 36, 37, 38–39; medicalised environment, child–parent relationship impact 32–33; parental anxiety, incompetency experience 33–34; parental identity, confidence forming 34, 37; voice-based baby bonding, communication 34–36, 37; *see also* neonatal care, UK (NHS); neonatal music therapy
remembering days, remembering events 67, 69
respite needs 13, 18–19, 42, 128
restoration-oriented behaviours 51
Rice, Anneke 20
Rickard, N. 94
Rickson, Daphne 114–129
rights-based approach 90, 145
Robin House Children's Hospice, Balloch 88, 89, 93
roles and role ambiguity/multitude in music therapy 42–43
Rosie's Rainbow Fund 68
Ross, Ricky 121, 127
Rowley, A. 15, 25
Royal College of Music Junior Department (RCMJD) 134, 135–136, 141
Royal Marine Association Concert Band 136
Royal Northern College of Music (RNCM) 137, 141–143, 144
Royal Philharmonic Orchestra 20, 23, 137
Royal Philharmonic Society's composers programme 143
Russell, Julie 1–9, 3, 11–27; *see also* Fraser, Julie and Ian Russell (client experience)

Schut, H. 51
scores, personalised 145
secure base concept 19
self-care, therapist 14–15, 23, 25
self-efficacy, parents 34–36
Shoemark, H. 101
Shooting Star Children's Hospices, Guildford 12–27; *see also* Fraser (Julie and Ian Russell, client experience)
Sibelius music software 135, 136
social isolation 16, 33, 63, 72–73, 82, 83, 133, 147
social model of disability 145; *see also* advocacy

Song from a Window (Heath) 56
'Songs of Kin' intervention (Loewy) 37
songwriting 46–48, 49, 56, 86–99, 116–129; *see also* 'Moving on With Music' project and research (NRS)
Sophie (Nguyen family, client experience) 42–54, *54*; Claire House Children's Hospice 42; collaborative song creation 46–48, 49; experience and emotional processing (Wendy, therapist) 44, 45, 46, 47, 48, 50–51; experience and impact (parents) 43, 44–45, 46, 48, 50; home session 46–47; hospice sessions 44–47; medical condition, impact 43–44; parental anxiety, acknowledgment problems 45, 46, 48, 49; post-bereavement sessions, grieving 48, 52, 53; role and focus ambiguity/multitude 42–43, 49, 50; self-expression, pleasure, child-guided focus 44, 46–47, 49; sessions planning and child-centred adaptation 45, 45–46, 47; 'Sophie's Wonderful World' song 53
'Sophie's Wonderful World' 45, 46, 47, 48, 49, 50, 53
Steinberg, Megan 144–146
Stroebe, M. 51
supervision, clinical 15, 25, 51, 111
Swan, Victoria 72–84

tactile scores 145
Taleisen 132
therapeutic relationships 3, 8, 14, 19, 22, 84, 104
therapeutic space 78–79, 107, 108–109, 127, 138
therapist support and self-care 15, 25; burnout, therapist's 15, 23, 25; clinical supervision 15, 25, 51, 111; compassion fatigue 25; guilt feelings 14
therapist–client relationship: client-centred approach 3; collaboration, 'fellow traveller' concept 3, 7; countertransference 14, 25, 50, 108; dual role (therapist–mother), potential and support need as 13–15; power balance 2–3
'This is happening' (Kathryn Williams, Sonia Allori) 145–146
Thompson, T. 6
thriving xi, 20
Titus, Mariam 31–40

Together for Short Lives charity 100
transitional care, paediatric to adult services 114, 116, 127; *see also* 'Moving on With Music' project and research (NRS)
transitional objects, legacy objects/music 39, 49, 98–99, 125–126, 136
Treloars School and College 133–134, 136–137, 140–141
Trevarthen, C. 13
Tsiris, Giorgos 24, 114–129

UN Universal Declaration of Human Rights 90
uncertainty (medical, future lives) 19, 20, 42, 43, 45, 84, 122–123
United Nations Convention on the Rights of the Child (UNCRC) 90
Universal Composition style 145
Universal Design for care environments 145
University College London Hospital (UCLH), Neonatal Intensive Care Unit (NICU) 31–40, 61
The University of West England (UWE) 100–101, 112
University of York 3, 4, 26

Varden, Steve 146
virtual music therapy groups (Demelza) 72–84; bereavement, dealing with (group, therapist) 75–76; communication/human connection (family–family–therapist) 73, 75–76, 76–77, 78, 81–82, 83; COVID-19 73–74; cultural, social consideration 81; group diversity and flexibility needs 75, 77–78, 81; Milly and Tom Grey, experience 74, 76–77, 78–79, 80, 81; music choice (pre-recorded vs live) 75; mute-management (therapist, group) 80; physical and virtual boundaries 79–80;

positive outcomes 82–83; session preparation (therapist, families) 75, 76; session running (therapist) 77–78; session type, structure, frequency 74
voice, defining 88

Wainer, Hilary 56
Watkins, Jocelyn 133, 134–136
'What a Wonderful World' 46, 53
When Professionals Weep (Katz) 25
Whitman, Abigail 146
William (Joanna Chambers, client experience) 100–101, 103–109, *107*, 110, 111–112; child and parent as session lead 103–105; dyad (mother–son) 100, 101, 104, 108; experience, impact, evaluation (Joanna) 106–108; initial sessions 103–104; later sessions 105–106; middle sessions 104–105; music therapy trios (mother–son–therapist) 104–105, 108; *see also* hospice–hospital link, music therapy linkage
Williams, Kathryn 145–146
Wilson, Anita, Ian and Lily 86
Wood, Jane 112, 136–137
Wood, S. 90
World Federation of Music Therapy 2
World Health Organisation (WHO) 1, 2

Xypolitaki, Elli 129

Yalom, I. D. 7
Young Adult Service, Prince and Princess of Wales Hospice, Glasgow 129
young adults, moving on from paediatric palliative care; *see* 'Moving on With Music' project and research (NRS)

Zoom 72, 75, 77, 79, 80; *see also* virtual music therapy groups (Demelza)

For Product Safety Concerns and Information please contact our EU
representative GPSR@taylorandfrancis.com
Taylor & Francis Verlag GmbH, Kaufingerstraße 24, 80331 München, Germany

www.ingramcontent.com/pod-product-compliance
Lightning Source LLC
Chambersburg PA
CBHW070309230426
43664CB00015B/2698